ANISH KAPOOR

ANISH KAPOOR
UNSEEN

ARKEN Museum of Contemporary Art

Published with generous funding from:

A.P. Møller og Hustru Chastine Mc-Kinney Møllers Fond til almene Formaal
Augustinus Fonden
Aage og Johanne Louis-Hansens Fond
Danish Arts Foundation
Furi Appel og Gunnar Niskers Fond til Almennyttige Formål

Preface

Infinite darkness, swirling black water, a sea of red pigment and a huge slab of blood-red wax: these things await us in ARKEN's galleries. *Anish Kapoor – Unseen* presents a selection of Anish Kapoor's most important large-scale works created during the artist's more than forty-year career. Extending across most of the museum from the 100-metre-long Art Axis into the adjacent galleries, the exhibition is the first in the history of ARKEN to take up so much space. Several of the works have been built into the architecture of ARKEN, at times interrupting the usual routes through the museum's spaces. *Memory* (2008) blocks the museum's foyer, the reflections in *S-Curve* (2006) expand and distort the surroundings, and *Destierro* (2017) creates a red pigment landscape which entirely occupies part of the museum, no longer permitting entry.

Anish Kapoor – Unseen is Kapoor's first major solo show in Scandinavia, and we at ARKEN Museum of Contemporary Art are very proud to present such a comprehensive exhibition featuring one of the world's leading artists. Born in 1954 in India, Anish Kapoor has worked out of the UK since 1973. He works with a wide range of media, from sculpture and architectural work to painting and drawing, using materials such as pigment, wax, stone, fibreglass, silicone and polished stainless steel.

pp. 8-9
From the left:
Random Triangle Mirror, 2017;
S-Curve, 2006;
Grave, 2019
Installation view,
ARKEN Museum of Contemporary Art, Ishøj

With his unique use of materials, shapes, colours and surfaces, Kapoor plays with our perception of reality. He gives what we cannot see – the absence and the void – palpable, sensuous form, as for example when water flows into an invisible abyss in *Descension* (2014), or when he lets us gaze into the darkness of the interior of *Memory*. Despite the impressive size of these works, something always remains hidden: something we can neither see nor fully understand. *Anish Kapoor – Unseen* addresses this paradoxical aspect of Kapoor's works and of art in general. We feel the effect of the works with our bodies and senses, yet there is always more at stake than we can immediately perceive.

In this book, the co-curator of the exhibition Sarah Fredholm takes the work *Descent into Limbo* (1992) as the starting point for a closer look at the affective impact that Kapoor's works have on the viewer. Cognitive scientist and poet Pireeni Sundaralingam focuses on the works' insistent physical presence in a hyper-technological and digital reality. In an interview, the artist offers insights into his work and its recurring themes. Professor of architectural history Mari Hvattum examines the trans-formative power of Kapoor's works with a particular focus on the version of *S-Curve* on display at the Kistefos museum's sculp-ture park in Norway. Anthropologist Mikkel Bille and contemporary archaeologist Tim Flohr Sørensen focus on Kapoor's artistic explorations of darkness, the void and the un-known. We are grateful to all the authors for their in-sightful contributions to this publication.

Our warm and heartfelt thanks go to Anish Kapoor for creating an absolutely exceptional exhibition for ARKEN. We are grateful and extremely pleased to be temporarily housing this sequence of major works from 1992 to the present day. The exhibition was created in close collaboration between ARKEN and Anish Kapoor Studio, and we would like to extend our thanks to Lucy Adams, Sophie Baker, Peter Lynch and Clare Chapman for an excellent collaboration. A big thank you also goes to Claus Robenhagen and Lisson Gallery for their collaboration on the exhibition. Finally, a warm thank you to Strandberg Publishing and graphic designer Claus Due for the great work on this publication.

A large number of foundations have contributed gene-rous and absolutely indispensable support to the exhibi-tion, enabling us to realise it in its full, ambitious scale. We would like to express our greatest gratitude to the A.P. Møller Fonden, Augustinus Fonden, Aage og Johanne Louis-Hansens Fond, Danish Arts Foundation and Furi Appel og Gunnar Niskers Fond.

On behalf of ARKEN and the exhibition team,
Marie Nipper, director

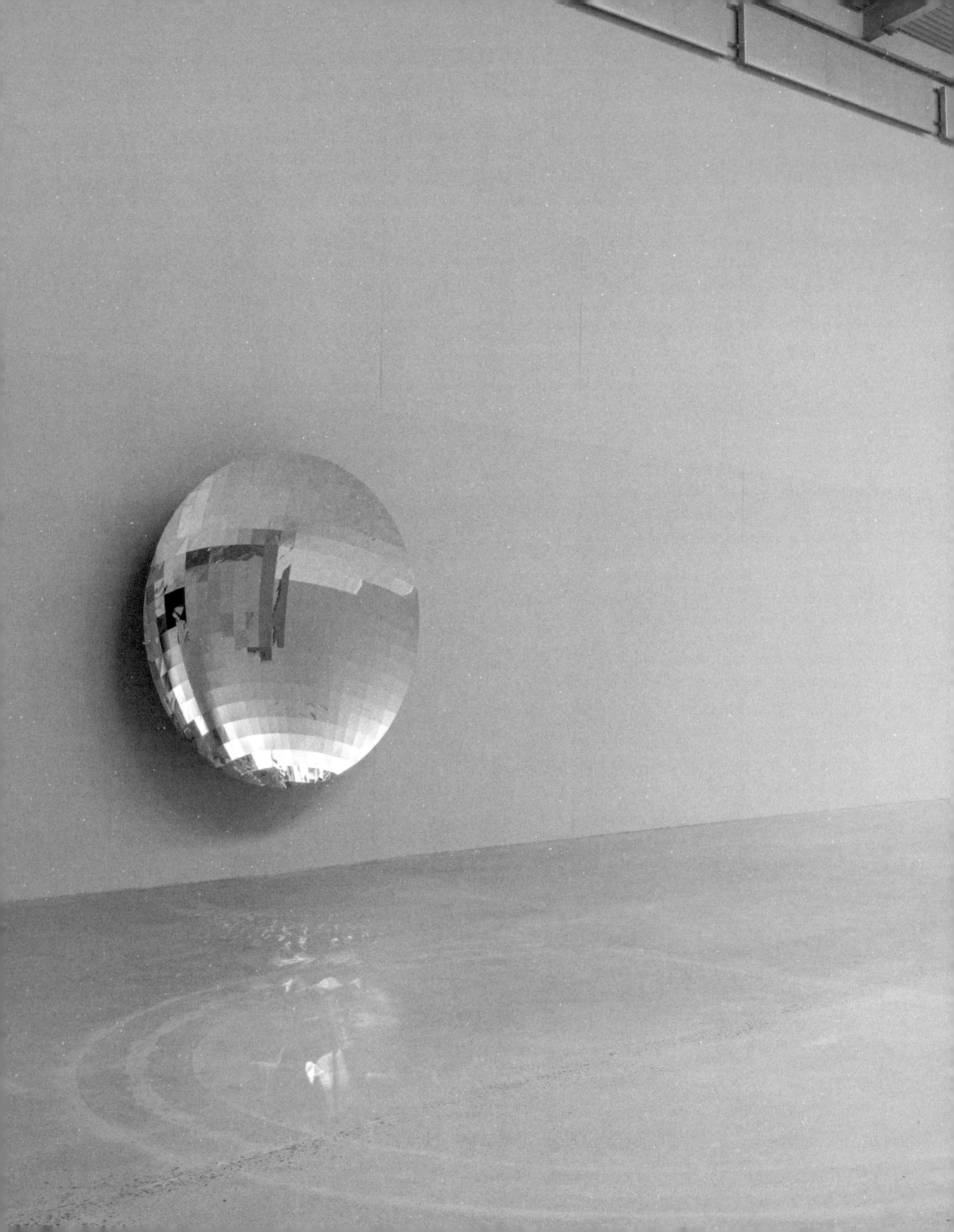

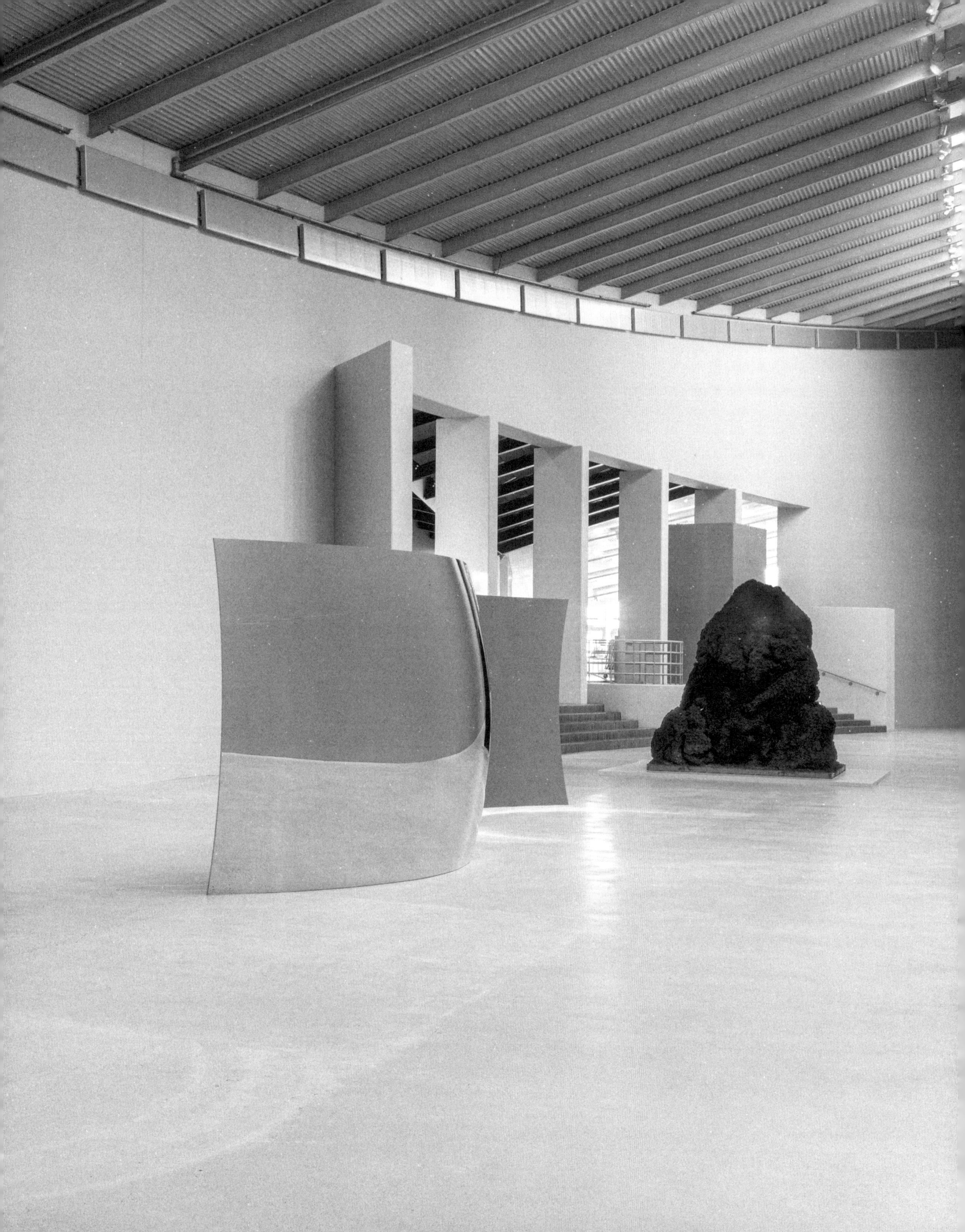

Facing the Void

Effect and Affect in Anish Kapoor's *Descent into Limbo*

Sarah Fredholm

Sarah Fredholm has been a curator at ARKEN since 2022. In addition to the Anish Kapoor show, she has curated exhibitions featuring Leonora Carrington (2022) and Eva Steen Christensen (2023). She holds an MA in art history from the University of Copenhagen and the Université de Paris 8 Vincennes-Saint-Denis, specialising in philosophical and critical angles on contemporary art.

There is something utterly dark before me. Not the kind of black I am used to seeing; this black contains a different sort of darkness. In fact, the colour is a very intense deep blue, but that is not how it immediately appears from a distance. Here, on the concrete floor at ARKEN, the darkness assumes the shape of a defined round field – simultaneously immaterial, tactile and difficult to define. I move around and lean over the field, trying to understand what I am seeing. I do not touch it, even though I want to know how the black feels. And I keep observing the darkness in an effort to come closer to understanding it.

The work is created by Anish Kapoor, and it was first exhibited in 1992. Its title, *Descent into Limbo* [pp. 107-109], instils in me the idea that the darkness extends *down* into the floor and is not 'just' on the surface of the floor, although it appears to be. My eyes cannot ascertain what is what. Feeling a growing sense of disorientation, I have to look away to avoid a dizzy spell. Turning my gaze back to the work, I feel a pull in my stomach. The hollow, as I have by now determined it to be, evokes a sense of standing by an abyss containing nothing but deep darkness. I stand before a void. Or at least that is what my senses tell me. The idea of emptiness, nothingness and infinity frightens me as I stand there in front of the work. Yet the darkness exerts a hypnotic pull, too, and I cannot tear myself away from the dark circle.

How are we to understand this work? And what is happening to me as I experience it? I am certainly affected – physically, sensorially, emotionally – by my encounter with Kapoor's *Descent into Limbo*. But what sort of meaning and significance can be assigned to the work's effect on me, to the experience of it?

This is the point of departure for the present text: in my disoriented experience of the work as it appears in ARKEN's exhibition *Anish Kapoor – Unseen*. I will examine this encounter with the void by focusing on the emotional or *affective* power that I believe Kapoor's works possess – with *Descent into Limbo* as a starting point.[1] What kind of potential resides in the work's effect on us as viewers? And in what ways is it meaningful to us?

The text begins with an introduction to Anish Kapoor's endeavours as an artist, including the art-historical landscape out of which his art has grown. Using affect as a theoretical lens, I will take a closer look at *Descent into Limbo* and the work's affective impact.[2]

BETWEEN WORK AND VIEWER
In *Descent into Limbo* Anish Kapoor plays with the viewer's senses in an exploration of the illusory qualities inherent in the material – the tactile, deep blue pigment that lines the hole in the floor, causing it to appear utterly black. Kapoor laid down the foundation for much of his later artistic work early in his career, in the late 1970s. For example, the first series of works he exhibited, *1000 Names* (1979–81) [p. 12], makes use of elements such as monochrome primary colours, pure pigments and minimalist, geometric shapes. It also explores what we cannot see: according to Kapoor, the sculptures in the series can be regarded as the tips of small icebergs that continue down below the surface of the room's floor. Thus, these works mark the beginning of the artist's exploration of illusion.[3] Another significant feature of *1000 Names* concerns the way in which the pigment extends directly out onto the floor. The sculptures almost merge with the exhibition space, which is otherwise traditionally understood as merely a setting, a framework separate from the work itself.[4]

During the first decades of the artist's endeavours, Kapoor's sculptures and installations grew increasingly monumental, often fully integrated into the space or architecture in which they were situated. The materials he utilises in his work ranges from pigment, wax, silicone and water to stone, steel, concrete and resin.[5] Regardless of scale, the artist's unique use of materials, surfaces, colours and space is what activates the senses, giving rise to the *affective* aspect.

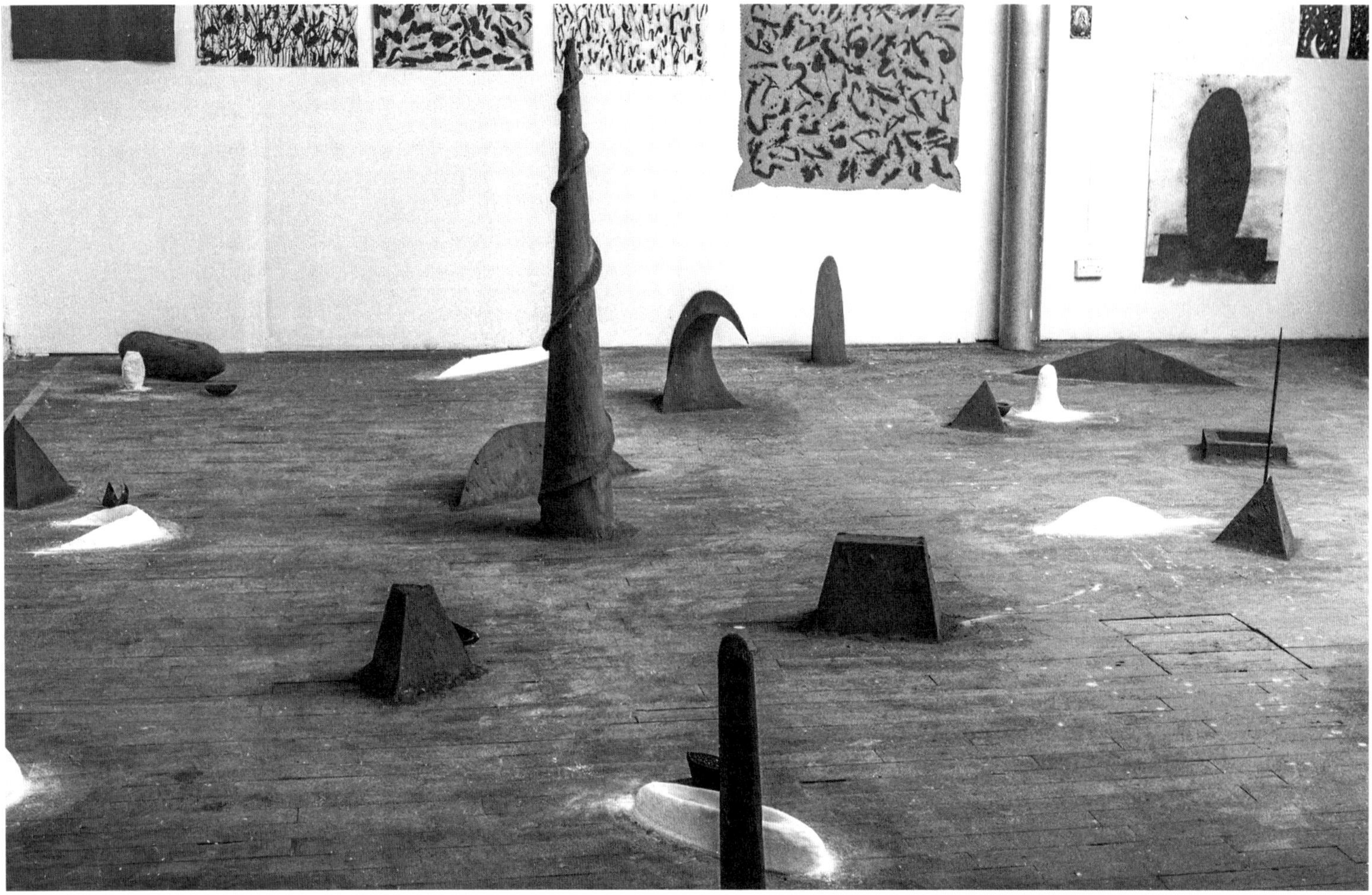

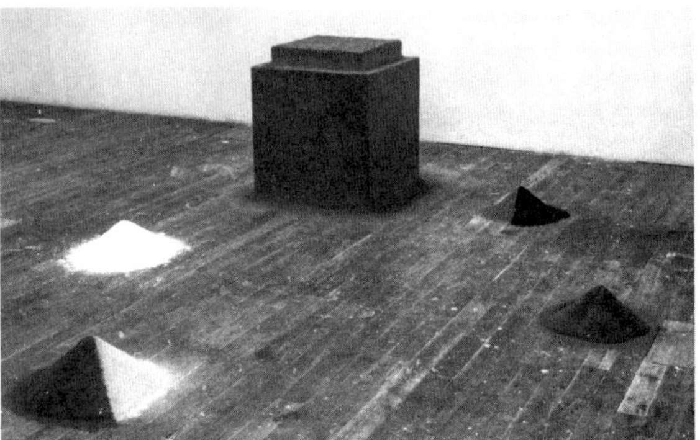

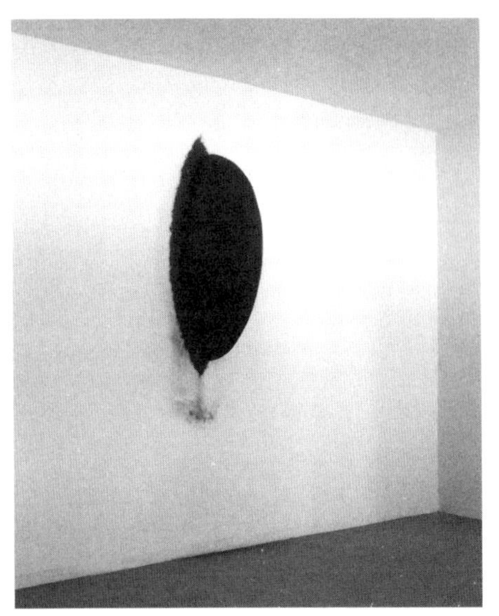

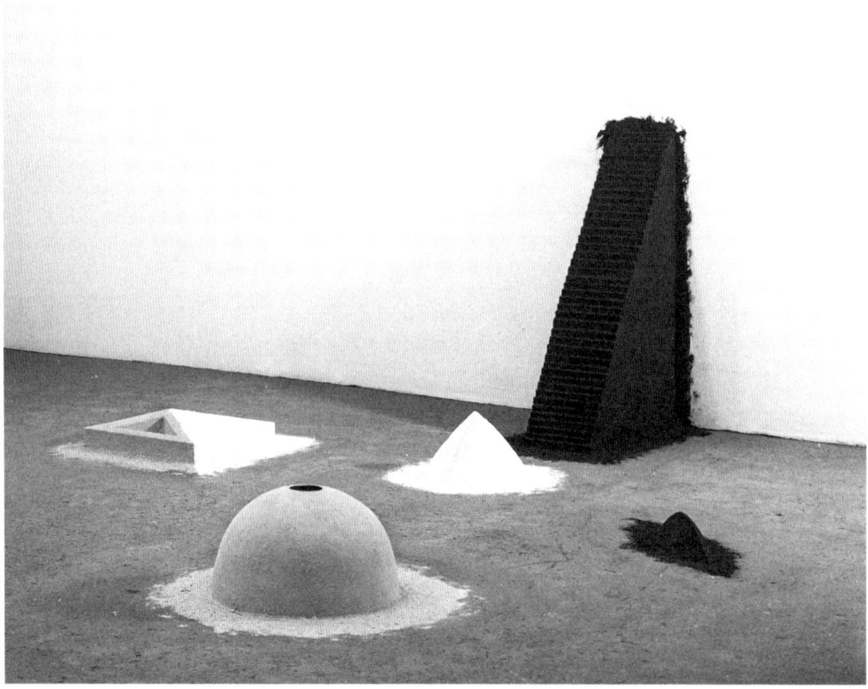

Anish Kapoor, *1000 Names*, 1979-83
Mixed media, pigment
Dimensions variable

When Anish Kapoor embarked on his studies in London in the 1970s, the British art scene was greatly influenced by the modernists' experiments with new materials and abstract sculptures.[6] At the same time, Kapoor became acquainted with the works of American minimalist artists such as Donald Judd (1928–1994) and Sol LeWitt (1928–2007) [see both on p. 15].[7] Thus, Kapoor's works also grew out of the innovative artistic movements arriving in Europe from the USA from the 1960s onwards: pop art, land art and, as mentioned, minimalism.[8]

The minimalists favoured sculptural formats of stringent simplicity and industrial materials devoid of any representation of reality or expression of emotions, ensuring that the sculptures could instead enter into a direct relationship with the viewer and the perceived reality. Free of symbolic content, a minimalist artwork could keep the viewer's attention focused on matters of time and space – in other words, on the physical aspects of the actual encounter with the work of art.[9] Minimalist artists were concerned with a viewer's experience of the works' material presence in the exhibition space. The approach was radical at the time: the minimalists changed the concept of sculpture, prompting a process of reconsideration and reinvention.[10] Minimalism did away with the dogmas of modernism, which dictated that the work of art should be self-reliant, cut off from the outside world and the viewer, and that it had to stick strictly to one artistic medium – either sculpture or painting.[11] In the eyes of the modernists, focusing on the viewer and the experience of the work in time and space was tantamount to blurring and mixing the media – and the temporal aspect was even considered *theatrical*.[12]

At the outset of his career, Kapoor operated in the wake of the minimalists' critical revolt against the modernist concept of the work of art. In his art, value is found *between* the work and viewer – in the effect of the work and in the experience thereof. At the same time, right from the outset Kapoor aimed for something other than the minimalists' cool, tightly composed 'specific objects', to use a term coined by Donald Judd about his own works.[13] Perhaps as a comment on this, Kapoor refers to his works as 'non-objects', meaning objects that are very insistently, physically present yet at the same time almost merge with the surrounding space.[14] *Descent into Limbo* is one such 'non-object', as are the works *S-Curve* (2006) [p. 91] and *Descension* (2014) [pp. 122-125] also featured in ARKEN's exhibition.

Furthermore, Anish Kapoor does not reject content or references in his works in the same way as, for example, Judd, and in this sense Kapoor's project has more of a kinship with post-minimalist artists such as Eva Hesse (1936–1970) [p. 15] and Richard Serra (1938–2024) [p. 16], whose works speak more directly to the body.[15] Both Hesse's and Serra's work is far more organic than that of the minimalists, and they take a more experimental approach to exploring the properties of their chosen materials. Hesse uses soft, organic materials that change over time and appeal directly to the viewer's body, while Serra's steel sculptures have a different physical effect on the viewer than the industrial sculptures made by the minimalists. Contrary to the minimalist credo, which, in the words of Frank Stella (1936–2024) [p. 16], reads "What you see is what you see",[16] Kapoor's works are *more* than what we can see. While the minimalist works referenced by Stella are nothing more than the colours, shapes, lines and surfaces that we immediately see, Kapoor's works occupy the tension-filled territory between what we can see and what we cannot see. Poised between the material and the immaterial, a work like *Descent into Limbo* invites an affective response in the viewer.

EMOTIONS IN ART
Anish Kapoor himself points out that his works have to do with the viewer's emotions and specific experience.[17] The point is borne out by my own emotional response in my encounter with the darkness in *Descent into Limbo*. But where did new art forms such as minimalism and

post-minimalism leave emotions as part of the art experience after the 1960s and 1970s?

In *Visualizing Feeling* from 2011, art historian Susan Best examines how the interpretation of art's 'affective dimension' can be considered a blind spot in art history – focusing particularly on late modern art from after 1960.[18] Of course, the notion that feelings and affect constitute a 'blind spot' in art history is open to discussion, and Best's claim could be nuanced by drawing on other discourses within art history regarding the impact of art on the viewer's body and mind. For example, phenomenological and performativity theoretical approaches take the viewers' bodily reactions into account in their analyses of works of art. However, Best also delimits her argument. She is not interested in works of art that clearly aim to express and evoke specific feelings – such as expressionist art, which, very briefly put, expresses the artist's psychological state and so can produce an emotional response in the viewer. Best is interested in artworks in which the affective dimension is more opaque and difficult to read. She believes that an understanding of this dimension requires efforts of attention and analysis that have generally tended to be devoted to new ways of representing or producing ideas in art.

Best explains that the issue of feelings in art received greater attention in the 19th and early 20th centuries, while art historians in the second half of the 20th century, with some exceptions, had little to say about the matter.[19] She also states that the 'blind spot' in the reception of art from the late modern period arose partly through the *conscious rejection* of emotion in minimalism, land art and conceptual art.[20] Minimalism is a good example, as the elimination of emotions in minimalist works does not mean that the works cannot arouse a viewer's emotions. Susan Best traces how contemporary art historians and critics actually emphasised emotional reactions in the encounter with minimalist works – describing them, for example, as 'boring', 'aggressive' and 'pleasant'. It just so happened that no actual analysis of these responses to the minimalists' works was carried out in the subsequent art historical discussions.[21]

According to Best, "feeling is at once spontaneous and obscure [...]. The affective dimension of art may be apprehended or felt immediately, but its meaning is not so readily apparent. This may be because this aspect of art is not part of the key methodologies that art history deploys".[22] She maintains that the art-historical conceptual apparatus does not traditionally associate feelings and the affective with meaning, and that the problem resides in a general tendency to subordinate the emotional and irrational to reason and the rational, thereby placing emotions and affect beyond the reach of interpretation.[23]

Within the theory of affect, which I will touch upon in the following section, we find a conceptual apparatus that facilitates an approach to art which takes a more immediate, sensory experience into account. Here, affect is considered *part of* the realm of the social, not opposed or subordinate to reason and the rational.[24] We will go on to see how this makes sense in relation to *Descent into Limbo*.

AFFECTIVE STATES

The aspects that are difficult to put into words regarding our encounters with Anish Kapoor's works – what happens when his art touches us on a deeper level – are often described in literature about his art as having to do with the sublime. In philosophy and art, 'the sublime' can be briefly explained as referring to something so overwhelming that we cannot comprehend it.[25] In other writings, the effect in Kapoor's works is described as a 'magical aura'[26] radiating from the works with almost spiritual power, or, referencing the psychoanalyst Sigmund Freud, as *unheimlich* or 'uncanny' instances of the familiar becoming alien and thus frightening.[27] Furthermore, much has been written about the perceptual and metaphysical dimensions of Kapoor's artistic work.[28] Affect theory makes it possible

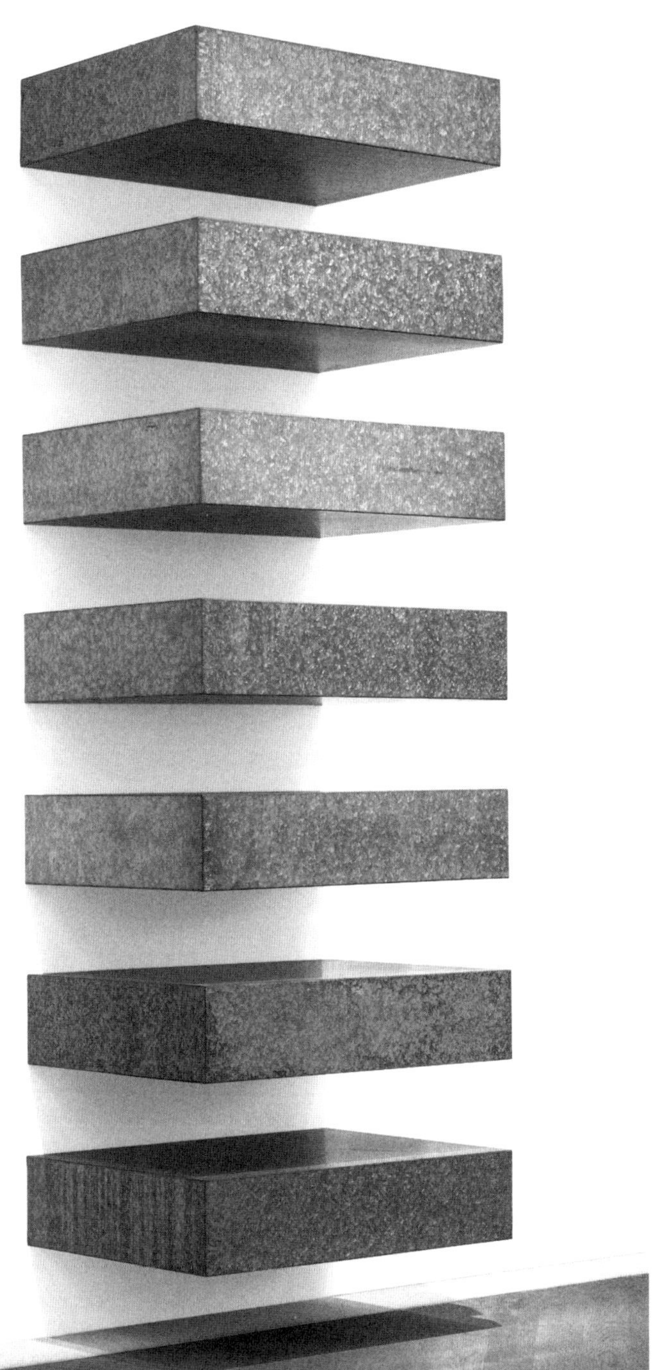

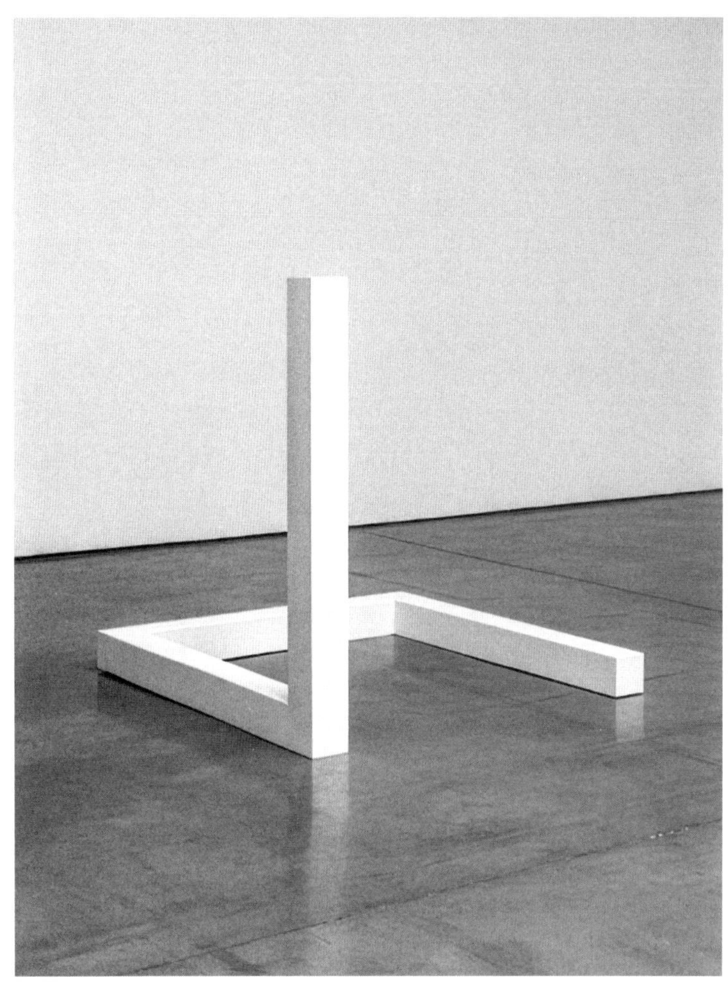

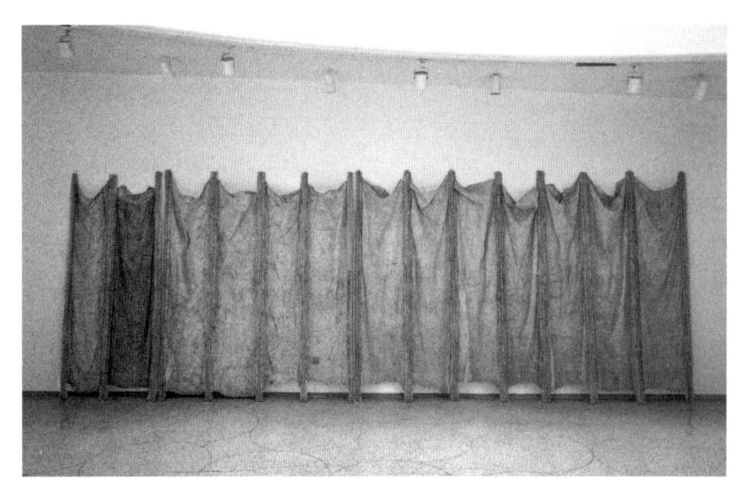

Donald Judd, Untitled, 1965
Galvanized iron; seven units, each 9 × 40 × 30"
[22.8 × 101.6 × 76.2 cm], installed vertically with
9" [22.8 cm] intervals.
Overall: 126 × 40 × 30" [319.2 × 101.6 × 76.2 cm]

Sol LeWitt, *Incomplete Open Cube 4/4,* 1974
Baked enamel on aluminium
106.7 × 106.7 × 106.7 cm

Eva Hesse, *Expanded Expansion,* 1969
Fibreglass, latex, cheesecloth
Installation variable, 3 units.
Overall: 3.1 × 7.6 m

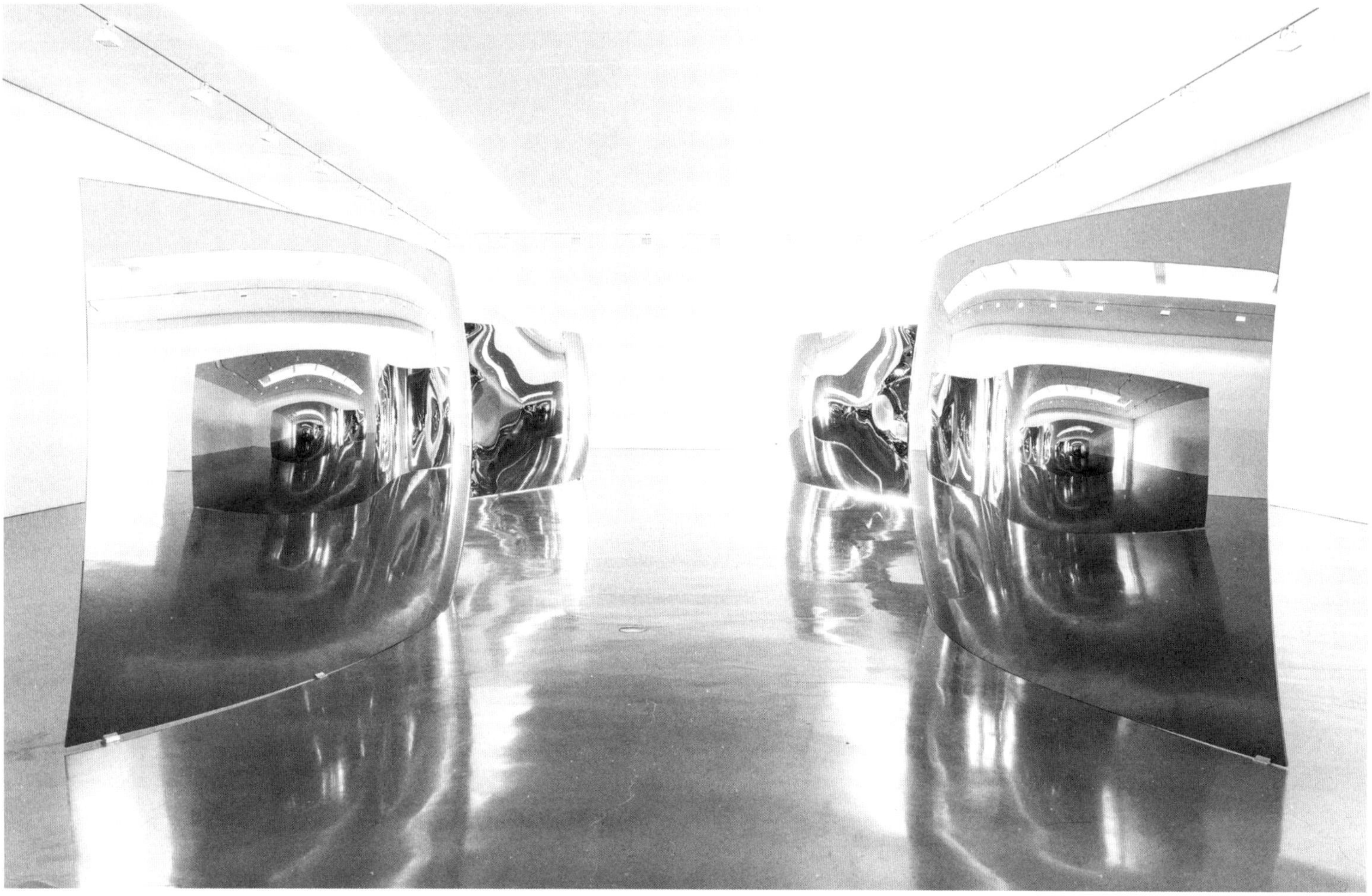

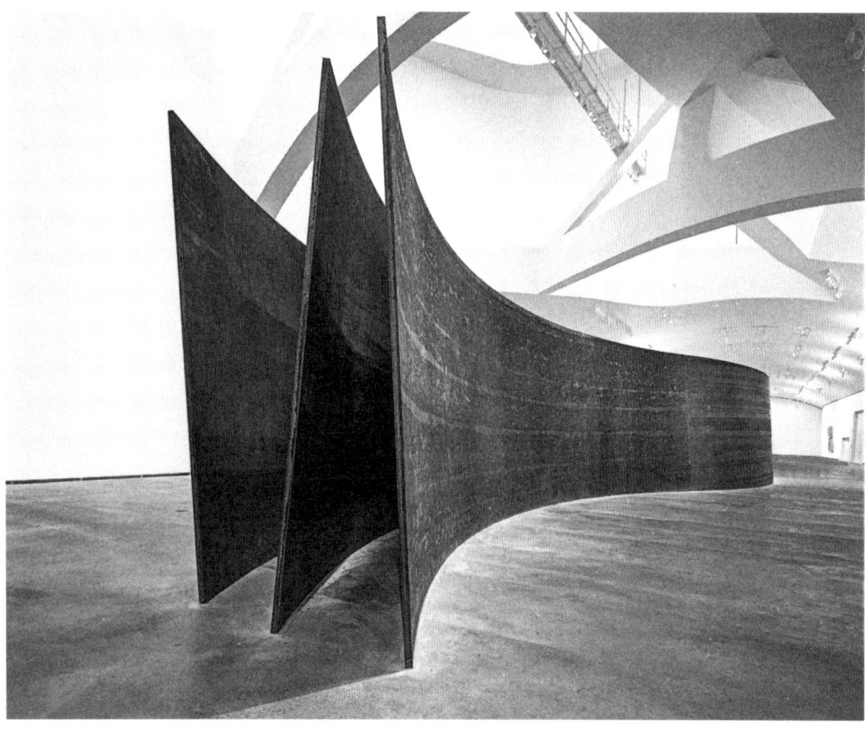

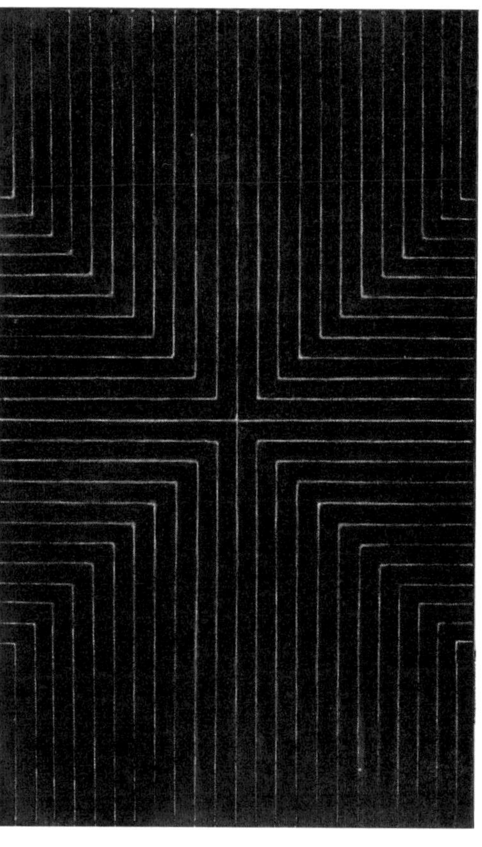

Anish Kapoor, *Double S-Curve*, 2019
Stainless steel
Dimensions variable

Richard Serra, *Snake,* 1994-97
Weathering steel
4 × 31.7 × 7.84 m

Frank Stella, *Die Fahne hoch!,* 1959
Raise the Flag!
Enamel on canvas
3.1 × 1.85 m

to more precisely describe the bodily sensations and states of mind that seem to arise in the encounter with many of Kapoor's works, thereby adding nuance to the more abstract phrases often used.

Since the 1990s, a large number of theories operating under the umbrella term 'the affective turn' have explored feelings and affect as phenomena and as objects of analysis.[29] It is here that we find a terminology that may help us understand how Anish Kapoor's art works affectively. An important point within affect theory is that affect and feelings are not internal, psychological states but rather something that arises in *relationships* in the social sphere.[30] This goes against the grain of our everyday perception of emotions as something you *have* and which come *from within.* Conversely, we speak about affect as something we *are in* – 'being in an affective state', which is closer to the point of view that links affect to relationships, contexts and events. Hence, 'affect' can be usefully used to describe what happens when you face *Descent into Limbo.*[31]

In my encounter with the work's indefinable, seemingly black void, I asked how we might understand its 'meaning' and our experience of the work. An obvious starting point would be to look at the title, with 'descent into limbo' denoting a movement down into a void, an intermediate state, or a transitional stage. The circle can be considered a representation of this, and perhaps the work deals with this limbo. Stopping the reading at this point would obviously yield only a superficial understanding that overlooks the effect the work has on the viewer. Doing so would pass by the affective dimension.

In the article "Affective Operations of Art and Literature",[32] art historian Ernst van Alphen distinguishes between an allegorical and an affective reading of art. The former strives to find a substantive explanation of what works are 'about' – the way I, in a somewhat caricatured manner, just tried to do with *Descent into Limbo.* According to van Alphen, the affective approach involves "a mode of reading that is sensitive to what I would like to call 'the affective operations of art and literature'". This pertains to another form of 'meaning' which cannot be as easily read as a sign or a symbol.[33]

Building on recent affect theory, it is interesting to examine what affect and emotions *do*, rather than what they *are*. And how affect and emotion are always already part of what we associate with rationality, thereby moving beyond the traditional opposition between reason and emotion.[34] Ernst van Alphen states the following about the affective encounter with art:

> Affects can arise within a person but they also come from without. They can be transmitted by the presence of another person, but also by an artwork or a (literary) text. They come from an interaction with objects, an environment, or other people. Because of its origin in interaction, one can say that the transmission of affect is social in origin, but biological and physical in effect.[35]

> This is to say that affect and feelings are not 'our own': they are transmitted by another person, by an object or by the surroundings in an interactive process. Van Alphen points out that this also applies when the transmitting agent is a work of art and not another human being, which challenges our usual understanding of the outside world. As he says, theories within humanism have instilled in us an idea that all materiality is passive and unconscious, and so we are not used to understanding objects as active 'agents'. But when we recognise material objects – and works of art – as potentially active, it becomes possible to describe what they can *do* to us, thus enabling us to see how works of art act affectively.[36]

BEING RESPONSIVE TO THE WORLD
Let us return to my encounter with *Descent into Limbo*. The agency of the work makes me, the beholder,

move around the dark circular shape in ARKEN's floor. The situation and the experience make me dizzy and disoriented; I also feel an uneasiness and something close to fear. Thus, the work's affective qualities affect me physically even as it sends my thoughts racing – evoking abstract notions of infinity, emptiness and nothingness. These ideas contribute to my affective response to the work. I enter into a relationship with the work, an interaction where my reactions might be called 'social' in origin – they arise in the context – yet physical in effect, to paraphrase Ernst van Alphen's description. The feelings of anxiety and fear that the work imposes on me come from outside.

The affective response and the thoughts and ideas evoked are closely entwined in the encounter with the work, meaning that it makes no sense to distinguish between something rational (my thoughts) and irrational (my affective response). What is more, this is a processual, fluid exchange that unfolds spatially.[37] The encounter takes place in a relational space that shapes and *affects* me. I am *in* an affective state rather than *having* the feelings. Kapoor's *Descent into Limbo* works in an affective manner insofar as the work turns into a state, a sensation or a mood that I feel physically. Thus, the work does not (only) function as an image of a void which we can try to read as a representation; it also exerts an influence through its materiality – the pigment's illusory play with the viewer's senses. I feel the work as a physical, sensual presence, an interlocutor that transmits affect.

The question is, then, what such an understanding of the work entails. What emerges when we shed light on the work's affective impact on the viewer? To explain this, Ernst van Alphen references philosopher Gilles Deleuze's idea of 'shock to thought':

The recognition of the role of the affective operations forces us to slow down – not shut down – the reading for meaning and our haste to reach that destiny. A hasty flight to (allegorical) meaning can only end up in the already known, in the recognition of conventional meanings, whereas the affective operations and the way they shock to thought are what opens a space for the not yet known.[38]

While an allegorical approach leads us to the already familiar, the affective approach paves the way for something new to emerge. The phrase 'shock to thought' implies that a potential change can occur in the affective encounter with the work.[39] Here, 'shock' should not be understood as something necessarily dramatic or violent. The Deleuzian affect theorist Brian Massumi speaks of 'micro-shocks' and describes them as "the kind that populate every moment of our lives. For example, a change in focus, or a rustle at a periphery of vision that draws the gaze towards it. In every shift of attention, there is an interruption, a momentary cut in the mode of onward development of life".[40] In my experience of *Descent into Limbo* this can be described as an insidious feeling of disquiet and disorientation which 'interrupts' my movement. The issue is not about clearly formulated *new* thoughts, a message or the like. In my encounter with the work, I am gripped by the work's agency – by what the work does, and what it makes me do, feel and reflect on. This is where the shift or 'micro-shock' occurs, my focus changes, and the speed of my reading of the work slows down, as Van Alphen describes it.

The affective encounter with the work holds potential for us to relate to the outside world as an open, dynamic network – and an intricate web of relationships, material elements, social actions, bodies and notions linked to this. Thus, affective art experiences like my encounter with *Descent into Limbo* may prompt us to glimpse how we are simply one material object among many, one subject among others. These are some of the *new* thoughts or sensations that can appear momentarily in the encounter with Kapoor's work, breaking away from conventional ideas about the passivity of the material world. The crucial aspect is that I feel the work affectively – more than just a representation of a void, it has active impact. The disorientation caused by the encounter even puts me quite literally out of my mind: the experience is beyond my control. Literary theorist Frederik Tygstrup describes the affective 'connection' as a responsiveness to the world, a willingness to listen.[41] In our encounter with the world – and all that is beyond our control – we are encouraged to be attentively open-minded.

MOVED AND CHANGED A LITTLE
The affective 'connection' will of course assume different forms depending on what we experience – and who is experiencing it. The same applies to the potential change and the breaking away from established thought patterns, which are also conditioned by the relationships and elements actualised in the relevant situation.[42]

In ARKEN's exhibition, Anish Kapoor's mirrored *S-Curve* meanders through the museum's largest gallery, the Art Axis. The sculptural 's' shape of the work reflects and distorts its surround-ings. Seen from one point my reflection is upside down, from another it is far too large, and as I move on the reflection of my body and the room appear distorted. The changeable mirror images in *S-Curve* embed themselves in my body – the work's agency or 'performance' sets me in motion. I feel a different kind of lightness here than when I faced the abysmal darkness of *Descent into Limbo*. Here, the interaction and exploration feel like play.

Kapoor's monumental *At the Edge of the World II* (1998) `[pp. 68-71]`, is also presented in the Art Axis. The dome-shaped structure hovers high above me, its underside covered in dark red pigment. The dome reaches almost all the way to the walls, so that the tactile red space envelops me as I stand below it. Looking up, I cannot tell where this space begins and ends. Thus, *At the Edge of the World II* delivers a sensory impact of yet another kind. In terms of material and effect, the work can be said to be reminiscent of the dark void in *Descent into Limbo*, but for me the sense of endlessness felt here is different. I become fascinated, and my movement through the exhibition comes to a halt so that I may stay in this feeling of infinity.

Anish Kapoor's works become transmitting agents for these states, affective-bodily sensations or moods which can pave the way for new thoughts and reflections – like 'micro-shocks' occurring in the periphery of my vision as I watch my own distorted reflection or stand transfixed at the spectacle of crimson infinity.

Just as no clearly formulated thoughts or insights arise out of the affective response, it should also be noted that it does not have a specific purpose. In her "Affect and the Participatory Event", art historian Camilla Jalving describes a form of *affective* participation in the art experience which challenges preconceived notions about *active* participation. She points out the impor-tance of not attributing any particular utilitarian value to affect in the experience of art, such as empowerment or critical thinking – we should abandon the idea that the viewer's (active) participation must lead to specific outcomes. While such ideals *may*, according to Jalving, be promoted in the affective encounter with the work, this will never be a clearly defined goal. The most important thing is that we feel affect, that we are *affected*: this is where the potential for 'the not yet known' arises.[43]

This is the potential that resonates in our encounters with Anish Kapoor's works. It is not about a change of attitudes or a critical awakening, but about a space of opportunity that paves the way for the unknown, allowing us to be moved and changed a little.

19

NOTES

1   Within affect theory, one of the major discussions concerns whether it makes sense to distinguish between affect, defined as physical-bodily experiences, and emotions, defined as psychological, inner states. Basically, both aspects, whether we call them affect or emotions, can be seen as part of a differentiated yet overlapping field of states of mind, moods, bodily experiences, etc. See Frederik Tygstrup, "Affekt og rum", in *Kultur&Klasse* 115, vol. II, 2013, pp. 17–19.

2   The different currents of affect theory can be divided into two overall 'schools'. One, inspired by the philosopher Gilles Deleuze, distinguishes between affect and feelings. The philosopher Brian Massumi is a central theorist within this direction. Here, affects are considered to be pre-linguistic, undifferentiated, directionless 'intensities', often regarded as physical-bodily phenomena, while emotions are considered post-linguistic, meaning that they are phenomena we can describe, categorise and linguistically distinguish from each other – such as 'hate' or 'joy'. The focus within this 'school' is on a 'reservoir' of fluid affects rather than on the specific, 'frozen' emotions. The other direction, of which the psychologist Silvan Tomkins is a particularly prominent representative, as is queer theorist Sara Ahmed, rejects the idea of a clear distinction identifying where affect ends and emotion begins. It does so based on the view that we can never have direct access to something pre-linguistic, pre-social. Within this camp of affect theory, the main focus is on what affect/emotions *do* – not on what affect/emotions essentially *are*. Thus, it can be considered an offshoot of, for example, performativity theory. See Mons Bissenbakker Frederiksen, "Styr dine følelser! En affektiv vending", in *I affekt: Skam, jubel og frygt som analysestrategi*, Mons Bissenbakker Frederiksen and Michael Nebeling Petersen (eds.), Varia, Center for Kvinde- og kønsforskning, vol. 9, 2012, pp. 4–18. In what follows I will subscribe to the latter 'school' while keeping an eye on Brian Massumi's approach to affect as outlined by affect and queer theorist Mons Bissenbakker Frederiksen in his review of the affect theory field. As he points out, speaking of two 'directions' runs the risk of being reductionist, yet this can be useful for our understanding of the currents. Bissenbakker Frederiksen, "Styr dine følelser! En affektiv vending", p. 6.

3   Clare Chapman, Lee Doonan, Tae Hyunsun et al. (eds.), *Anish Kapoor / Objects*, Leeum, Samsung Museum of Art, 2012, p. 22.

4   Chapman, Doonan, Hyunsun et al., *Anish Kapoor / Objects*, pp. 21–22.

5   Nicola Jacchia, Marie Nipper, and Anne Mette Thomsen (eds.), *Yves Klein, James Lee Byars, Anish Kapoor*, Cudemo, 2012, p. 124.

6   Chapman, Doonan, Hyunsun, et al., *Anish Kapoor / Objects*, p. 21.

7   In addition to the minimalist artists highlighted here, Kapoor was also inspired by figures such as Joseph Beuys, Marcel Duchamp, Walter de Maria, Paul Thek and Paul Neagu. See David Anfam (ed.), *Anish Kapoor*, Phaidon, 2009, p. 493.

8   Anne Ring Petersen, *Installationskunsten – mellem billede og scene*, Museum Tusculanums Forlag, 2009, p. 63.

9   Petersen, *Installationskunsten – mellem billede og scene*, p. 73.

10 One of the theorists who addressed the new departures taking place with minimalism and land art was the art critic Rosalind Krauss. Krauss does not consider the new types of works to be sculptures, responding to this change by formulating a number of new concepts to encompass the works emerging from the 1960s – sculpture in an 'expanded field'. Rosalind Krauss, *Sculpture in the Expanded Field*, The Viking Press, 1977.

11 Camilla Jalving, *Værk som handling*, Museum Tusculanums Forlag, 2011, pp. 36–37.

12 A seminal attack on the minimalists' new departures was made by the art critic Michael Fried. He favoured the modernist concept of the work of art, yet despite his critical starting point he very accurately summed up what minimalism was about. In *Art and Objecthood* from 1967, Fried describes minimalist works as 'literalist', meaning that they are not expressive or symbolic. They create a 'theatrical' effect which takes place over time "in a situation – one that, virtually by definition, *includes the beholder*". Taking a modernist point of view, Fried advocates the opposite of this – the work of art must, according to him, be autonomous and genre-specific. Michael Fried, *Art and Objecthood*, University of Chicago Press, 1998, p. 153.

13 Fried, "Art and Objecthood", p. 150.

14 Nicholas Baume, *Anish Kapoor: In conversation with Nicholas Baume*, 2008, https://anishkapoor.com/772/in-conversation-with-nicholas-baume (last accessed 31 January 2024).

15 Anish Kapoor Studio, *Anish Kapoor: Make New Space. Architectural Projects*, Steidl Verlag, 2020, pp. 557–558. In the 1980s, Anish Kapoor was also part of the New British Sculpture group, which reacted to the predominance of minimalism and conceptual art. See Anfam, *Anish Kapoor*, p. 495.

16 Bruce Glaser, "Questions to Stella and Judd", in Gregory Battcock (ed.), *Minimal Art: A Critical Anthology*, University of California Press, 1995, p. 158. Originally *Artnews* 65, no. 5, 1966.

17 Baume, *Anish Kapoor: In conversation with Nicholas Baume*, 2008, unpag.

18 Susan Best, *Visualizing Feeling: Affect and the Feminine Avant-garde*, I.B. Tauris & Co Ltd, 2011.

19 Best, *Visualizing Feeling*, p. 30.

20 Best, *Visualizing Feeling*, pp. 1–2.

21 Best, *Visualizing Feeling*, pp. 41–43.

22 Best, *Visualizing Feeling*, p. 7. In *Visualizing Feeling*, Best's purpose in pointing to the blind spot in art history is to examine four artistic practices from the 1960s–1970s, specifically those of Lygia Clark, Eva Hesse, Theresa Hak Kyung Cha and Ana Mendieta. Her analyses of the affective dimension in the work of these artists take a different form than my study of Anish Kapoor's works; only her introductory considerations form the basis of the present text.

23 Best, *Visualizing Feeling*, pp. 4–5.

24 Bissenbakker Frederiksen, "Styr dine følelser! En affektiv vending", p. 7.

25 See, for example, Chapman, Doonan, Hyunsun et al., *Anish Kapoor / Objects*, 20; Anthony Vidler, *Anish Kapoor Whiteout*, Charta, 2004, p. 8; Donna De Salvo, "Interview with Anish Kapoor", in Anfam (ed.), *Anish Kapoor*, p. 403; Vidal, "The Return of the *Aura*", p. 54; Anish Kapoor Studio, *Anish Kapoor: Make New Space*, pp. 560, 565.

26 Vidal, "The Return of the *Aura*", p. 41.

27 Vidler, *Anish Kapoor Whiteout*, p. 10; Christopher Bollas, "Materialising the unthought known: Reflections on the work of Anish Kapoor", in *Works, Thoughts, Experiments*, Museu de Arte Contemporanea de Serralves, 2018, p. 2.

28 Anish Kapoor Studio, *Anish Kapoor: Make New Space*, p. 557. Other approaches often seen in the treatment of Kapoor's art include the phenomenological (see, for example, Vidler, *Anish Kapoor Whiteout*) and psychoanalytical (see, for example, Bollas, "Materialising the unthought known"). Delving into greater detail on these issues falls beyond the scope of this article.

pp. 22-23
Foreground:
At the Edge of the World II, 1998
Background:
Untitled, 2022
Installation view,
ARKEN Museum of Contemporary Art, Ishøj

29   See note 2.

30   Bissenbakker Frederiksen, "Styr dine
     følelser! En affektiv vending", p. 7; Tygstrup,
     "Affekt og rum", p. 23.

31   Tygstrup, "Affekt og rum", pp. 18–19.

32   Ernst Van Alphen, "Affective Operations of
     Art and Literature", *Res: Anthropology and
     Aesthetics*, no. 53/54, The University of
     Chicago Press, 2008.

33   Van Alphen, "Affective Operations of Art and
     Literature", pp. 26–28.

34   Bissenbakker Frederiksen, "Styr dine
     følelser! En affektiv vending", pp. 8–12.

35   Van Alphen, "Affective Operations of Art and
     Literature", p. 23.

36   Van Alphen, "Affective Operations of Art and
     Literature", pp. 23–26. The 'affective turn'
     is akin to the 'performative turn' – where
     performativity is understood as an art-
     theoretical term for the work's performance
     and its aesthetic effect: both 'turns' focus
     on what objects *do* rather than on what they
     represent. Thus, in both 'turns' the focus is
     shifted away from meaning to the situation
     created by the work. See Camilla Jalving,
     "Affect and the Participatory Event", in
     ARKEN Bulletin, The Art of Taking Part,
     vol. 7, ARKEN Museum of Modern Art, 2017,
     p. 122.

37   As Frederik Tygstrup writes, the idea of *the
     spatial* is also a quality which affect theory
     attributes to the affective response: "When
     we speak about affect as an external reality:
     as something atmospheric, something
     ambient, meaning as something you 'are
     in' rather than something you 'have', we
     have already invested affect with spatial
     characteristics". Tygstrup, "Affekt og rum",
     pp. 24–26.

38   Van Alphen, "Affective Operations of Art and
     Literature", p. 30.

39   Deleuze's idea of 'shock to thought' is
     part of his broader philosophical project
     – a deconstruction of the oppositional
     relationships between philosophy and art,
     thoughts and emotions which pushes back
     the boundaries of traditional philosophy
     and opens up new possibilities for
     understanding and experiencing the world.
     Van Alphen, "Affective Operations of Art and
     Literature", p. 22.

40   Brian Massumi, quoted in Camilla M.
     Reestorff, "From Art-Work to Net-Work:
     Affective Effects of Political Art", in Britta
     Tim Knudsen (ed.), *Affective Methodologies:
     Developing Cultural Research Strategies
     for the Study of Affect* Palgrave Macmillan,
     2015, p. 12.

41   Tygstrup, "Affekt og rum", pp. 21–22.

42   Tygstrup, "Affekt og rum", pp. 21–23.

43   Jalving, "Affect and the Participatory Event",
     p. 128.

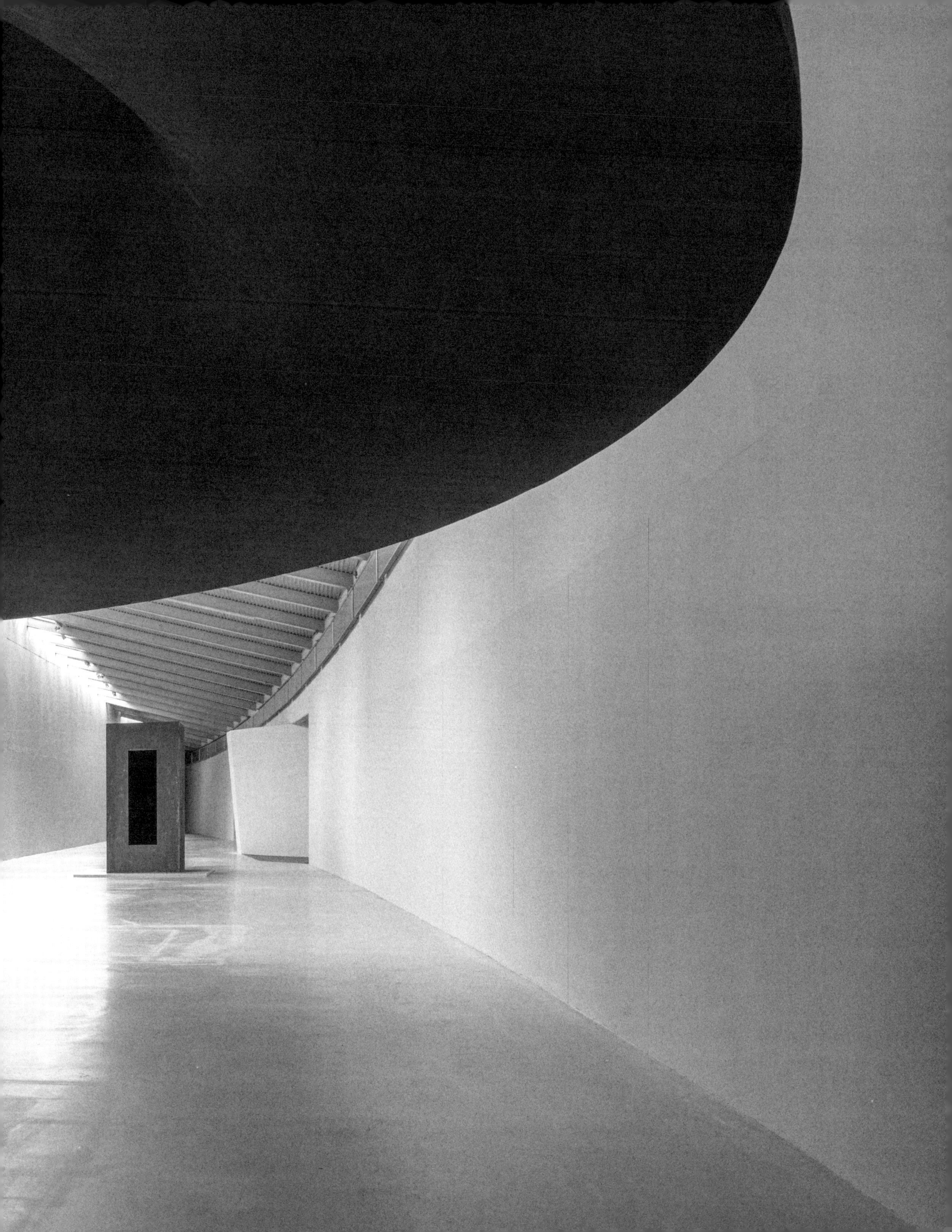

"Great art hovers in the space between meaning and no meaning"

Anish Kapoor in Conversation with Marie Nipper

This interview was conducted in February 2024 by Marie Nipper, director of ARKEN.

Marie Nipper
Your show at ARKEN spans forty years of artistic practice. How do you see your work as having evolved over the past four decades?

Anish Kapoor
I have a practice which is a daily reality for me. Out of my practice ideas and issues occur and reoccur.

I have often said that I have nothing to say as an artist. By this I mean that I have no message to give in the work; instead my work is a physical medium, through which I seek to explore what is unseen or half seen – the unseen half known in me. It surprises me that the questions that arise in my practice are recurring and are, over long periods of time, more or less consistent.

MN
You venture into this exploration through a variety of materials. Can you tell us about this vocabulary of materials that runs through your practice, for instance your work with stainless steel and pigment?

AK
One of the questions that has arisen for me and that I have explored in my practice is the entity I call the 'non-object'. The object that is void, or less than present, or both present and absent. I have explored this in many ways: pigment, concave stainless steel, painting, stone, the blackest black, etc. Polished stainless steel mirror in concave form is surprising and contradictory, it requires perfection, and when this is achieved it turns the world upside down and fills the space up with mirror, confounding the eye and the hand. Pigment, on the other hand, is fragile and ephemeral – I have sought to work with this. To touch is to destroy it. I see these objects as icebergs emerging, with most of the object hidden below the floor or behind the wall.

Andrea Mantegna
Descent into Limbo, 1492
Tempera and gold on panel
38.8 cm × 42.3 cm

Anish Kapoor
Adam, 1988-89
Sandstone, pigment
239 × 120 × 104 cm

Gian Lorenzo Bernini
Ecstasy of Saint Teresa, 1647-52
Marble
Height 150 cm

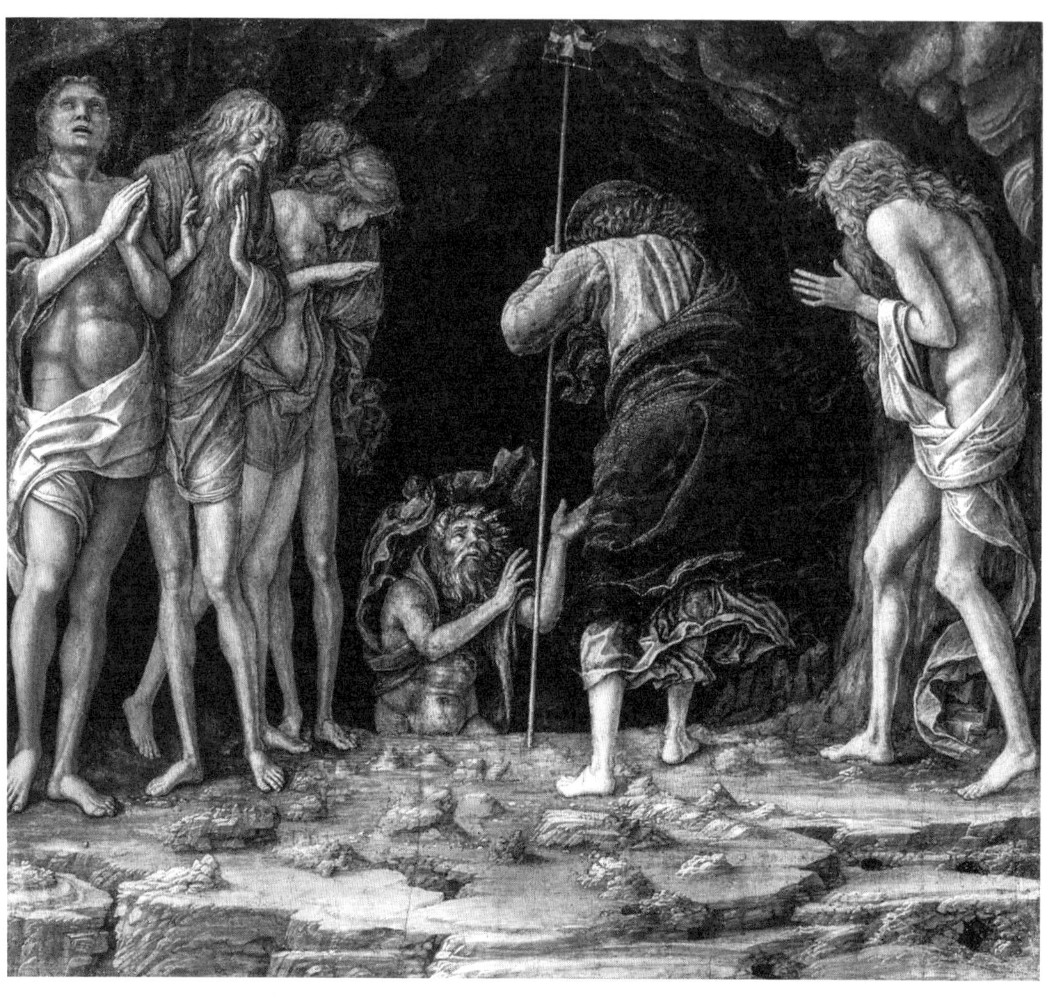

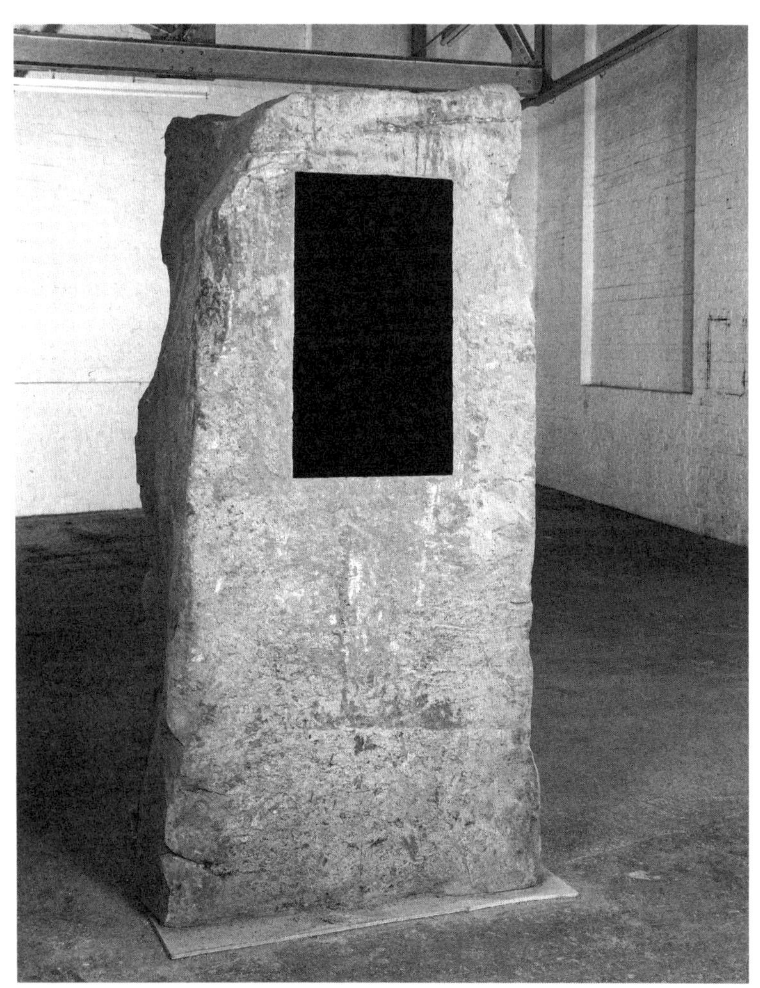

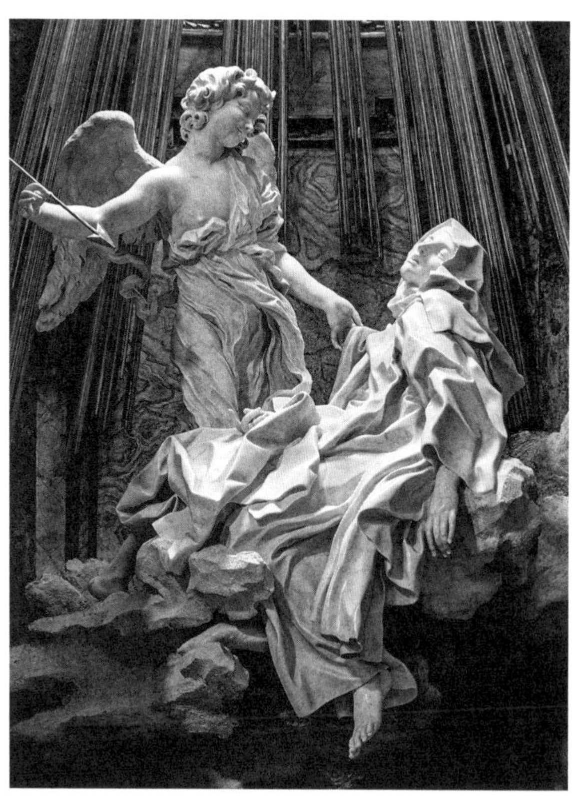

MN

Descent into Limbo (1992, ed.) [pp. 107-109], is a good example of a work where you use dark pigment. What does the void mean to you?

AK

The void works made with pigment fill space with darkness. They are empty objects full of darkness.

The black works propose four-dimensional objects. To explain, in the Renaissance there were two great discoveries: perspective, and the fold – the fold of fabric, the sign of being of the body. If this black material is put onto a fold the fold disappears, it can't be seen. It is therefore my contention that this takes the object beyond being – beyond body, into the fourth dimension.

Descent into Limbo takes its title from Mantegna.[1] In his painting Christ holds a staff and is at the precipice of a dark cave. He is about to descend. Dante is of course present.[2]

My *Descent into Limbo* is a void in the floor filled with darkness. It is as if there is a black carpet on the floor. I am interested in the tension between empty and full. The Kantian sublime has it that beauty is linked to oblivion.[3] At the edge of the precipice, falling into infinite darkness.

MN

You have a work called *Memory* (2008, ed.) [pp. 50-55], in the exhibition. We need to move around this work – a 24-tonne Corten steel tank – and use our memory to understand the full scale and shape of the sculptural form. Is it your way of telling us to put more effort into the act of seeing?

AK

No. As I say, I have no message to give and nothing to teach. *Memory* is an object with two aspects that are separated from each other by a wall. On one side of the wall is the large

Corten object and on the other is the empty interior of the same object. They are the same and completely different. The interior is bigger than that which contains it.

MN

Many of your works seem to require a perception that takes place over time. What role does time play for you?

AK

Time is a mysterious thing.
In poetic moments of wonder time stands still.
That is what I am after.

MN

The site-responsive work in the exhibition often obstructs the normal pathways through the museum or modifies the exhibition spaces – how do you relate to the architecture in which your works are presented?

AK

Sculpture is to do with space. It is not just the display of an object but the interaction between object and space that is of essence. Of course the body is implicit in this conversation.

There can be poetic resonance when the conversation between the object and the architecture is right. Sometimes this requires the space to be disrupted or interfered with.

MN

Your work seems to range freely among religious, mythological and intellectual traditions. What role does religion or spirituality play in your work?

AK

I don't believe that we can set out to 'make' something spiritual. Paul Celan (1920–1970, ed.), the great poet, said: "A bad poem is one which falls into meaning." Falls into meaning … Great art hovers in the space between meaning and no meaning. When this condition of a thing is present, it is art, and I dare say it is spiritual. The mysterious space of unknowing or half knowing.

The universe is dual: light and dark, inside and outside, male and female. We have constructed our moral universe around this reality. It is my understanding that because of this moral duality that is always in our consciousness, we human beings have unavoidable religious leanings. We are religious beings. Science is unable to tell us much about consciousness and gives no clue to questions like 'Where was I before I was born?' or 'Where do I go after I die?' In poetry and in art we can speculate about consciousness and the big questions of life and death – we must do no less. These are not acts of knowledge, they are linked to long cultural traditions and intuitive speculations – poetic acts.

NOTES

1 Renaissance artist Andrea Mantegna (c. 1431–1506) created his *Discesa al Limbo* in 1492.
2 The first part of the Italian poet, writer and philosopher Dante Alighieri's (c. 1265–1321) 14th-century work *The Divine Comedy* is called "Dante's Inferno".
3 See the German philosopher Immanuel Kant's (1724–1804) *Beobachtungen über das Gefühl des Schönen und Erhabenen* (Observations on the Feeling of the Beautiful and the Sublime), 1764.

Transcendence

Pireeni Sundaralingam

Pireeni Sundaralingam is a cognitive scientist and poet. Educated at the University of Oxford and at MIT, she has held a variety of posts, including Principal Advisor on Human Potential at the unrealised UN Museum, Copenhagen, and Poet Laureate at University College, Oxford. She consults worldwide for governments, cultural institutions and major film studios on human flourishing and neuro-resilience.

We live in an era marked by seismic renegotiations of the body's boundaries: a time of deepfakes, selfie tsunamis and an increasing number of virtual realities where we can slough off our physical selves as if leaving crumpled clothes at the edge of a sterile pool. There is an increasing tension between our conscious selves and the materiality of our physical bodies. Even as for-profit groups offer us the chance to leave behind our bodies, shed our skins and travel to their sparkling new worlds, our interactions with digital technologies are downgrading our corporeal selves. The more time we spend staring at digital screens, for example, according to emerging research, the more that the hardware and software of our own visual system degrades and the less we are able to see the world around us.[1] We become near-sighted, both literally and metaphorically.

Against the backdrop of this neo-cartesian nightmare, in which our consciousness is artificially being pulled apart from our physical selves, Anish Kapoor's works assume a fresh urgency. From the dialogic surfaces of the mirror works, to the sensory hyperpresence of installations such as *My Red Homeland* (2003) [pp. 136-139] and *Descension* (2014) [pp. 122-125], and the interrogative scale of pieces such as *At the Edge of the World II* (1998) [pp. 68-71] and *Memory* (2008) [pp. 50-55], these are interrogations that call the human body back into the room. Here are works that demand a viewer's real and solid presence moving through the gallery space, assembling meaning through dynamic interactions with each object. And ARKEN's architecture playfully destabilises this experience even further, making conscious the fragmented acts of perception through which our moving bodies construct our understanding. There is an echo here of the foundational experiments conducted into visual development, those that demonstrated that it is the physical experience of actively moving through the world (rather than passively being fed visual information) that is crucial for humans developing the ability to see.[2] It is in the call and response with our physical environment that we make ourselves.

Yet we live, these days, within highly engineered flat spaces. Adults currently spend nearly seven hours a day on average staring at the virtual walls of their phones,[3] while 45% of a representative panel of teenagers in the US report being online continuously.[4] Even our young children spend twice as much time interacting with flat screens than interacting with their three-dimensional parents.[5] Addicted to the certainty of swift, simplistic answers, we spend our days within the rectangular cages that we hold within our hands, trapped on the treadmill of the endless scroll.

SENSORY CAJOLINGS
The term 'anthropos' (Greek for 'human') can be translated to 'the one who looks up', and the pieces in the Anish Kapoor exhibition at ARKEN force us to look up, look out and rethink the scales through which we are moving our bodies and rewiring our brains. In an age in which our spaces of engagement have become constrained to a few inches from our face, works such as *At the Edge of the World II* create a brooding overhead pressure, daring us to look up and confront the spaces left empty by our vanished gods, those powerful spaces where our earthbound bodies formerly addressed and dialogued with the divine.

We are called back into the living, physical world, moreover, by the sensory cajolings of the pieces of Anish Kapoor: the echoes of air current across our skin as we walk between volumes and voids, the shifts in sound waves as we circumambulate the works. It is not just the presence of senses that has a profound impact, but also their absence. A terrible vertigo arises when these senses are denied. In *Destierro* (2017) [pp. 148-151], for example, we are presented with a vast, turbulent terrain that has been censored from our touch. What is it to stand and smell and see, yet not be able to touch?

The undulating landscape of *Destierro* is cordoned off from physical contact with our human bodies, even as a hungry machine squats squarely in its midst, asserting its gaping claw. Earth and air, water and light: we have the chance to observe our bodies changing across the compass points of the elements, our journey through the gallery space a voyage of call and response. Here is an opportunity to interrogate our bodies, to come to terms with the fact that we are, in turn, mere sacks of water and clay, spirit and breath.

Although our bodies are approximately 60% water,[6] we tend to overlook even this most fundamental of elements, its personality, its behavioural tics. All too often we see water as something contained, a controlled domesticated colourless liquid in our cups and glasses, the tame fluid that flows from our taps. We interact with water throughout our daily lives, bathing in it, drinking it, cooking and cleaning with it, and yet what do we really notice of its presence? How many times have we all seen water spill onto a nearby surface, and yet what have we actually seen, in all our many years of looking? Ask someone what happens when you spill water onto a flat tabletop and, invariably, they describe water forming a flat sheet, flowing off the table until all of it is on the floor. And yet water cannot, does not, lie flat in this way. Pour a little water onto a tabletop and it forms into fat droplets that do not lie flat but bulge and swell, sticking fat bellies out away from the table's surface. Even when water does pour off an edge, there is no single simple movement of water flowing in one direction: there's a pull and push between, on the one hand, gravity dragging water downwards, and on the other, the electrostatic forces inherent in water, resisting gravity and keeping the water in place. Yet the cognitive auto-correct of our neural systems all too often trips us up, getting in the way of us seeing what lies in front of us.

The magnificence of Kapoor's *Descension* at the ARKEN exhibition is that it reinvigorates our relationship to the most fundamental elements in our surroundings. The sheer scale of its power and unpredictability encourages us to enter a deeper level of dialogue with the materials of the installation, the gallery and the transience of our own fragile flesh. We cannot look away. Through sound and smell, through the groaning of the waters, we are called back into the room, and into our corporeal selves, the fractured components of our physical selves conjured and consolidated, like wayward asteroids pulled into orbit by the gravity of a larger, astral body. *Descension* calls us back into the room. We are placed in a position of homage, looking on at the cogitations of a thunderous, elemental force. Instead of searching skywards, we now find ourselves gazing downwards, confronting the immanence of the spaces lying beneath our feet. The void is no longer silent but instead calls ferociously, summoning us into its presence, pulling us back into our physical bodies, insisting on new dialogues.

INVERTING OUR ATTENTION
In Greek mythology, the Erinyes (the Furies) would punish erring mortals by amplifying their inner monologues, making each person conscious only of their own voices and worries: cutting off their awareness of those around them, of relationships, of their identity as an embodied self in dynamic relationship to the sky, the ground, the people around them. Anish Kapoor's works force us to confront other, more difficult forms of discourse. They invert our attention. They insist we return to the full capacity of our bodies in relationship. They inveigle us to renounce our narcissistic desire for control and containment, and instead open ourselves up to more nuanced forms of dialogue with our three-dimensional selves and our physical surroundings, to pause and reconsider.

Kapoor's works stand in exuberant contrast to the algorithm-driven spaces in which we spend so many of our waking hours, the for-profit digital spaces that have deliberately been built to amplify certainty, simplicity and speed, but at the most terrible cost to our nuanced, multi-dimensional selves. Our neural systems are predisposed towards imposing binary categories, especially under conditions of threat or time pressure. The faster we are forced to think and act, and the more that we scroll down digital lists, the more that our perceptual and cognitive systems become recalibrated at a neurological level towards being able to see only simple answers, parsing the world into heroes and villains, linear causalities. We may be training AIs but they, in turn, are training us, to lose our capacity for nuance, as well as our ability to navigate the ambiguity that allows the human brain to spark extraordinary ideas and take fire.

As is the case at ARKEN, Kapoor's installations invert the status quo, complicating the easy solution of simple answers, catapulting us into spaces of ambiguity. It is through such spaces of uncertainty that we transcend the fury of our modern repeating monologues, where we can again encounter the ineffable, and once more find our sense of self.

NOTES

1 Jiaxing Wang, Ying Li, David Musch et al., "Progression of Myopia in School-Aged Children after Covid-19 Home Confinement", in *JAMA Ophthalmology* 139, no. 3, 2021, pp. 293–300.
2 Kathryn Rose, Ian Morgan, Jenny Ip et al., "Outdoor Activity Reduces the Prevalence of Myopia in Children", in *Opthamology* 115, no. 8, 2008, pp. 1279–85; Ezequiel Di Paolo, Thomas Buhrmann and Xabier Barandiaran, *Sensorimotor Life: An Enactive Proposal*, Oxford University Press, 2017.
3 See https://www.statista.com/statistics/1380282/daily-time-spent-online-global/ (last accessed 13 February 2024).
4 Monica Anderson and Jingjing Jiang, "Teens, Social Media & Technology", Pew Research Center, 2018.
5 Laura Donnelly, "Children Spend Twice as Long on Smartphones as Talking to Parents", in *The Telegraph*, 7 February 2019.
6 See https://en.wikipedia.org/wiki/Body_water (last accessed 13 February 2024).

pp. 34-35
Destierro, 2017
Earth, pigment, mechanical digger
Dimensions variable
Installation view,
ARKEN Museum of Contemporary Art, Ishøj

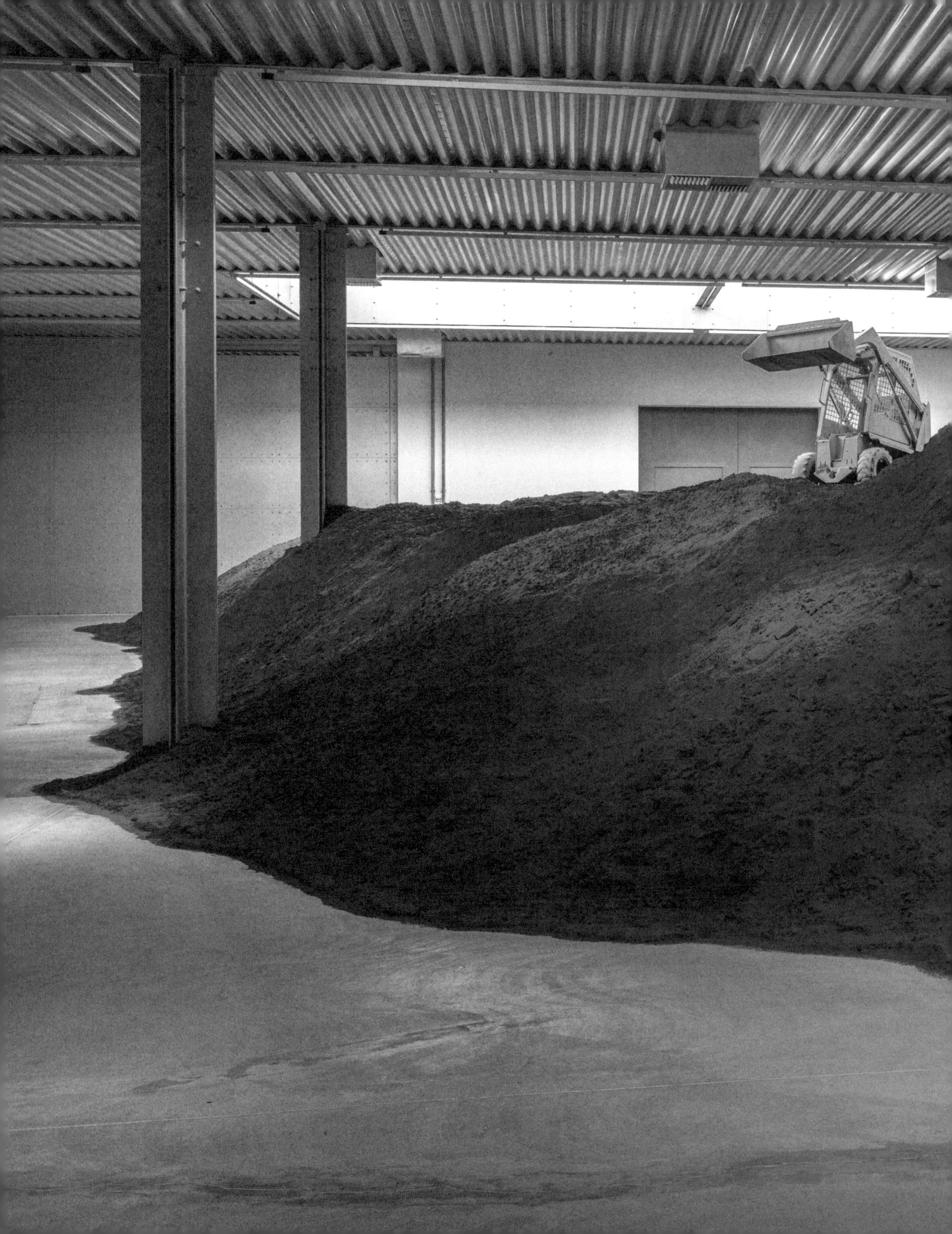

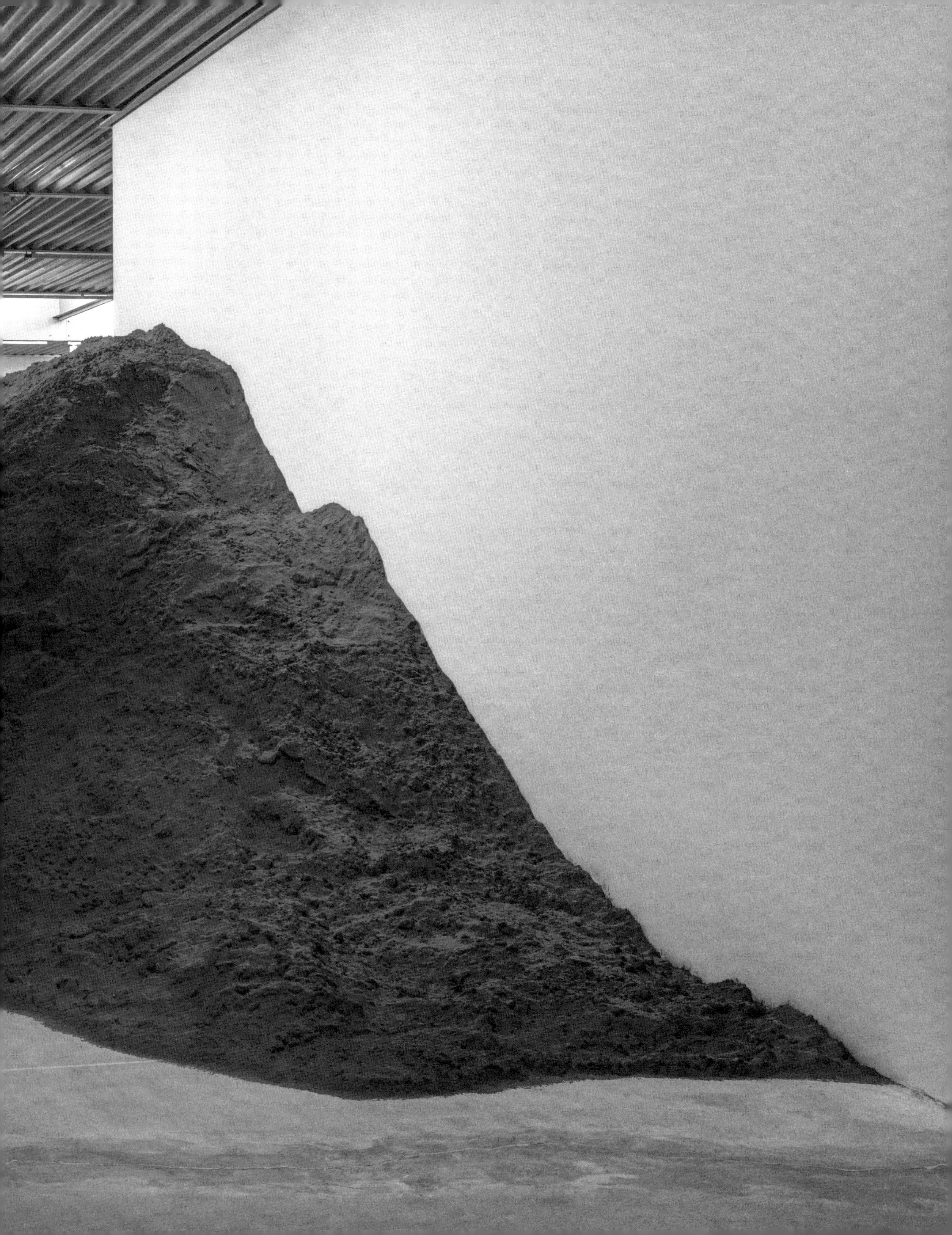

S-Curve Submerged

Anish Kapoor and the
Art of Changing Place

Mari Hvattum

Mari Hvattum is an architect and architectural historian. She is a professor at the Oslo School of Architecture and Design and a specialist in nineteenth-century architectural thinking. Her latest book is *Style and Solitude. The History of an Architectural Problem* (2023).

In August 2023, south-eastern Norway suffered the extreme weather named 'Hans' – five days of extreme rain followed by heavy flooding. One of the areas hit the hardest was the Randselva region, where towns, roads and farmsteads were flooded, including the pulp-mill-turned-sculpture-park Kistefos where Anish Kapoor's *S-Curve* (2006) [p. 38] normally sits peacefully but prominently on an artificial island in the river. During Hans, however, the peace dissipated. If, in normal times, the hyper-reflecting, gently undulating steel sheet presents a playful and captivating view of the world upside down and back to front, the flood rendered it, literally, a mirror of destruction. Submerged in the dirty rapids, it seemed to reflect a truly upended world.

Anish Kapoor is a master of transformation and metamorphosis. Materials, objects, and spaces – even people – are altered by means of reflection, levitation, colour and depth into something subtly but distinctly different. One of the targets for this almost alchemical transformation is place itself. While some of Kapoor's works may appear to augment and confirm their sites – like the way *Cloud Gate* (2004) [pp. 94-95] seems to make Chicago even more Chicago-like, or *Sky Mirror* (2001) wraps the city of Nottingham in an eminently recognizable upside-down image of itself – more often than not the artist operates by estrangement and surprise. The shockingly bright piece of sky taken down into the shaft-like space of the Rockefeller Center courtyard momentarily changed Manhattan, creating, for a few weeks in the autumn of 2006, a new place. The cuts and cavities evoked in works such as *Descent into Limbo* (1992) [pp. 107-109] and *Memory* (2008) [pp. 50-55] open up other worlds, hinting at unfathomable depths lurking beneath the veneer-like surfaces of the modern interior. And the utter weirdness of encountering a gurgling, foaming maelstrom inserted into an otherwise unremarkable floor (*Descension*, 2014 [pp. 122-125]) replaces for a second the 'actual' gallery space with an array of imaginary places. It is as if the incompatibility of the artwork with its surroundings produces a peculiar form of displacement; that the shock of finding water where there should be none alters both the water itself and the space into which it is inserted.

This intriguing oscillation between the place-confirming and the place-defying belongs to a long tradition. Eighteenth-century landscape theorists spoke about *fabriques*, defined by Jean-Marie Morel in his 1776 *Théorie des Jardins* as "all those constructions which human ingenuity adds to nature for the embellishment of gardens".[1] Follies in the eighteenth-century landscape garden played a double role. On the one hand, they augmented and expressed the character of their place, like the way a gothic hermitage might intensify the melancholy of a pine thicket or a classical temple augment the beauty of a woodland clearing. On the other hand, the pavilions, bridges, sculptures and grottos dotted about in the eighteenth-century landscape garden would also alter their places altogether, transporting the visitor from, say, a boggy Wiltshire in the South of England to a mythical Arcadia in ancient Greece. Ovid's *Metamorphoses* was a key reference in these gardens, where transformation – of substances as well as souls – was enacted through architecture, sculpture and landscape. Descending into the grotto at Stourhead in the UK, for instance, is like entering a human-made version of Ovid's 'deep world' in which sleeping marble nymphs and furious river gods negotiate between this world and the ones beyond. Heavy-duty engineering and subtle visual trickery go in tandem to create the perfect, place-defying illusion.[2]

Kapoor's work carries all the ambiguity of eighteenth-century *fabriques* and plays cunningly on the theme of metamorphosis. As the soft turns hard, the light turns dark, and voids turn to substance (and vice versa), the viewer is transported to different times and places. The

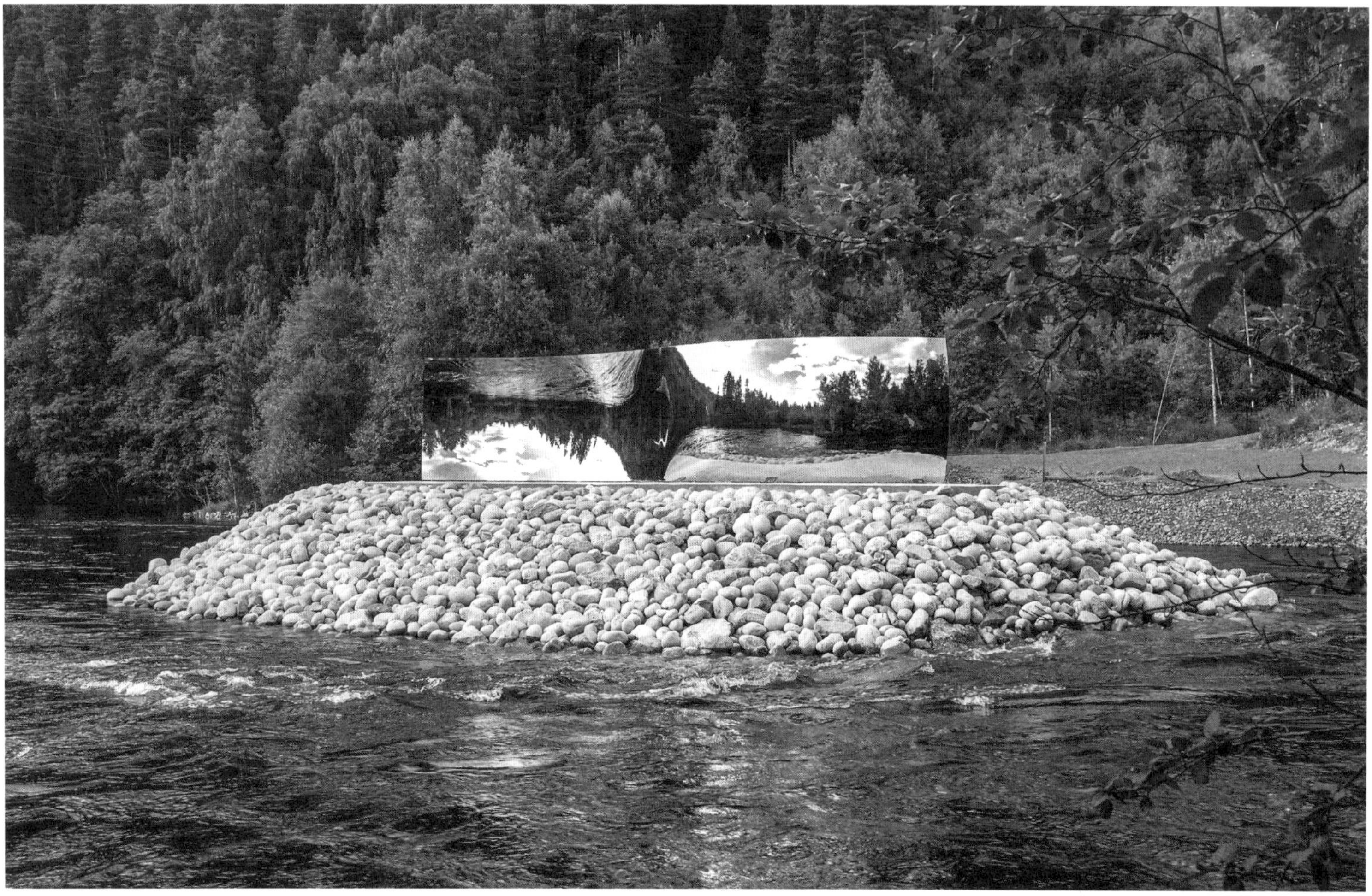

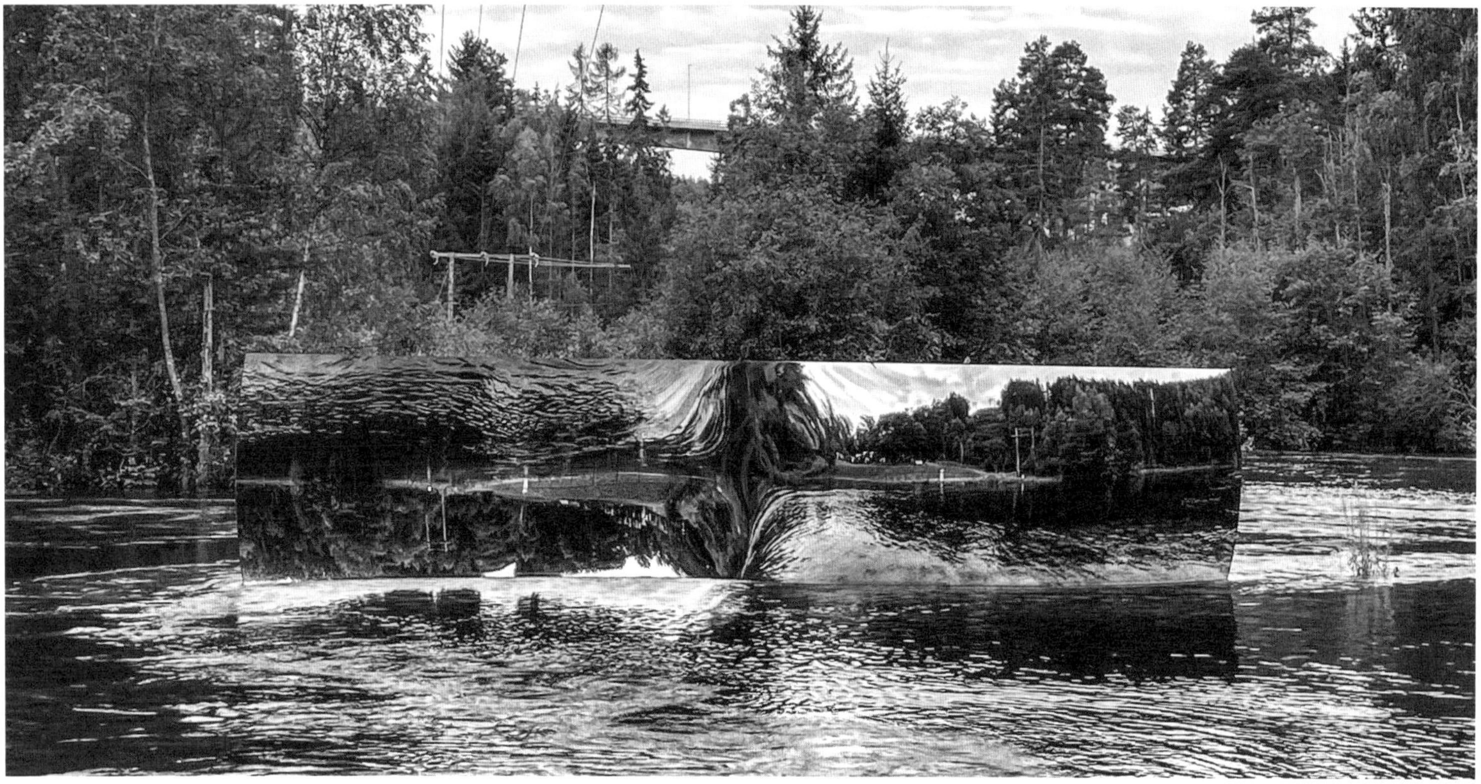

Anish Kapoor, *S-Curve*, 2006
Stainless steel
216.5 × 975.4 × 121.9 cm
Kistefos Museum before and
after the great storm in August 2023

S-Curve at Kistefos is a case in point. At first glance, it sits politely on its cobble island, projecting a benign if slightly skewed image of its surroundings. But unlike most mirrors, *S-Curve* does not reflect a stable environment existing prior to and independent of its reflection, nor is the reflection itself reliable and constant. Rather, the shiny steel against the moving water and the make-shift modernity of its industrial surroundings create a strangely unsettling scene where both the artwork and its surroundings seem to be in flux. During the storm at Kistefos, that flux was violently physical, threatening property and life. But even within the sleek non-place vibe of an art-gallery, *S-Curve* seems to move, and to move its place with it. Kapoor does not confirm old places, he invents new ones, made up from a thick debris of memories of places we might have known.

NOTES

1   Jean-Marie Morel, *Théorie des Jardins*, Pissot, 1776.
2   Ovid, "Orpheus and Eurydice", Book 10, *Metamorphoses* (1st century AD), Penguin, 1955.

Between Work and World

Mikkel Bille

Mikkel Bille holds a PhD in anthropology from University College London and is a professor of ethnology at the University of Copenhagen. He is the author of the books *The Atmospheric City* (with Siri Schwabe, 2023), *Living with Light* (2019) and *Materialitet* (with Tim Flohr Sørensen, 2019), as well as a large number of articles on light, atmosphere, architecture, cultural heritage and urban studies.

Tim Flohr Sørensen

Tim Flohr Sørensen is an associate professor of contemporary archaeology at the University of Copenhagen. He has previously held positions at Aarhus University and the University of Cambridge. His research mainly revolves around archaeology's theory of ideas with a focus on posthumanism and feminism. He is the head of the The Hub for Speculative Fabulation upon Incidental Observations.

Ever since the Enlightenment, the Western world has seen knowledge as an unconditionally positive quality. To 'enlighten' and to 'illuminate' have been associated with clear-sightedness, truth and knowledge in the realms of science and religious thought alike. You have insight or knowledge if you have been 'enlightened' or 'have seen the light'. Conversely, you may be said to 'be in the dark' if you do not have relevant information. Ambiguous matters occupy a 'grey zone', and institutions carry out 'blackouts' if they want to keep something out of the public eye.

Thus, metaphors for knowledge often revolve around light and darkness, but darkness is not only a metaphorical expression of a lack of knowledge. Darkness also imbues the unknown with a sensuous and spatial fullness. In several works, Anish Kapoor has worked to create a sense of depth where in reality there is only a surface. To create this effect, he uses densely saturated surfaces of black or dark colours that reflect a minimum of light. This may cause the viewer to be uncertain whether the black surface is in fact a deep hole, as for example in *Void Field* (1989) and *Void Pavilion VI* (2018). Other works, such as *Building for a Void* (1992) and *Descent into Limbo* (1992) [see all on the two following spreads], actually do feature holes into which viewers look down, but the dark surfaces of their walls create an impression of infinite depth, even though the holes are 'only' a few metres deep.

Anish Kapoor does not simply stage light and dark as a form of *chiaroscuro*, the kind of strongly contrasting opposition of light and shadow seen in the work of artists such as Rembrandt (1606–1669) or Caravaggio (1571–1610) [see both on p. 44]. Rather, he brings out the particular qualities of the dark, using darkness as a sensuous material in its own right. The works investigate, challenge and materialise what might be called 'the darkness of darkness' or 'the dark in the dark'. That is precisely what we are confronted with in our encounter with his works – and perhaps in this darkness we are also confronted with ourselves? As the Danish-Icelandic artist Olafur Eliasson and the Danish author Tor Nørretranders state in their book *Light!* (2015): "The darkness tells us something about ourselves: basically, what we see when it is pitch dark are our own hallucinations. We see spectres we ourselves invoke."

In this way, darkness acts as a mirror that not only shows passive reflections, but also actively helps to transform our perception of and insight into ourselves. In 2016, a similar effect was created within the field of sound at the Orfield Laboratories in Minneapolis, USA, where a team of design researchers focus on the human senses. Sound engineers designed a so-called anechoic chamber, which absorbs 99% of the sound in the room. No reverberations are generated inside the chamber, so the sound of footsteps, speech or breathing disappears completely. All that remains is your own internal sounds: the heartbeat, little noises from the stomach, the lungs, tinnitus. In this way, the anechoic chamber becomes a sound mirror of yourself. Reportedly, for most people who have been inside the chamber, it created an unbearable, disorienting and anxiety-provoking sense of emptiness – like Narcissus on a bad trip.

In a corresponding fashion, Kapoor has experimented with many different colours and shapes to prompt a sense of viewing pure emptiness, for example in *Void* (1989). In 2015, Kapoor bought the exclusive rights to use the colour Vantablack S-VIS in artistic contexts from the manufacturer Surrey NanoSystems. Vantablack is a version of black that absorbs more than 99% of the light that hits its surface. In practice, this means that it does not reflect light: at the time, Kapoor himself stated that Vantablack is the blackest material in the universe after black holes, and that it looks as if you could disappear into it.[1] When light is practically not reflected from a surface, that surface loses its visual contours; the topography of the object becomes invisible. However, creating this effect does not require

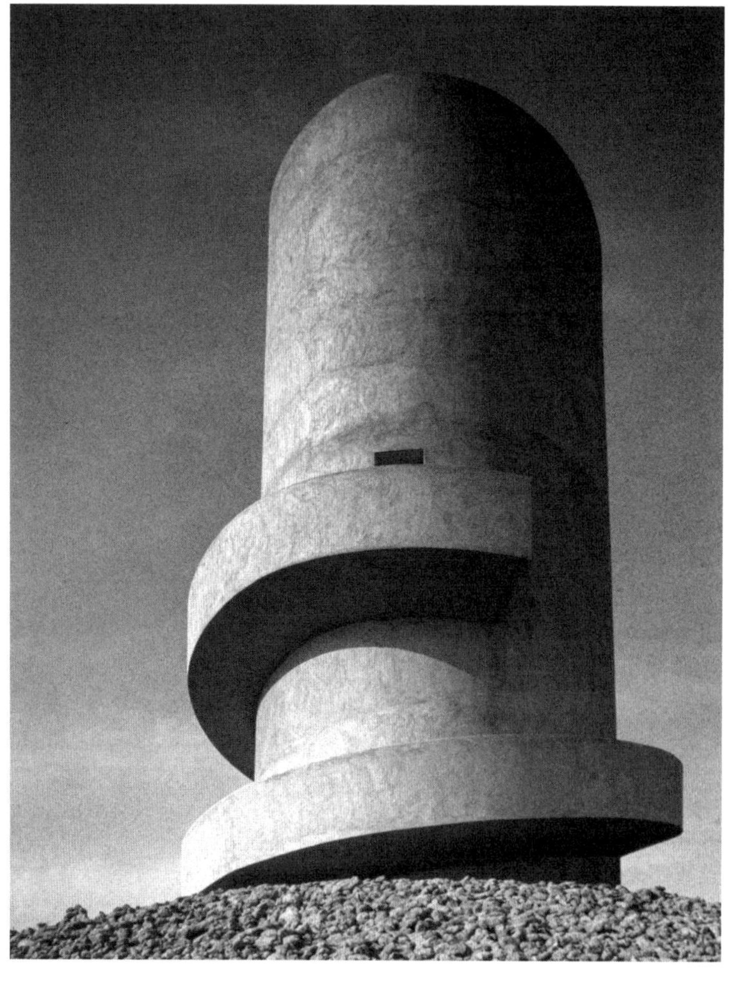

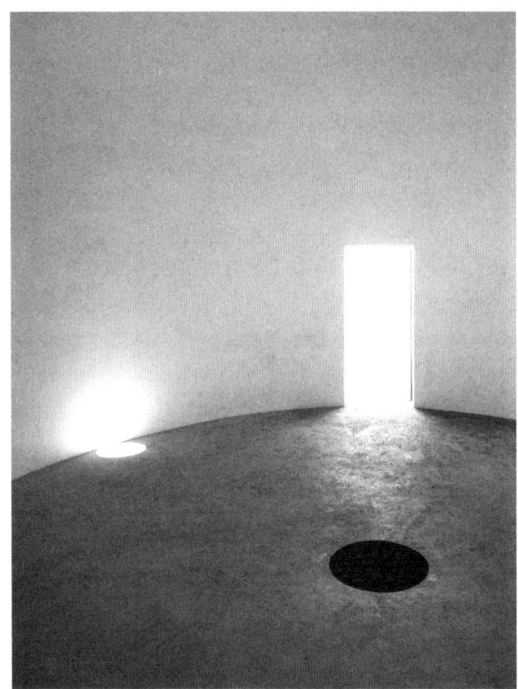

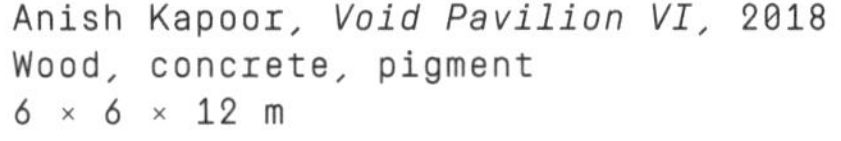

Anish Kapoor, *Void Pavilion VI,* 2018
Wood, concrete, pigment
6 × 6 × 12 m

Anish Kapoor, *Building for a Void,* 1992
Concrete, stucco
15 m
Seen from the inside and outside, respectively

an extreme technological product, as is demonstrated by the work *Descent into Limbo* which is a hole, two and a half metres deep, coated with Prussian blue pigment. "It looks like a black carpet on the ground, not like a hole, but it is a space completely brimmed full of darkness," Kapoor says of the work in an interview, adding: "It is frightening, very frightening, because it's a bloody deep, dark hole, but it's also an object and not an object."[2] When the work was exhibited in Porto in Portugal in 2018, a visitor accidentally fell into *Descent into Limbo*, apparently mistaking the hole for a black surface. The dark colour made the contours invisible, allowing Kapoor to make the void deceptive even as it is also quite material and real. Thus, it would be a mistake to regard Kapoor's voids as pure or merely optical illusions, as games played with the audience or as a teasing quest for effect and spectacle.

Just as light is used in the works of Rembrandt and Caravaggio to prompt emotions in the viewer and not just to reveal the world, the power of darkness also resides in evoking an atmosphere by obscuring the visible. Darkness creates an absence of the visually perceptible, but this very absence can be so present that it intrudes even more insistently upon you than an illuminated work could ever do. In a manner of speaking, the presence of absence is the essence of the meaning found in the darkness: we do not quite know what is in the dark – indeed, whether anything is there at all – and this uncertainty becomes a vivid sense of something unclear and unresolved. The presence of darkness is a visceral experience that may not be unambiguous but is nevertheless intrusive. Thus, the dark-ness of darkness and the question of the presence of a 'something' – or a 'nothing' – can arouse feelings such as wonder, anxiety or uneasiness. When you stare into the darkness, you may doubt whether there is anything there at all. Is the darkness a drapery hiding some unseen being, an unknown force? Or is it merely what you see: darkness and nothing else?

Kapoor's works force us to confront the darkness, to feel the encounter with the unseen and unknown as a sensual experience where we gently lean into an unknown spatial form. This movement constitutes a way of *approaching* this uncertainty or something as yet unknown and unrecognised.

Anish Kapoor's works – such as *Not Eve* (1989) and *Black Absence* (2021) [see both on the following spread] – fundamental questions about our need to distinguish clearly between what is present and what is absent – or between 'something' and 'nothing': do we need to seek clarification of what lies in the dark? Perhaps Kapoor suggests that the question of whether there is indeed something in the dark can be answered with a 'maybe?' or 'I'm not *entirely* sure about that'.

Uncertainty is thus a legitimate cognitive state in the encounter with Kapoor's works, which offer us a place to dwell on doubt rather than having to find absolute answers and seek clarification. Thus, in these works, the question of seen or unseen cannot be resolved by simple visual confirmation. Rather, seeing is feeling. An interesting aspect of Anish Kapoor's works, aptly illustrated by the unfortunate visitor to the exhibition in Porto, concerns their marking of the boundary between the work and the outside world. One can undoubtedly point to darkness as a central part of this endeavour, but Kapoor takes various approaches to the transition between work and world. Some works, such as *Descension* (2014) [pp. 122-125], have a clear boundary between the work and the rest of the world. In other works, such as *Mother as a Mountain* (1985) [p. 74], the boundary is fluid, while in *Memory* (2008) [pp. 50-55] the transition is a central part of the movement around and in the work. Here, the work is intended to ensnare the viewer and absorb the audience in the dark. The separation between the work and the surrounding world is not just a boundary in a physical space, but also a state, something created through the interaction with the work's shapes and colours.

43

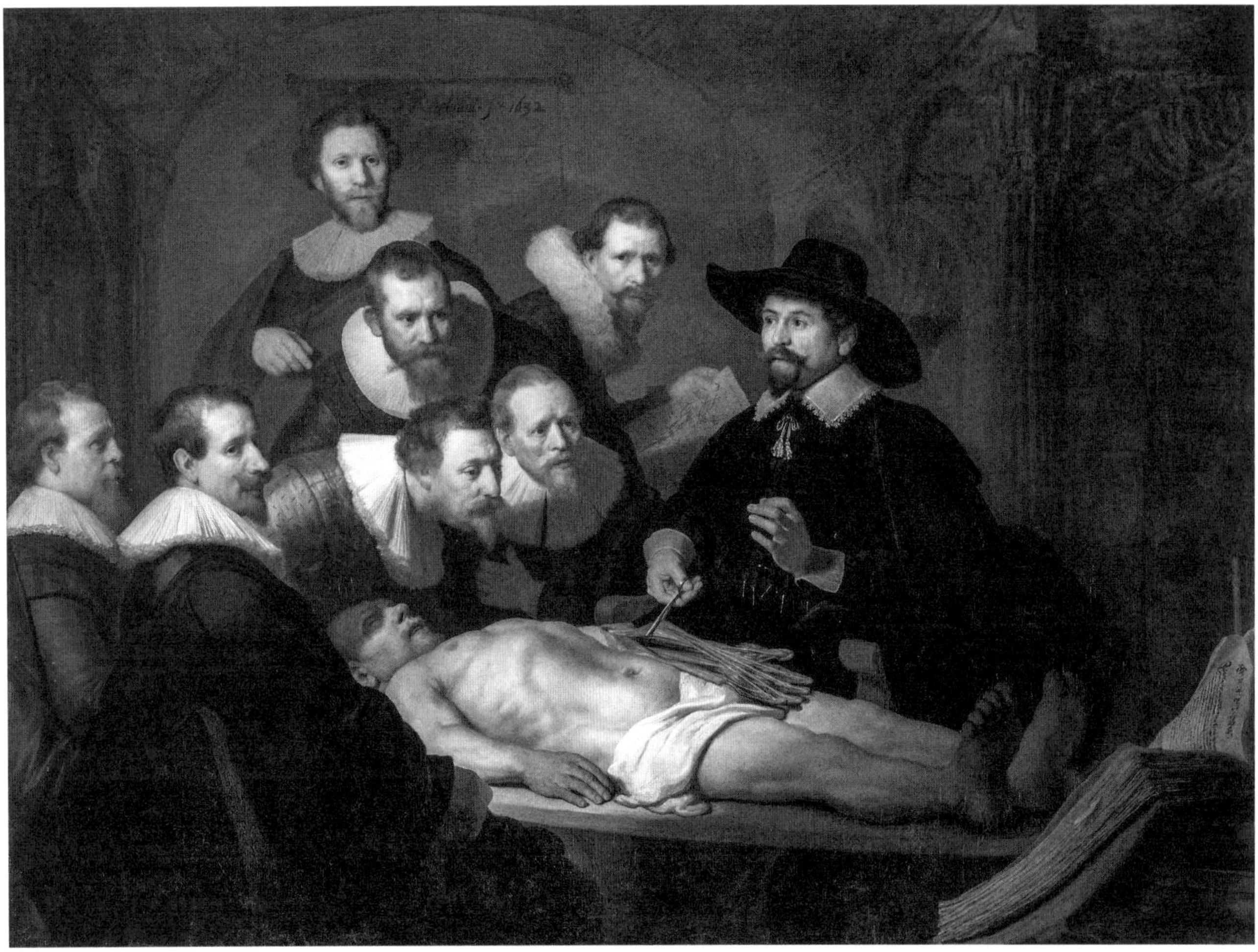

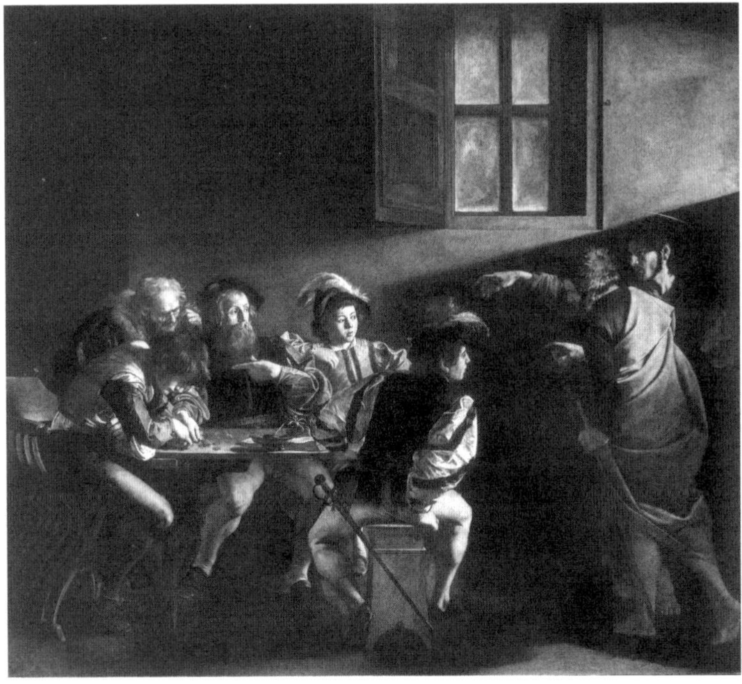

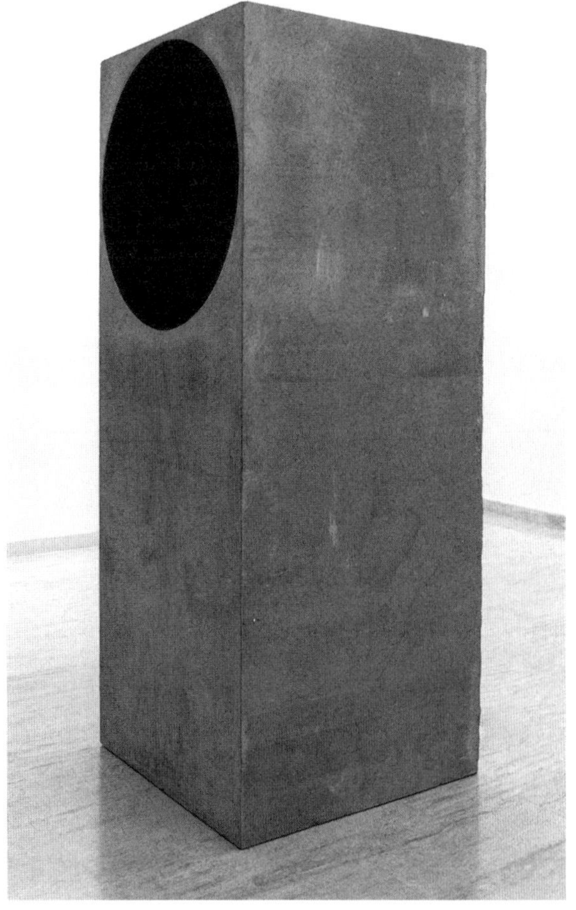

Rembrandt van Rijn
The Anatomy Lesson of Dr Nicolaes Tulp, 1632
Oil on canvas
169.5 × 216.5 cm

Caravaggio
The Calling of Saint Matthew,
c. 1600
Oil on canvas
322 × 340 cm

Anish Kapoor
Not Eve, 1989
Sandstone, pigment
213.5 × 85 × 86 cm

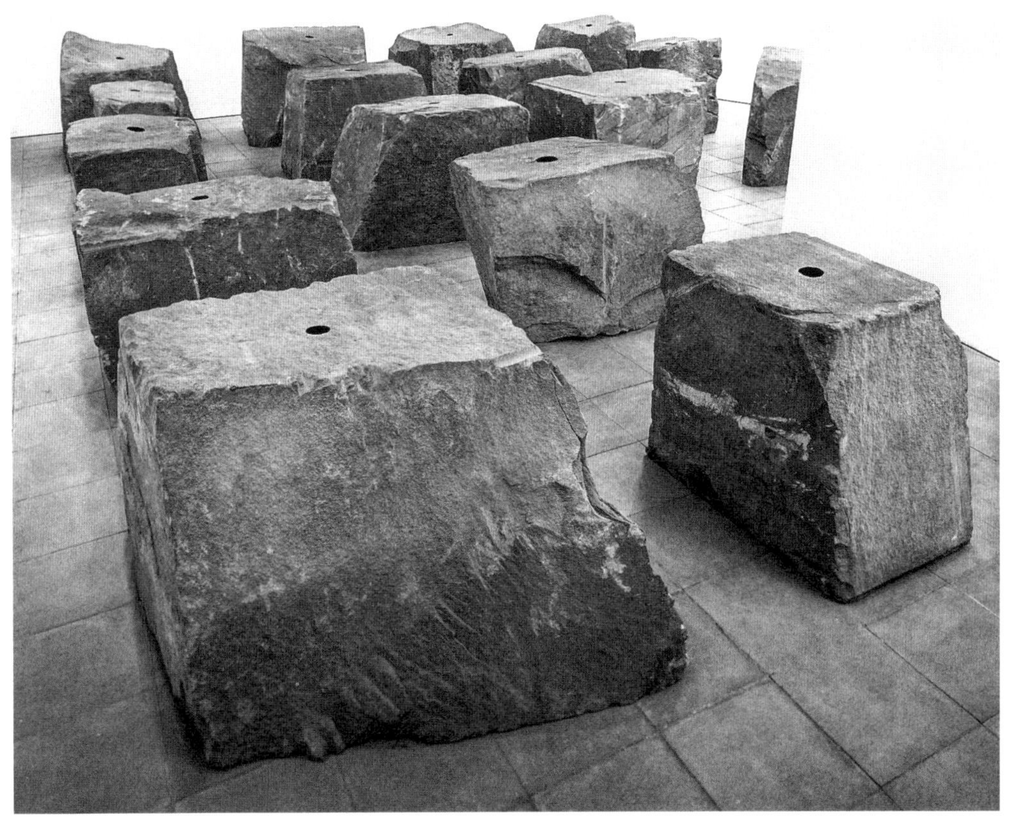

Anish Kapoor, *Void Field,* 1989
Sandstone, pigment
Dimensions variable

Anish Kapoor, *Black Absence,* 2021
Resin, paint
254 × 245 × 40 cm

Other works move in the direction of darkness and the void through means other than an all-consuming blackness. *Descension* is a water installation taking the form of a pool in which a swirling vortex creates a movement towards a void into which the foaming water is sucked. The opposite holds true for *At the Edge of the World II* (1998) [pp. 68-71], a red fibreglass sculpture suspended above the audience. Shaped like a gigantic funnel, the sculpture seems to grow gradually darker as you look up inside it. The work has an ascending depth suggesting that we are being pulled up into a potentially infinite space. We stand on the edge of the world, feeling as though we might fall out into space. Being in the vicinity of this kind of uncertainty, in the darkness and its fullness, is not without its hazards. In limbo – in the liminal intermediate state – we risk something. A sinking. A fall. A transition. Being sucked into a black hole. If you let yourself get carried away, that is.

Nothing can escape a black hole, not even light. In a cosmological sense, black holes pull in everything with the most radical and brutal gravity. They are often depicted as voids, nothingnesses, but they should rather be understood as objects or places of extreme mass and complete fullness. While Kapoor's works do not constitute black holes in a cosmological sense, they nevertheless absorb light and prevent most of it from being reflected. They also absorb our attention, although this is not quite comparable to the aforementioned anechoic chamber, where one may certainly speak of emptiness. In Kapoor's art, the darkness becomes a fullness, but the question remains whether we perceive this fullness as a silence or a roaring turmoil. Perhaps Kapoor's darkness reminds us of the American avant-garde composer John Cage's (1912–1992) composition *4'33"* (1952), where an orchestra remains silent for the entirety of the four minute and thirty-three second piece. Here, silence becomes a fullness. Layer upon layer of silence. Or perhaps Kapoor's darkness is comparable to *See Through Negative* (2014), an eight-minute-long album by the Danish grindcore band Dead Instrument, composed as an uncompromising, sonically swelling mass of down-tuned and distorted instruments and vocals that fill the entire soundscape.

So how do we lean into Kapoor's darkness? Into its stillness or into its uproar? Is it solely a visual optical illusion, or is there a 'something' in the darkness that, in its visual absence, lures us in as a way of approaching something unseen or as yet unrecognised? If the viewer is drawn in, where and when does this take place? On the edge of the void, we are confronted with the work. So, move closer. Or perhaps we need a certain distance to the work in order for its beauty, brutality or meaning to break through? Like standing at a distance, watching the rainbow unfold against a dark sky streaked with rain and sun.

NOTER

1 Brigid Delaney, "'You could disappear into it': Anish Kapoor on his exclusive rights to the 'blackest black'", interview in *The Guardian,* 26 September 2016, https://www.theguardian.com/artanddesign/2016/sep/26/anish-kapoor-vantablack-art-architecture-exclusive-rights-to-the-blackest-black (last accessed 12 February 2024).
2 Rebecca Mead, "Anish Kapoor's Material Values", interview in *The New Yorker*, 15 August 2022, https://www.newyorker.com/magazine/2022/08/22/anish-kapoors-material-values (accessed 12 February 2024).

ANISH KAPOOR
UNSEEN

WORKS

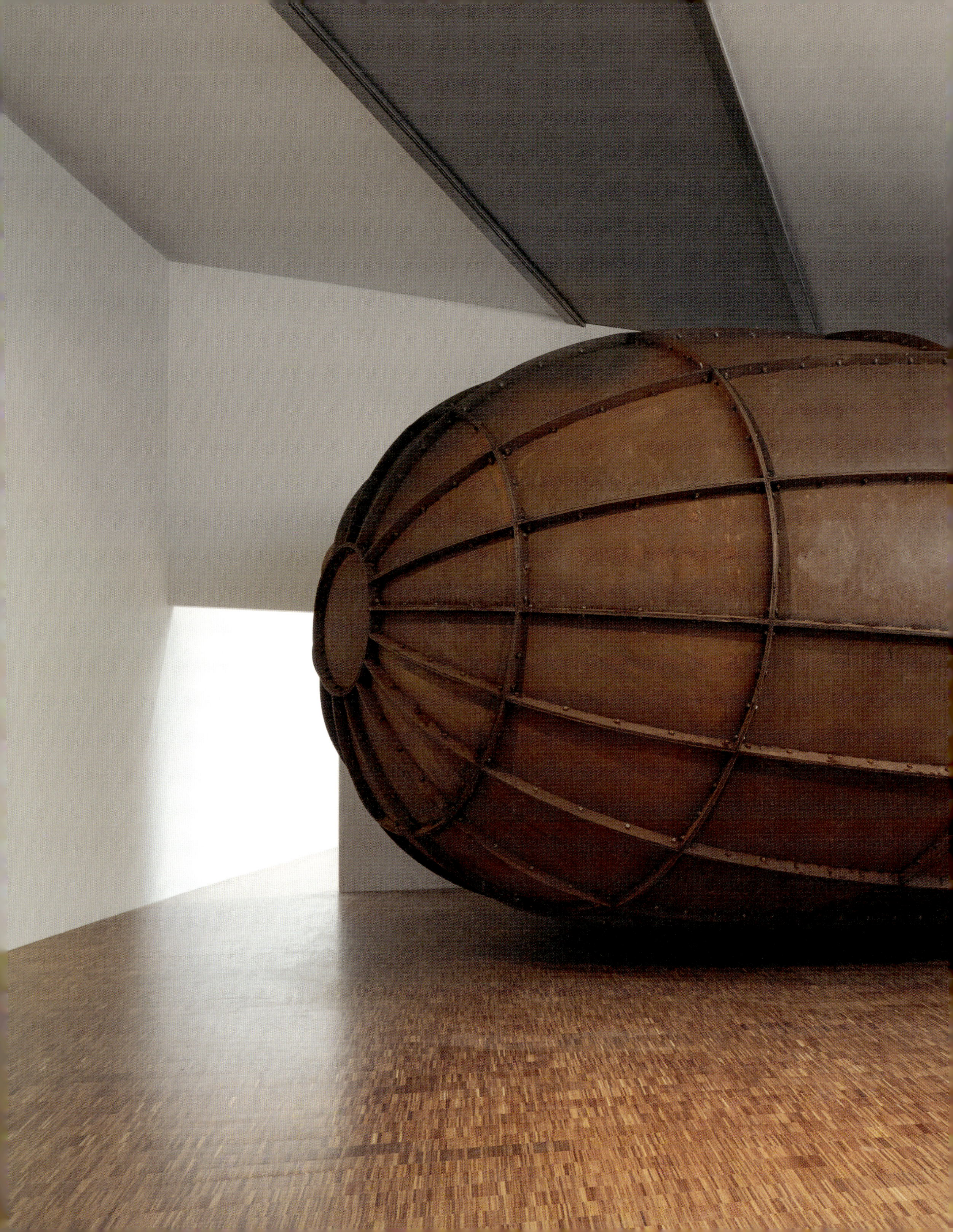

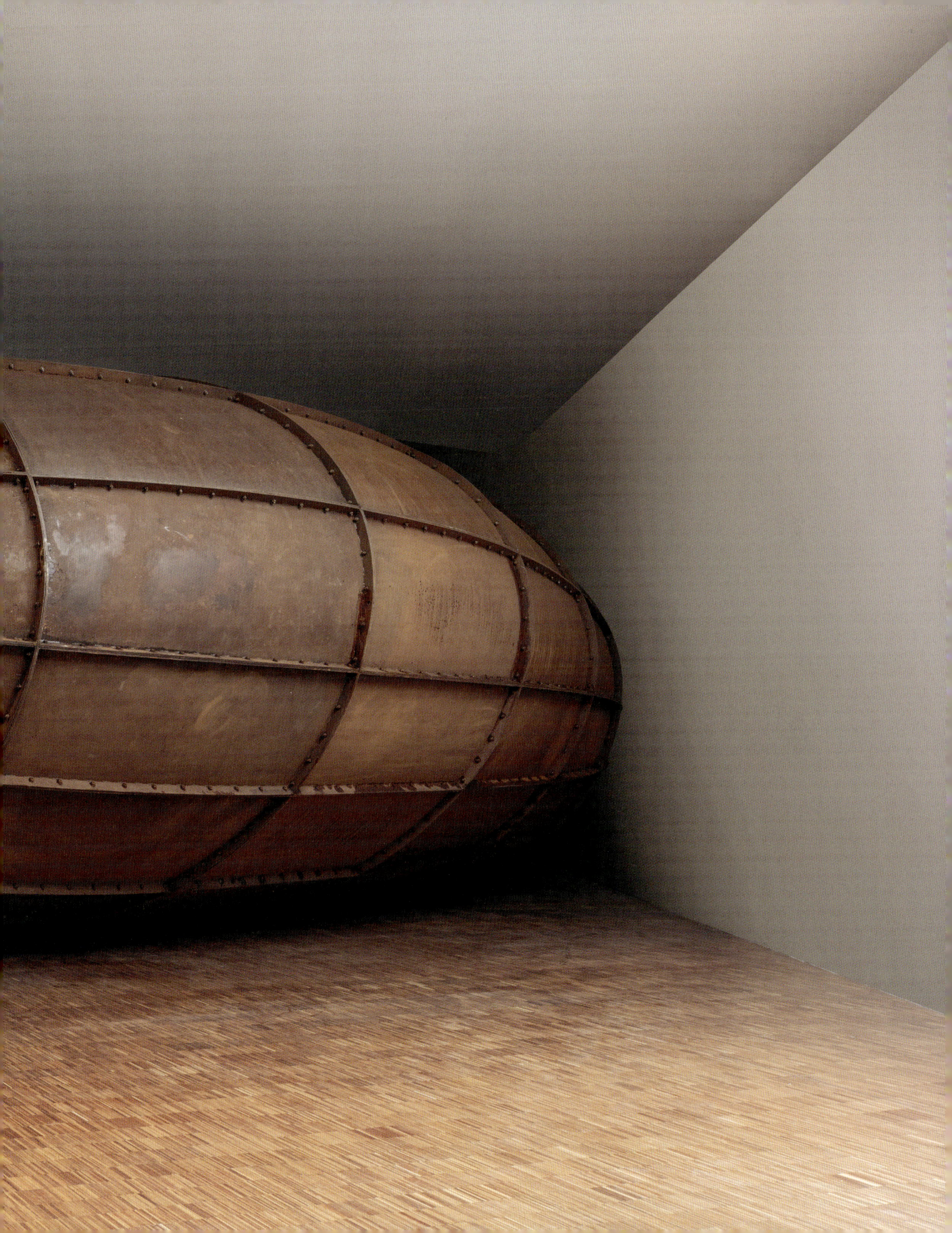

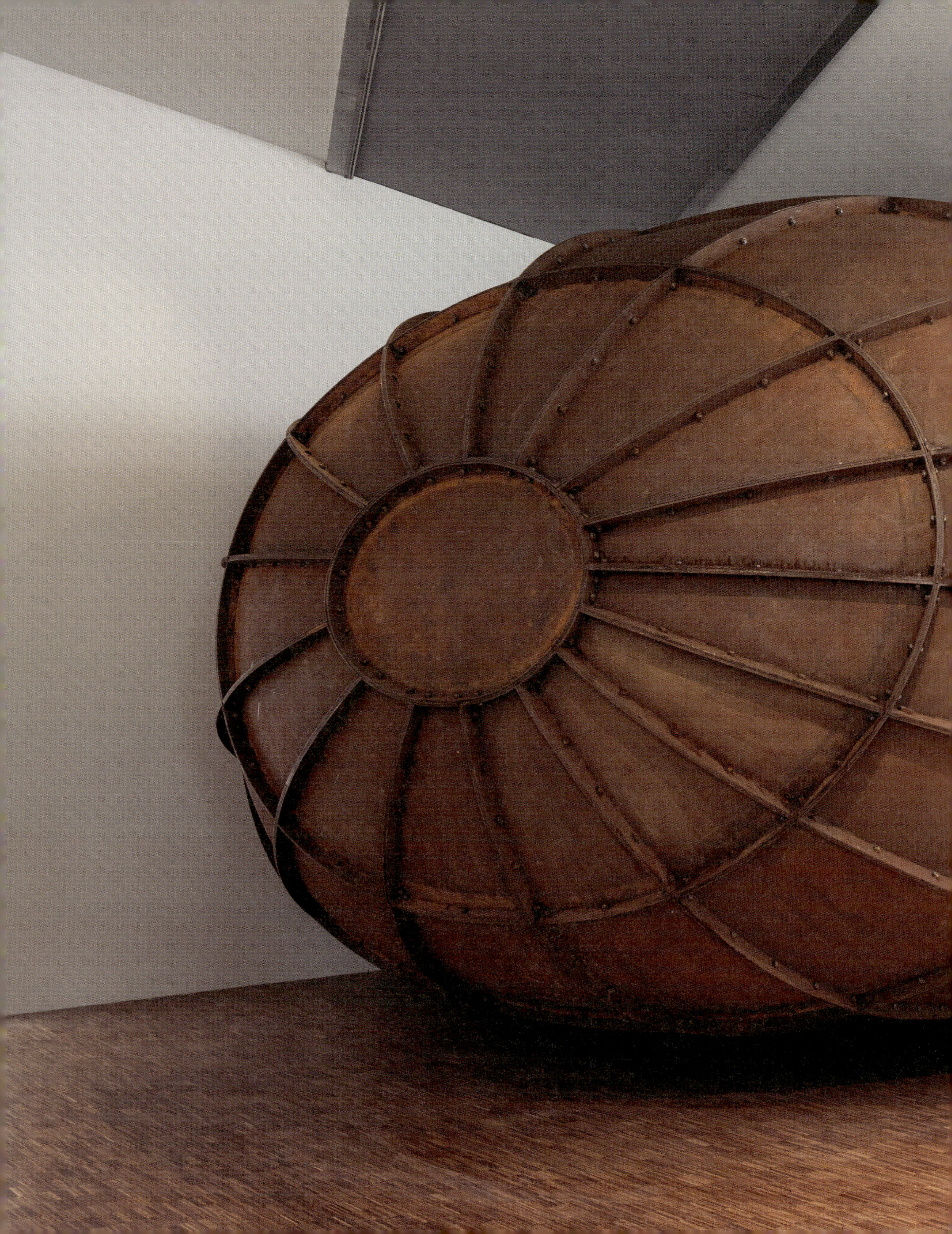

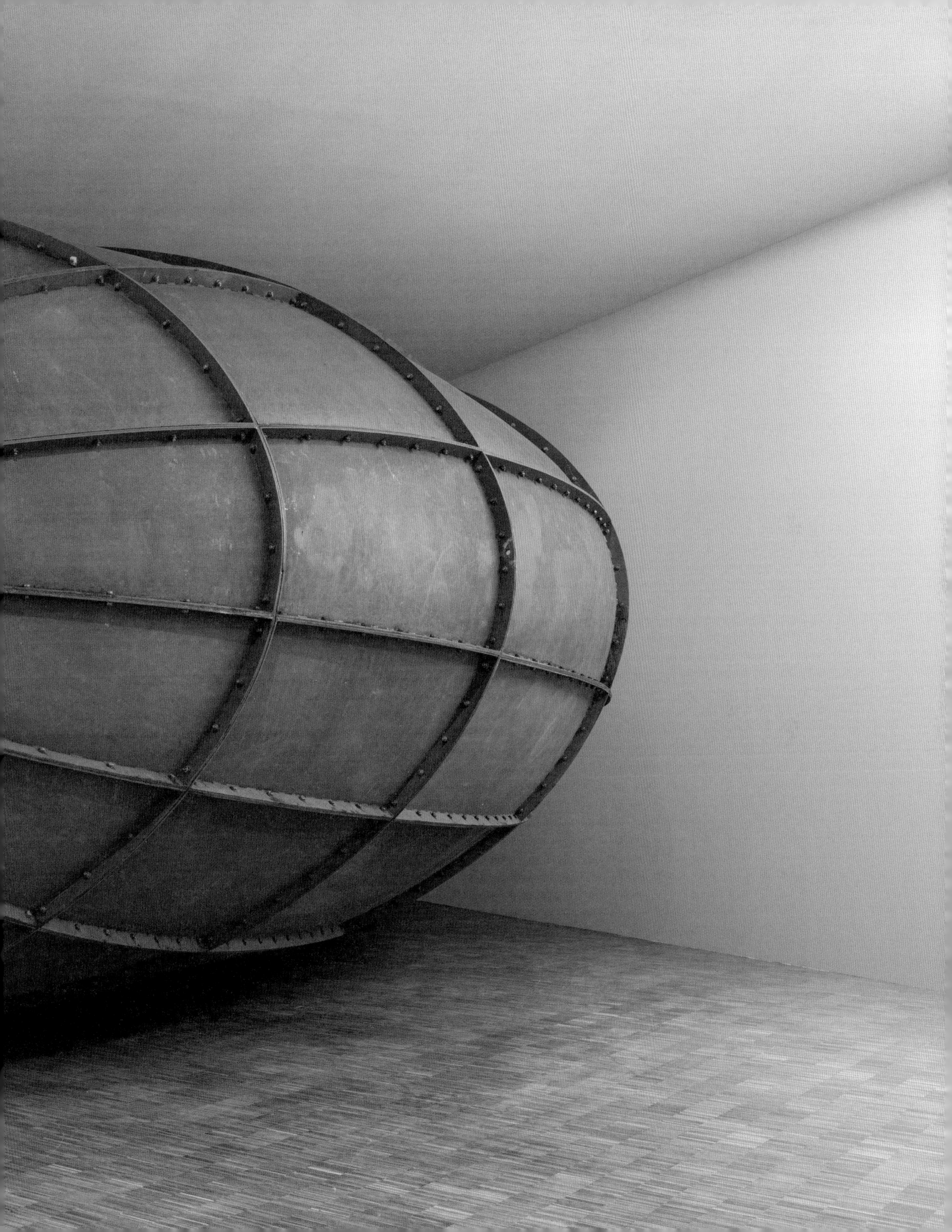

This and the two preceding spreads
Memory, 2008
Corten steel
14.5 × 8.97 × 4.48 m
ARKEN Museum of Contemporary Art, Ishøj

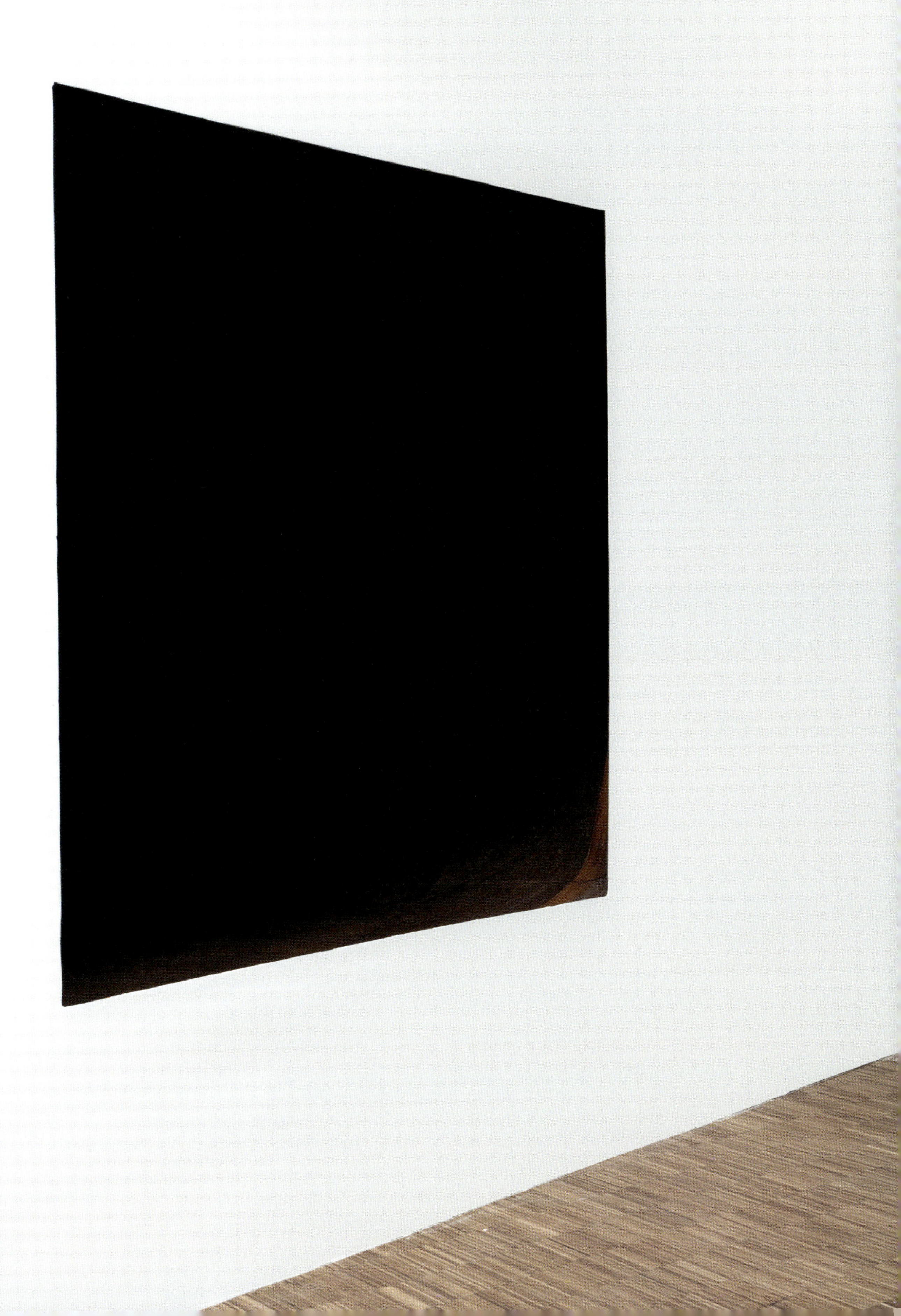

Pregnant White Within Me, 2022
Mixed media, paint
Dimensions variable

Underground, 2005
Concrete, iron
825 × 400 cm

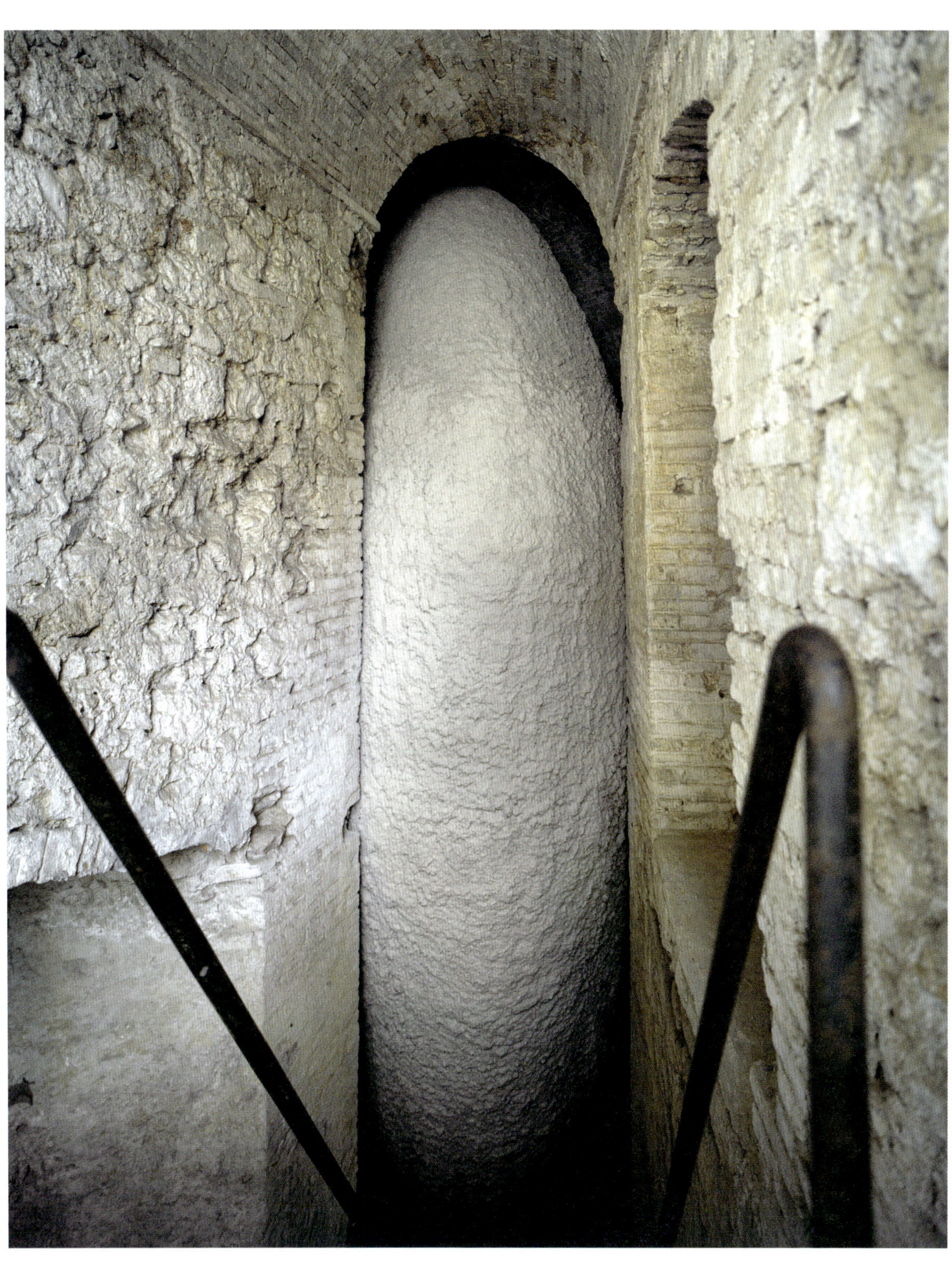

Turning the World Inside Out, 1995
Stainless steel
148 × 184 × 188 cm

L'Origine du monde, 2004
Concrete, pigment

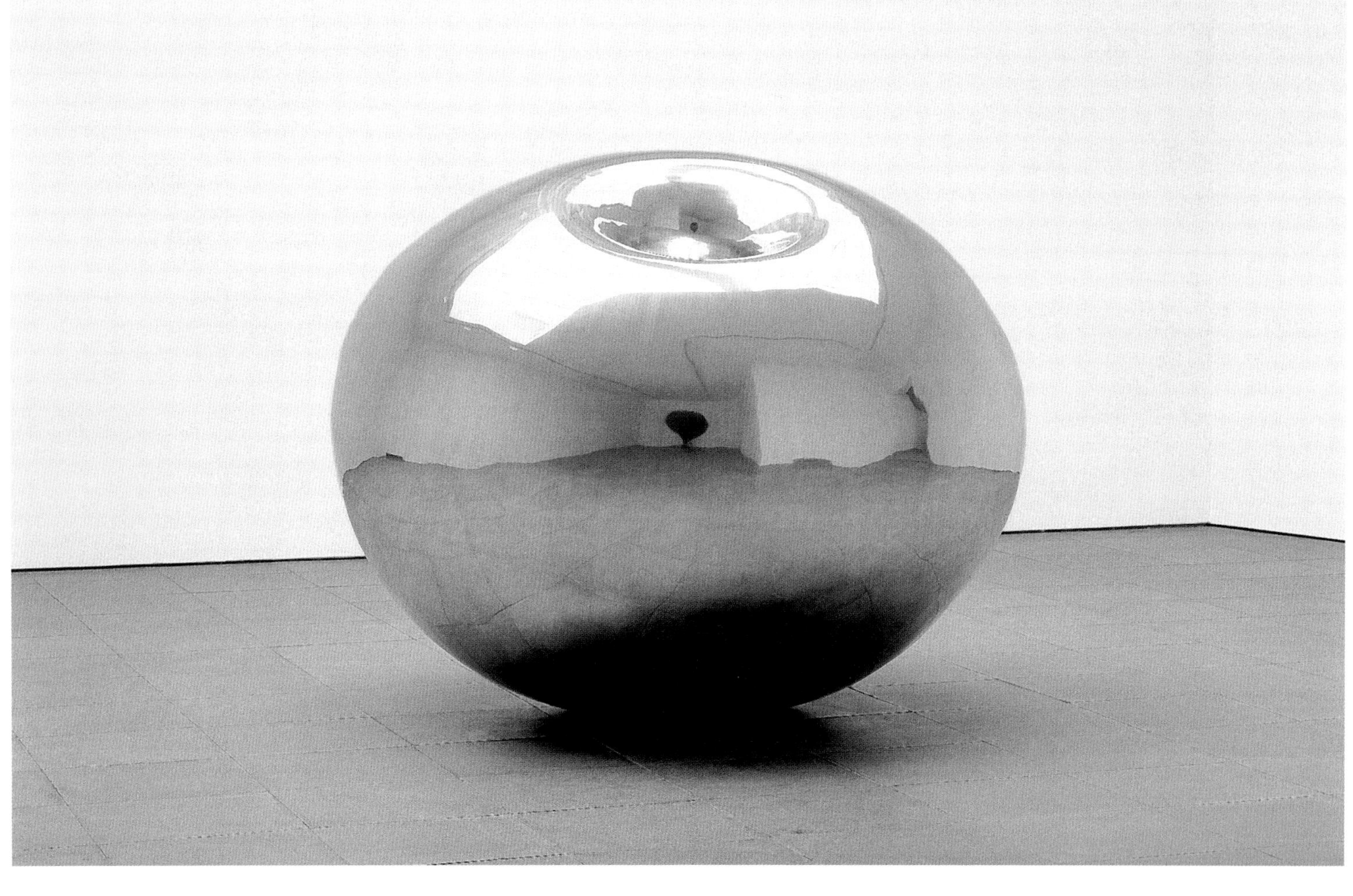

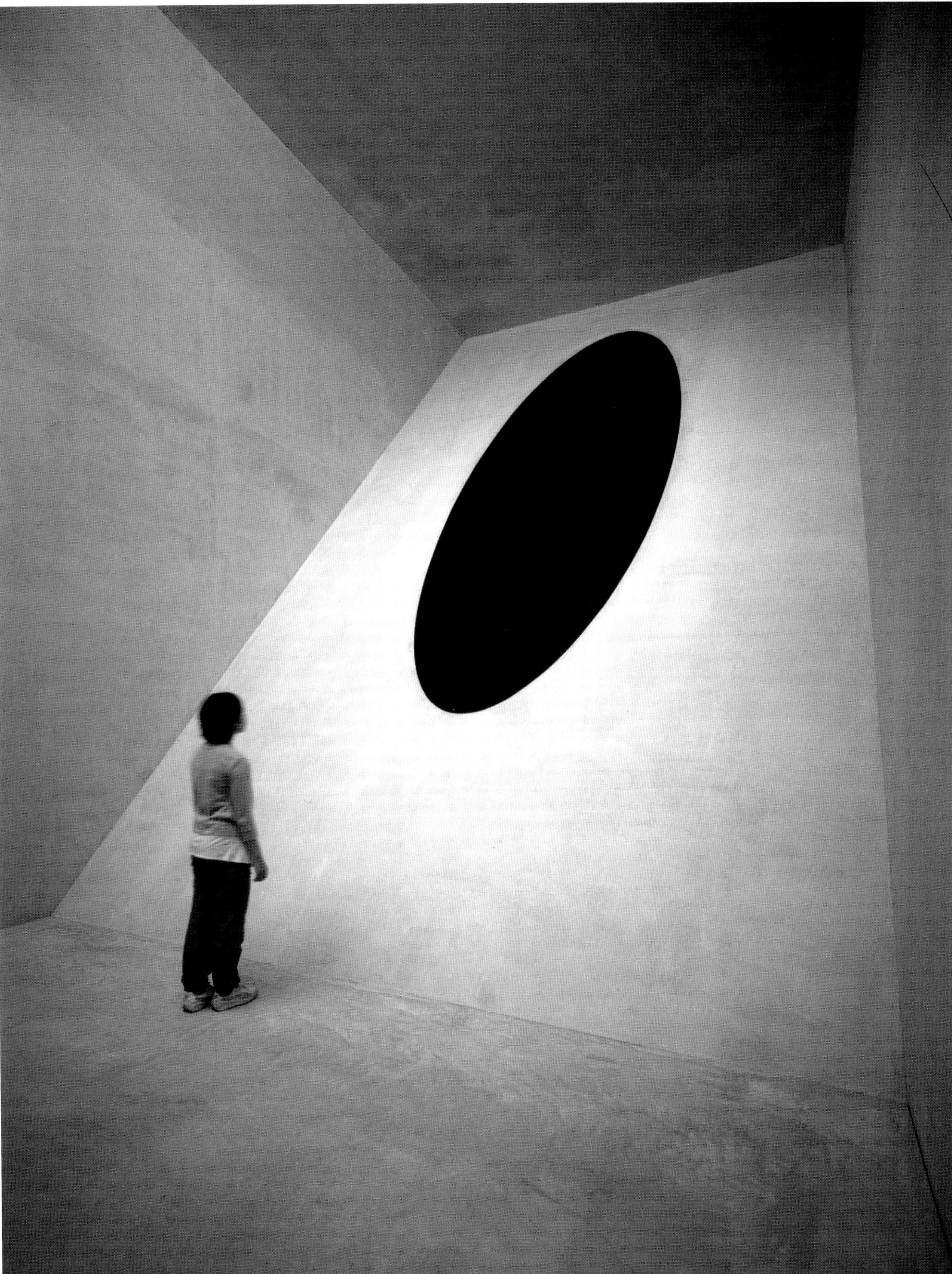

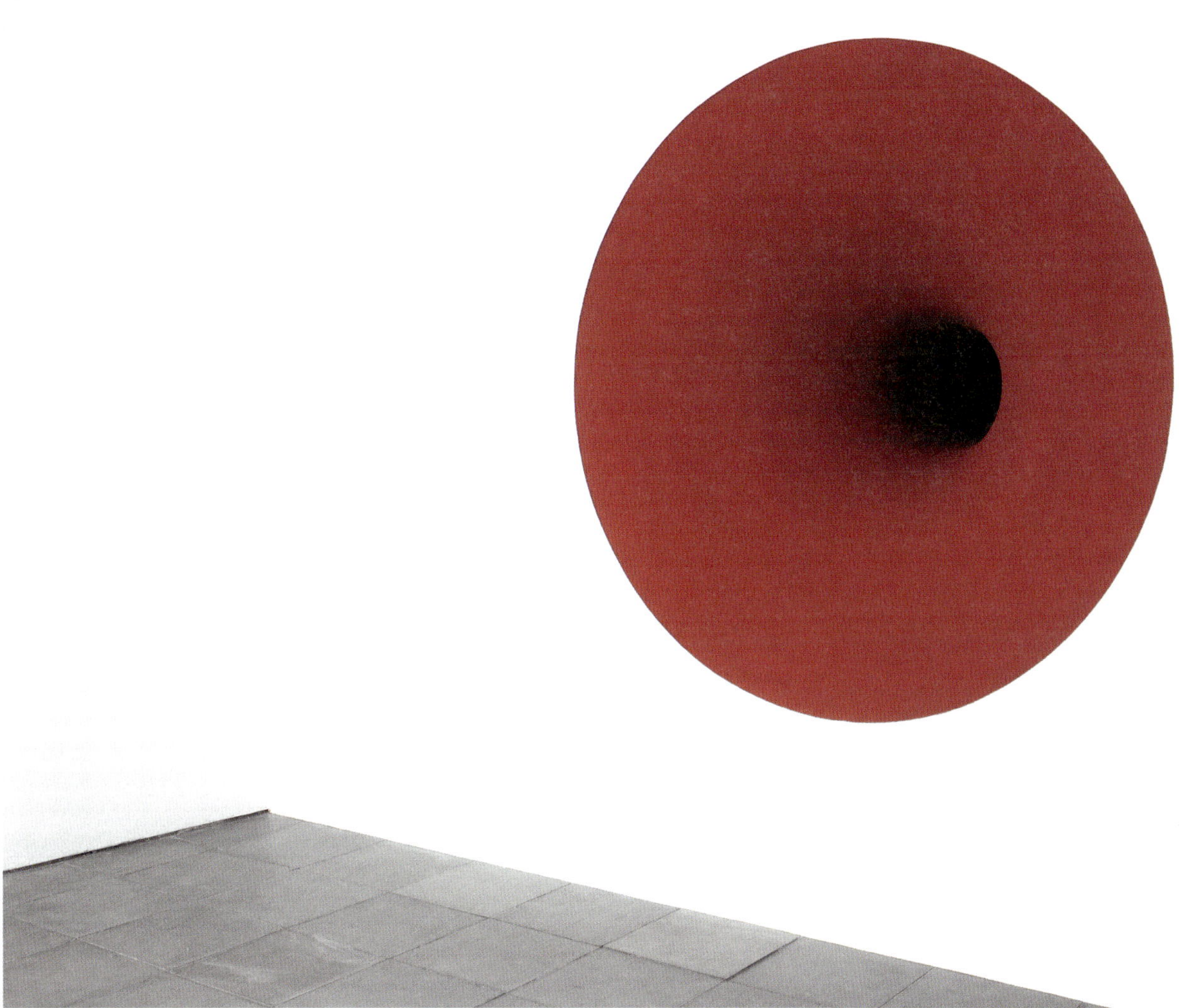

When I am Pregnant, 1992
Fibreglass, paint
Dimensions variable

Untitled, 1995
Fibreglass, pigment
Diameter 202.5 cm

pp. 62-65
Leviathan, 2011
PVC
33.6 × 99.89 × 72.23 m
Grand Palais, Paris

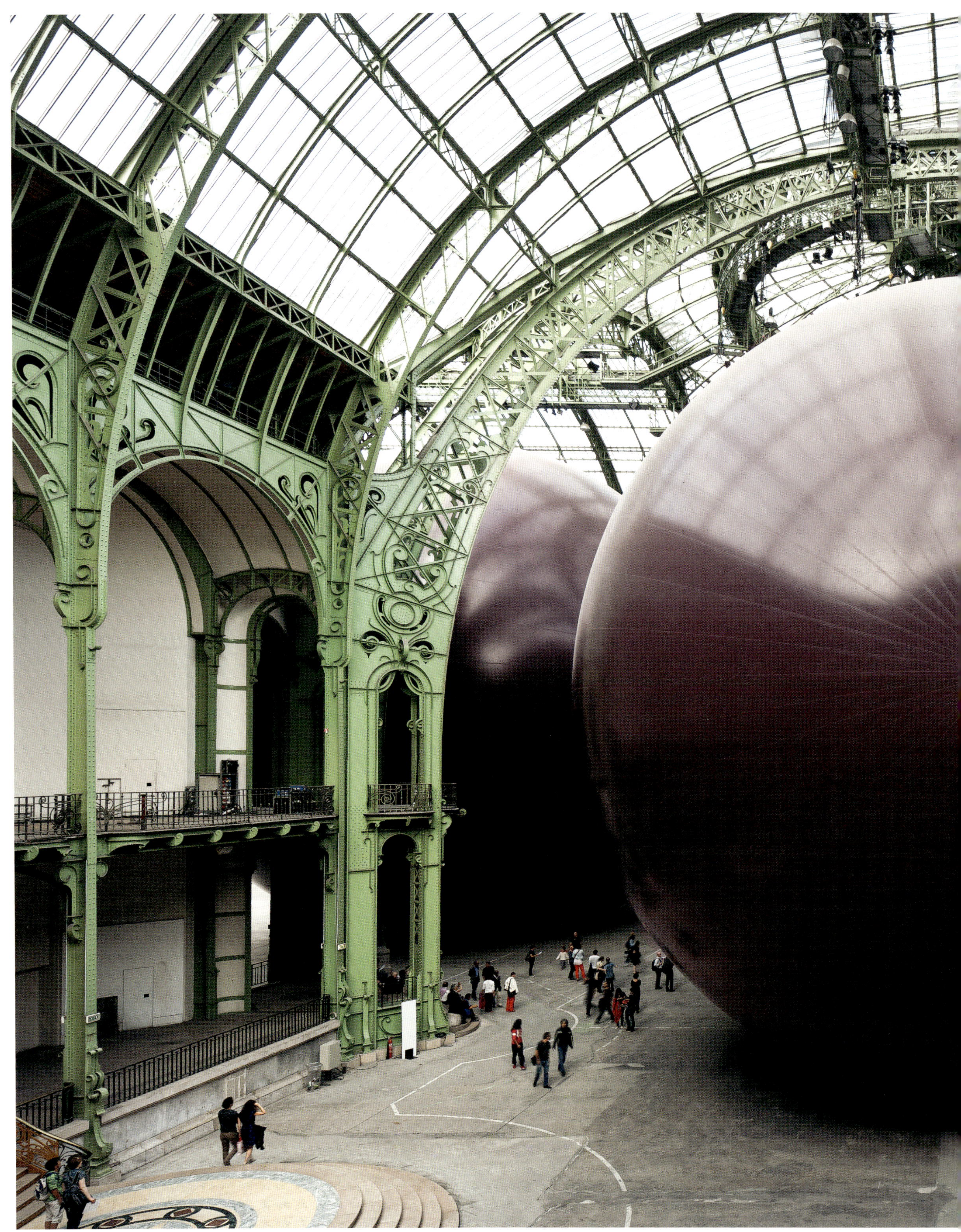

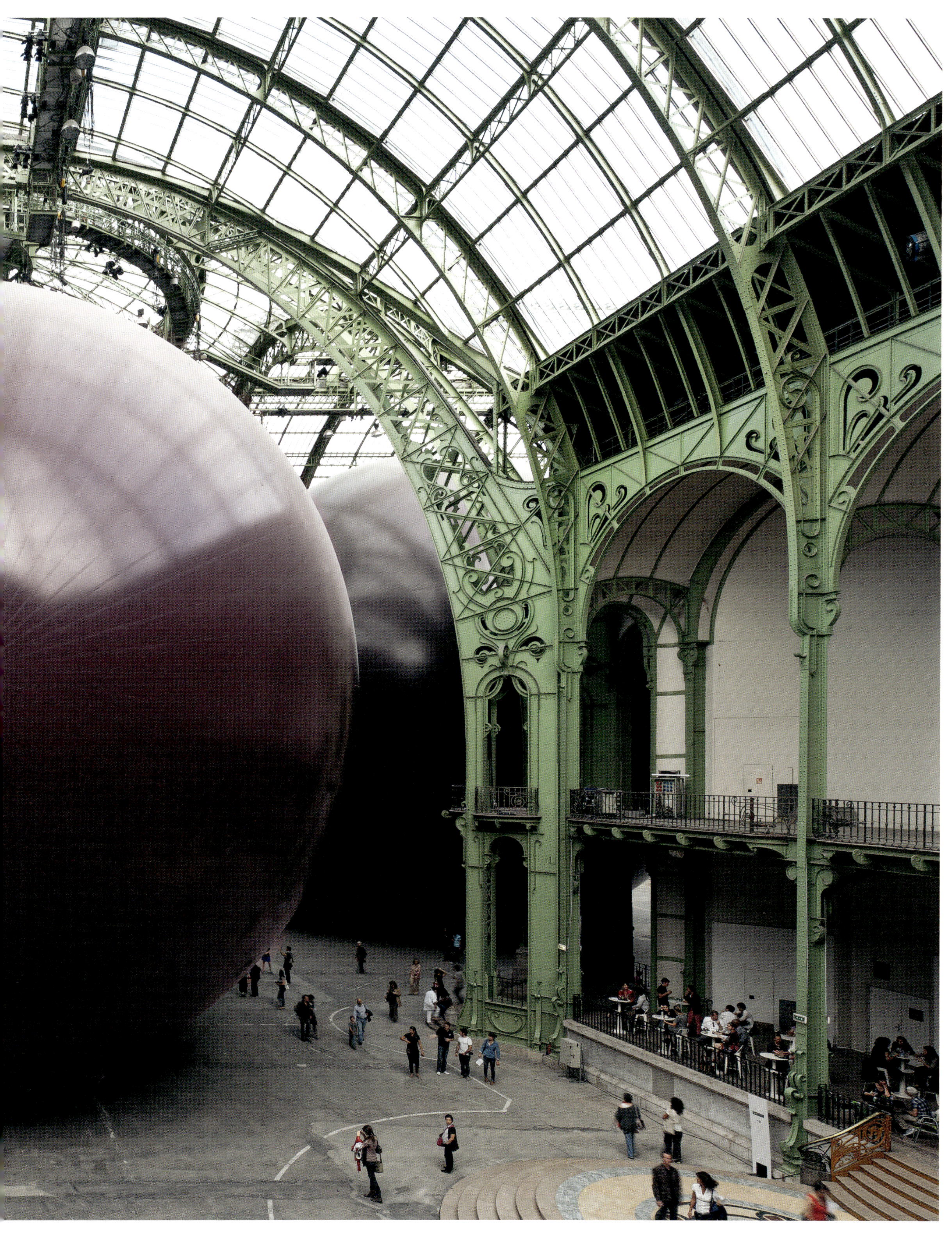

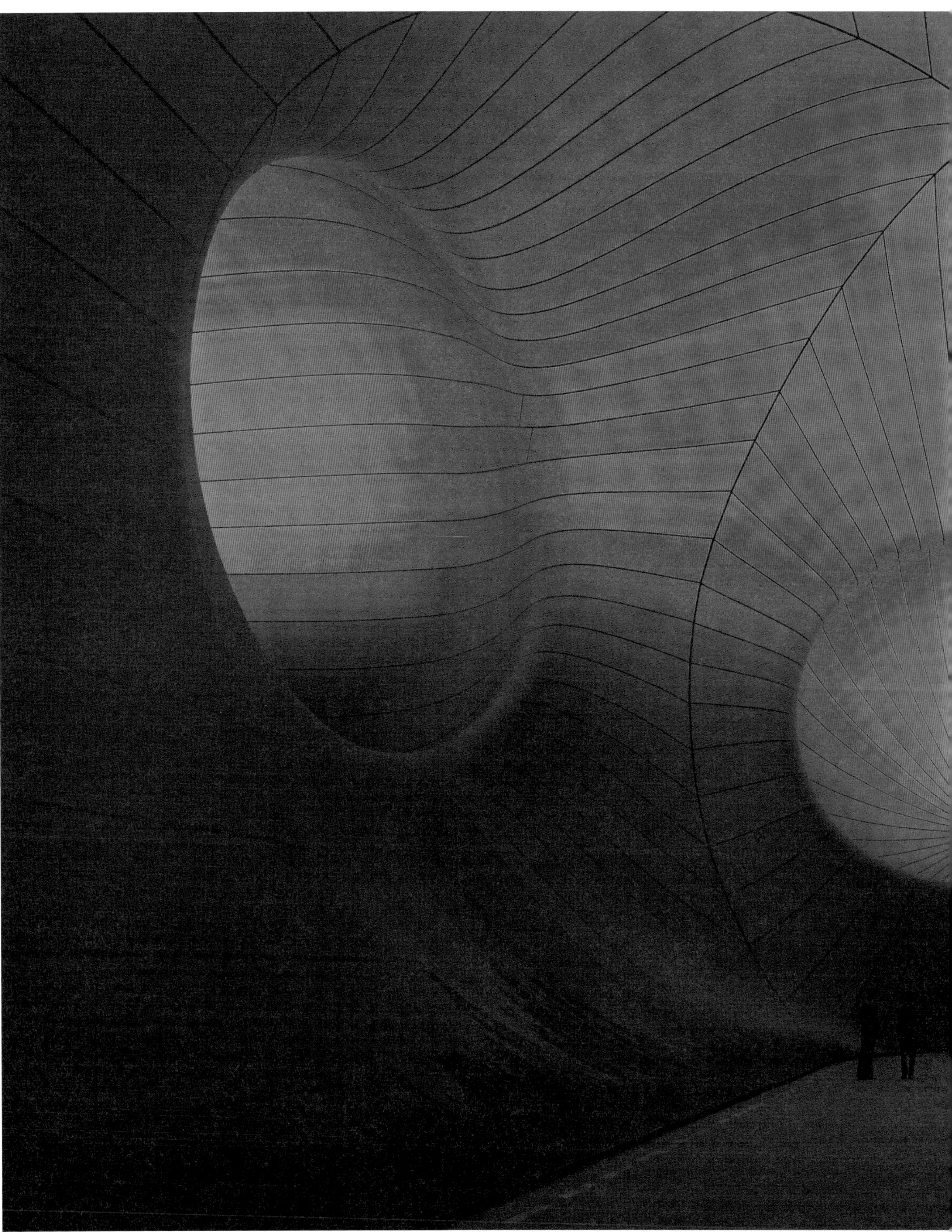

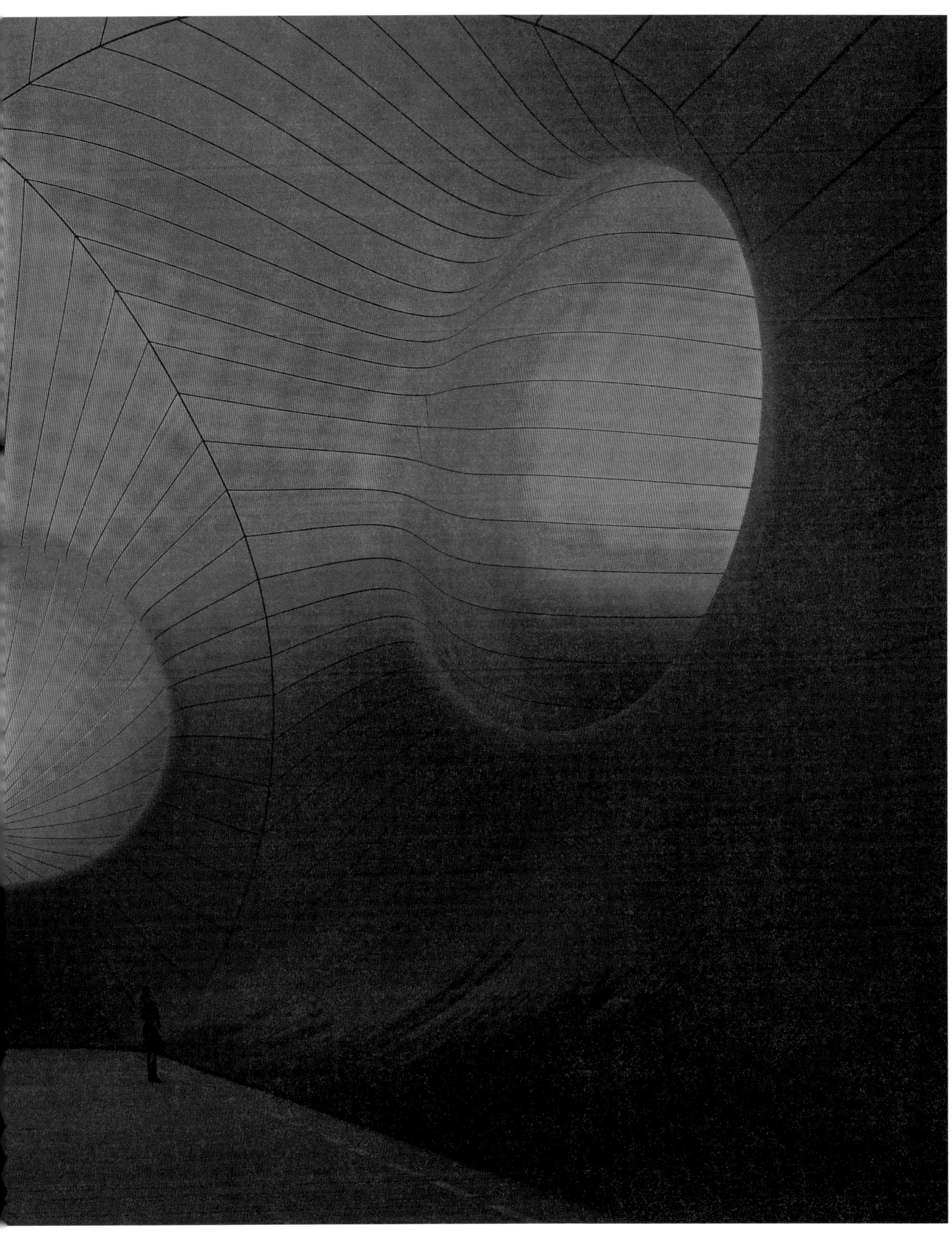

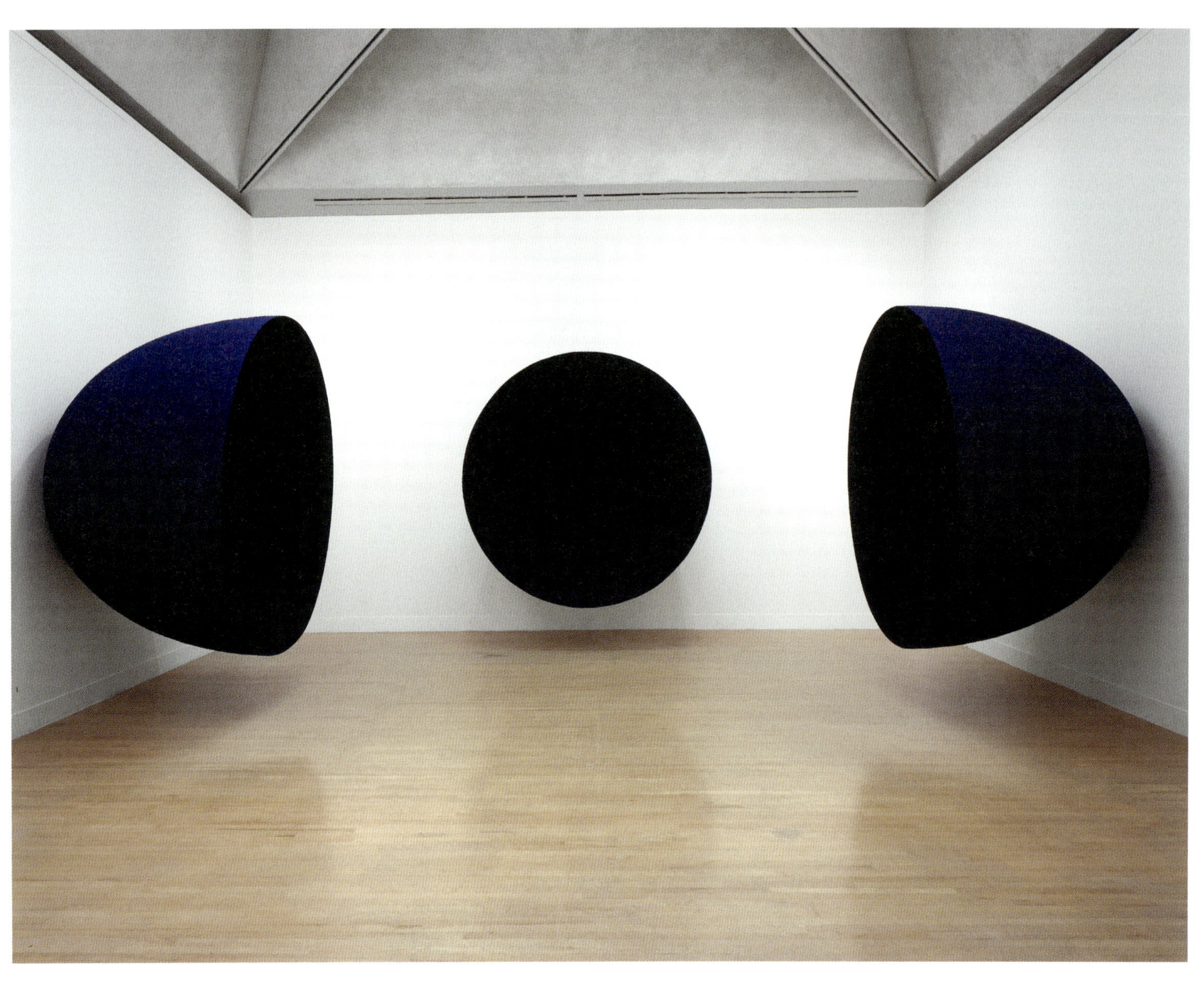

Untitled, 1990
Fibreglass, pigment
Dimensions variable

Healing of St. Thomas, 1989
Mixed media, pigment
Dimensions variable

pp. 68-71
At the Edge of the World II, 1998
Fibreglass, pigment
300 × 800 × 800 cm
ARKEN Museum of Contemporary Art, Ishøj

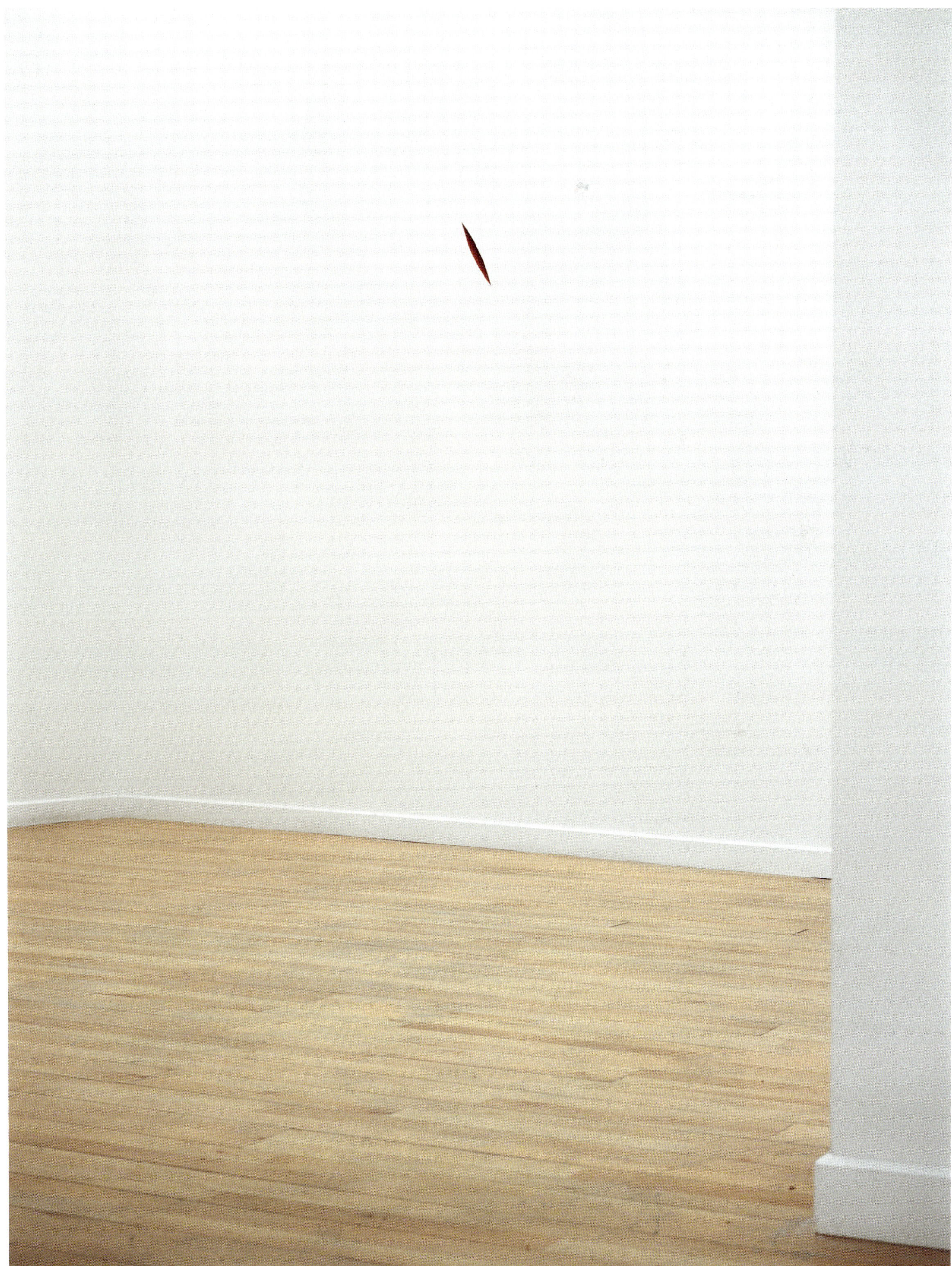

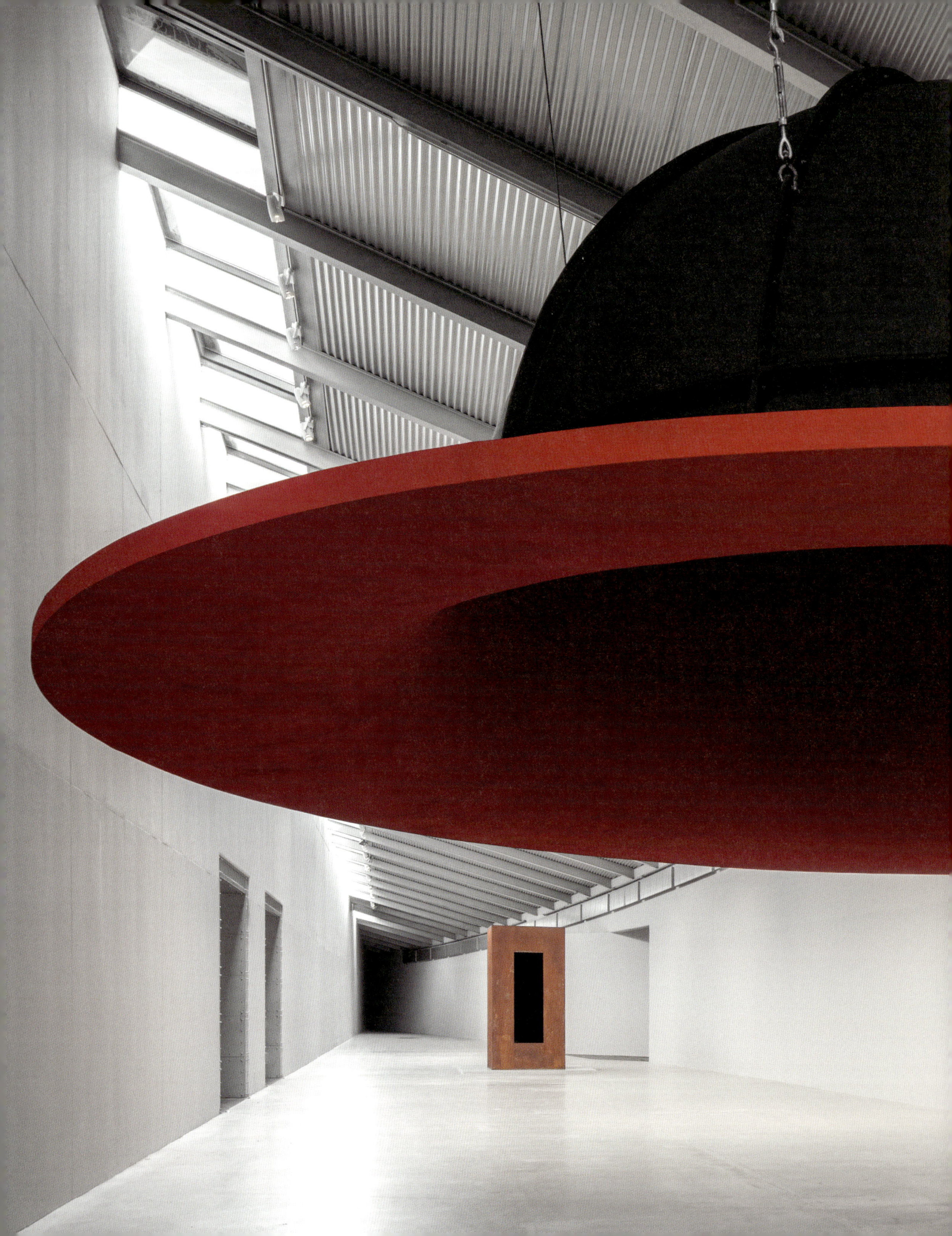

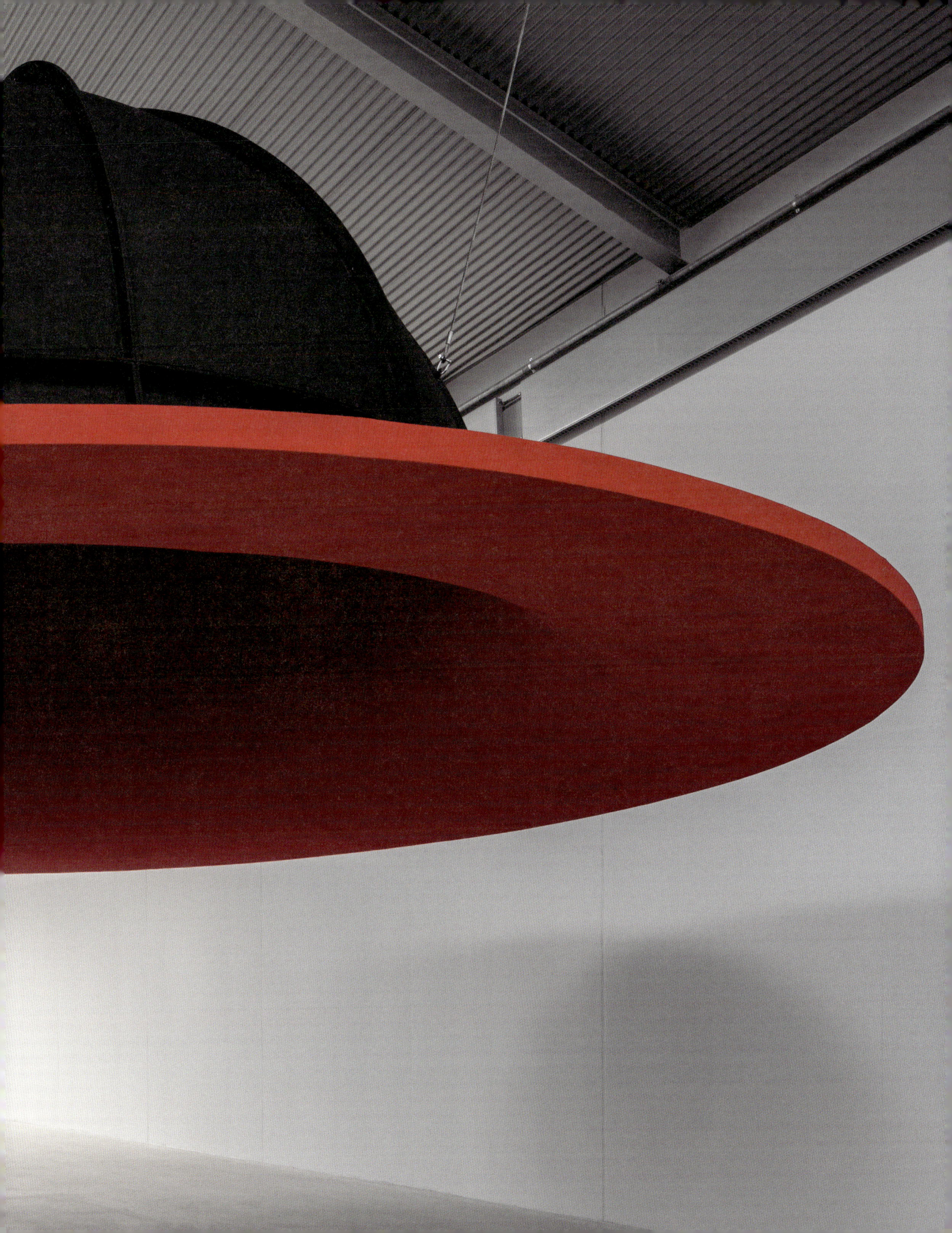

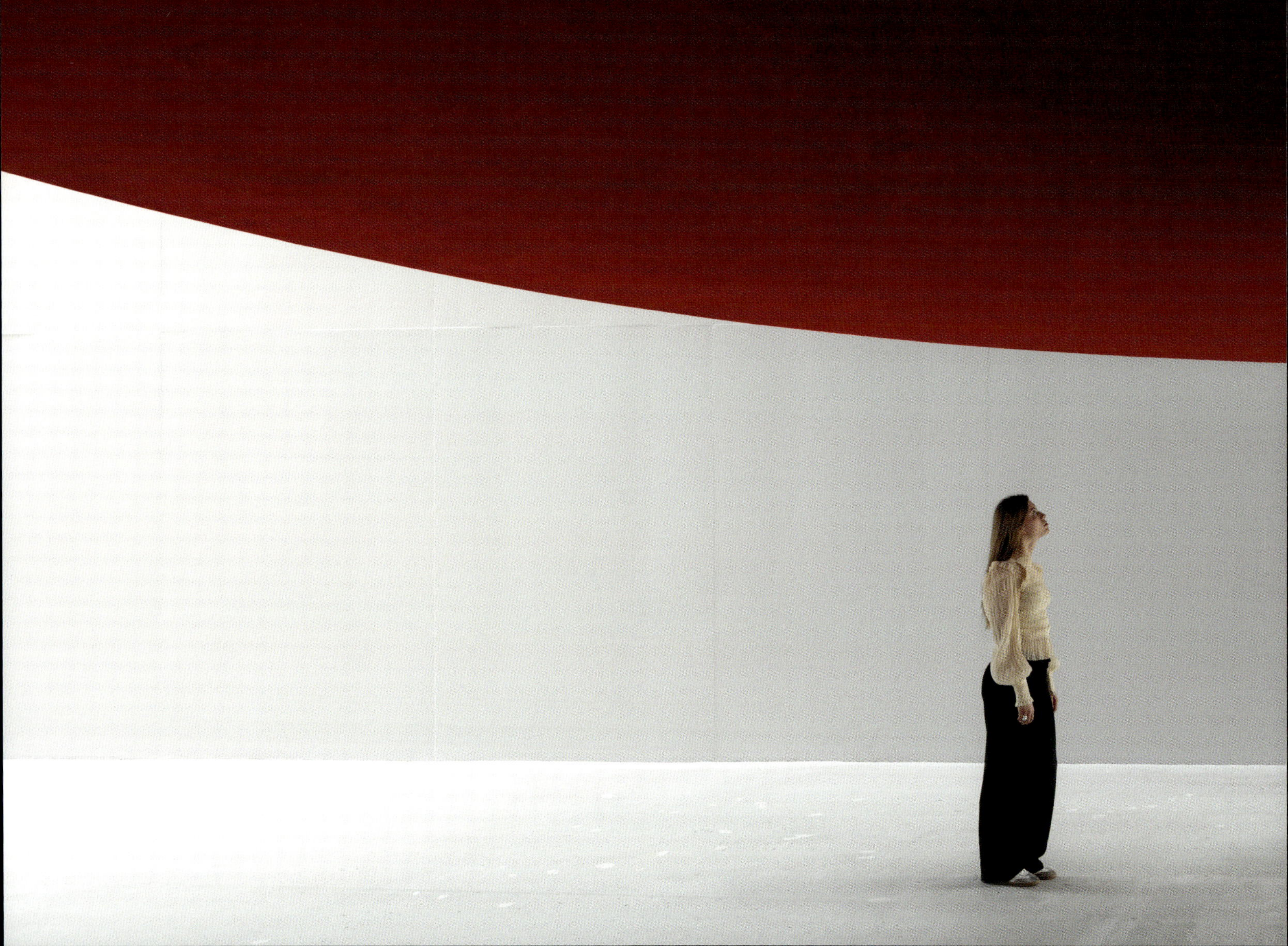

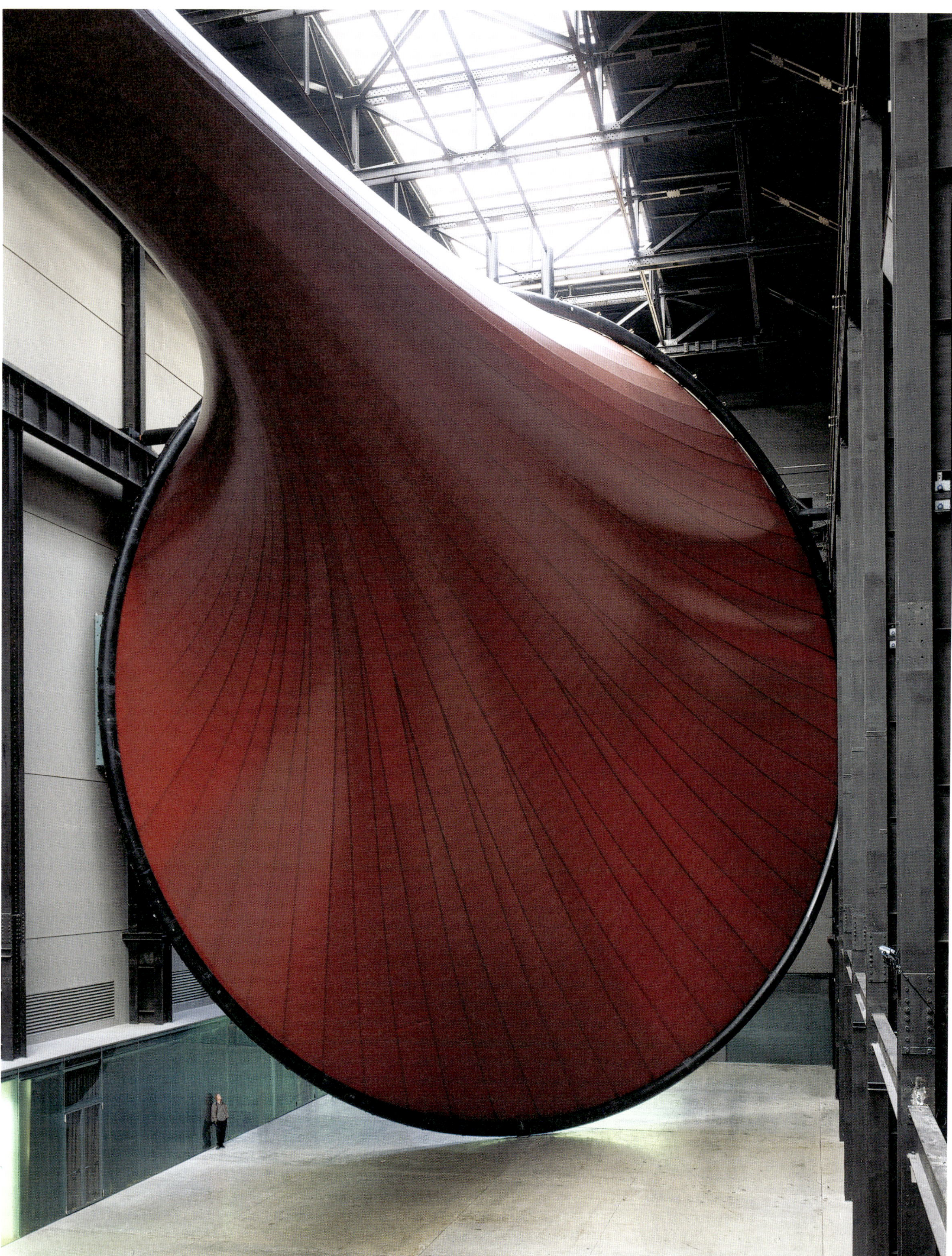

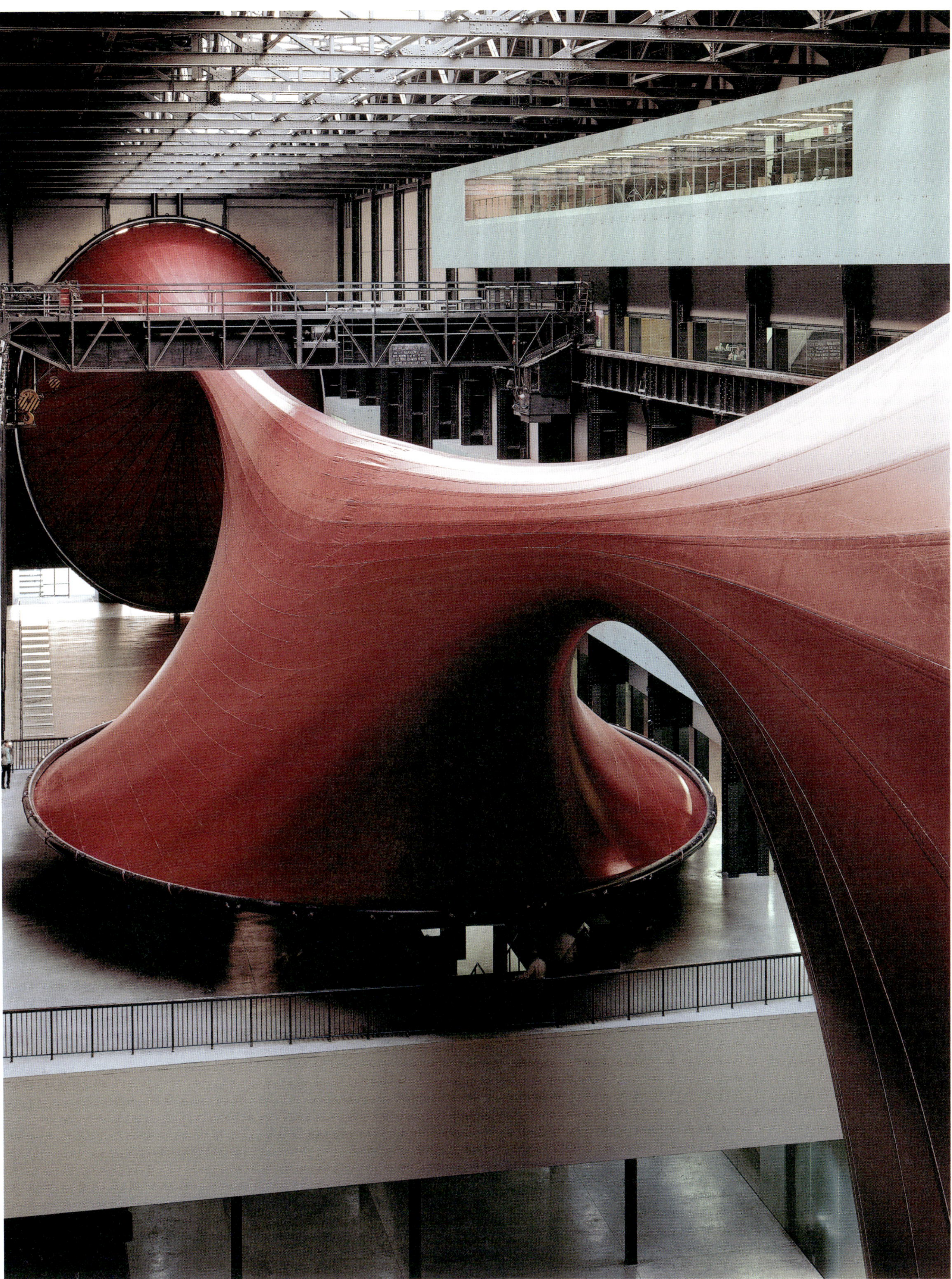

74

pp. 72-73
Marsyas, 2002
PVC, steel
35 × 23 × 155 m
Tate Modern, London

Mother as a Mountain, 1985
Mixed media, pigment
140 × 275 × 105 cm

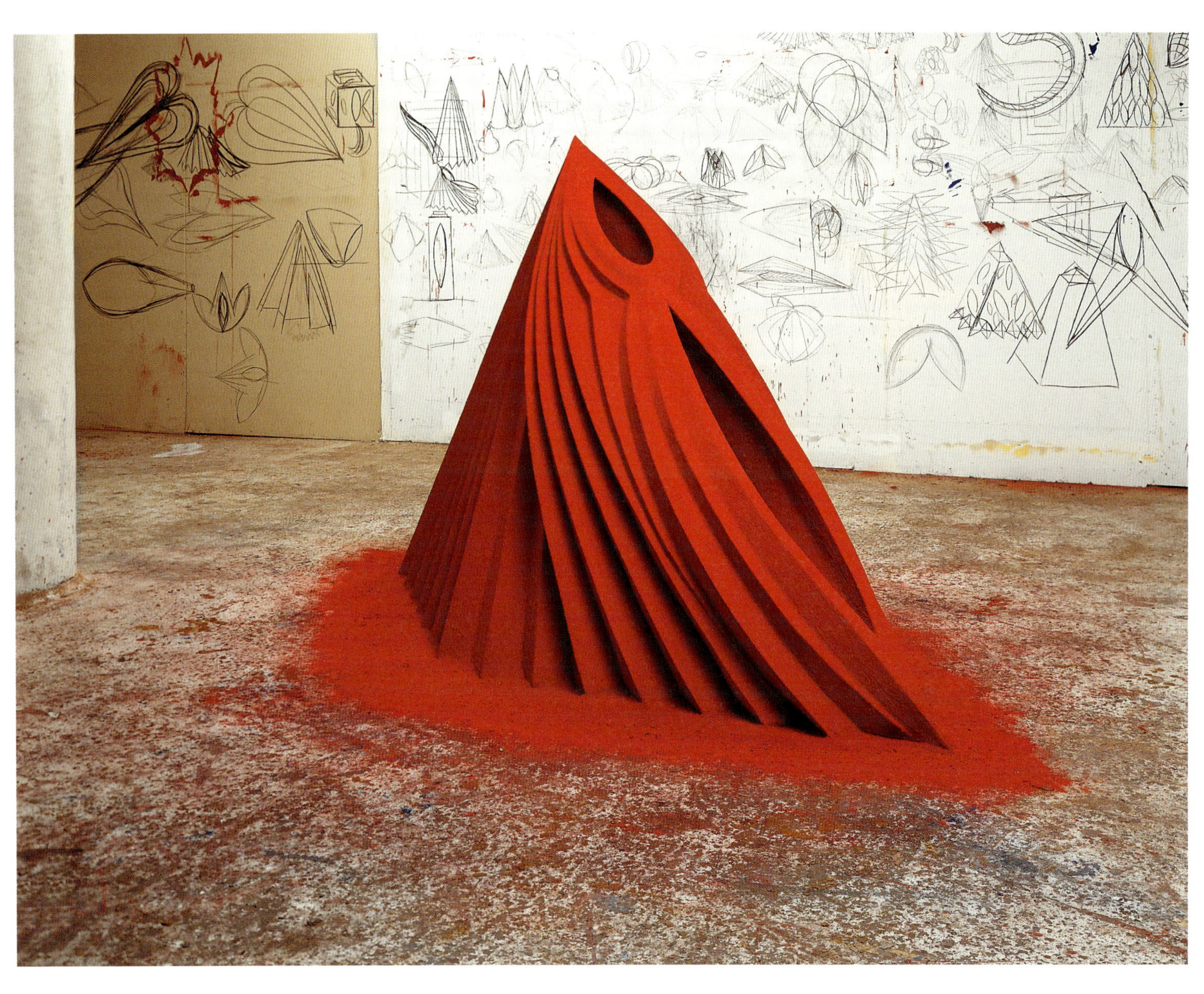

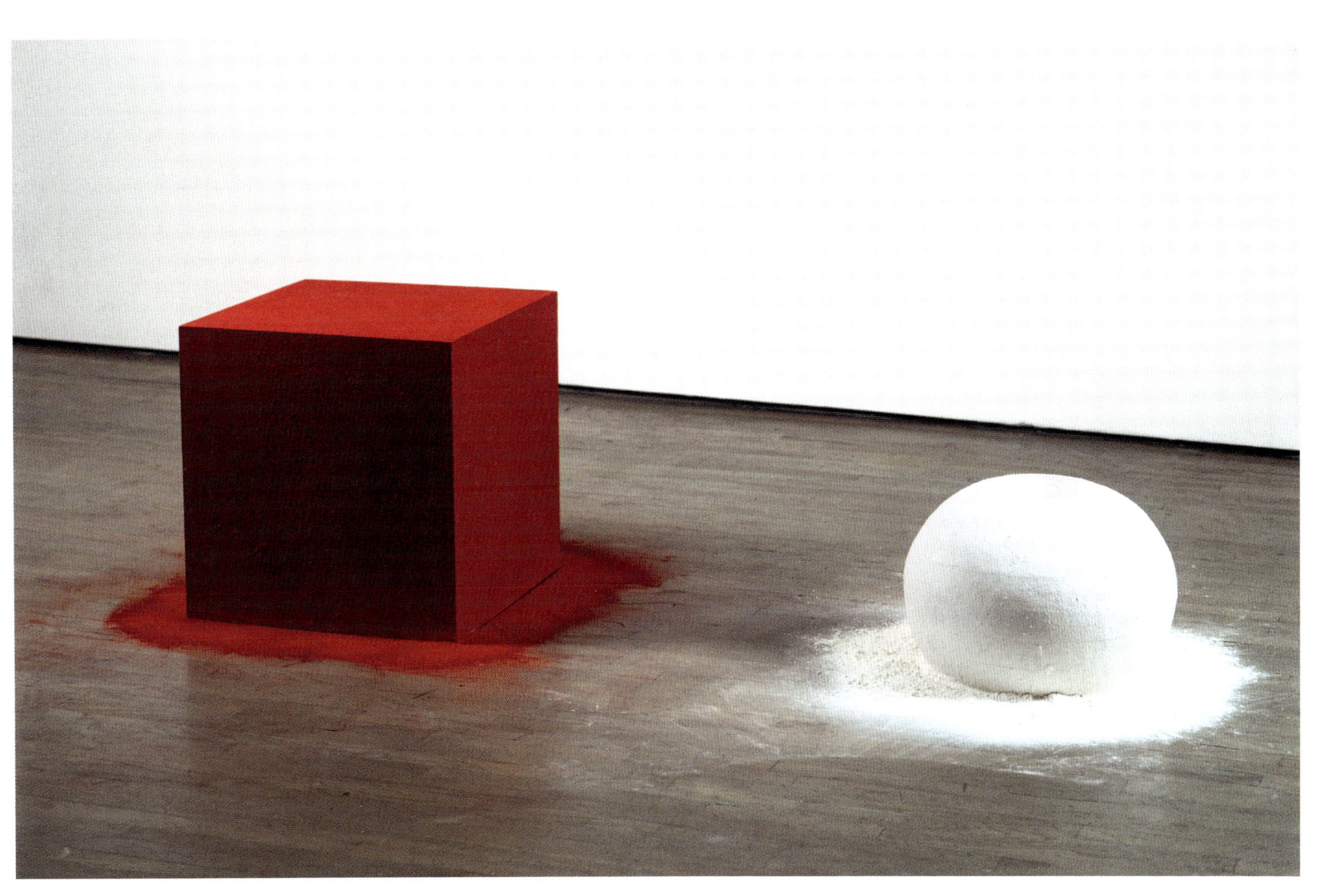

1000 Names, 1979-80
Mixed media, pigment
Dimensions variable

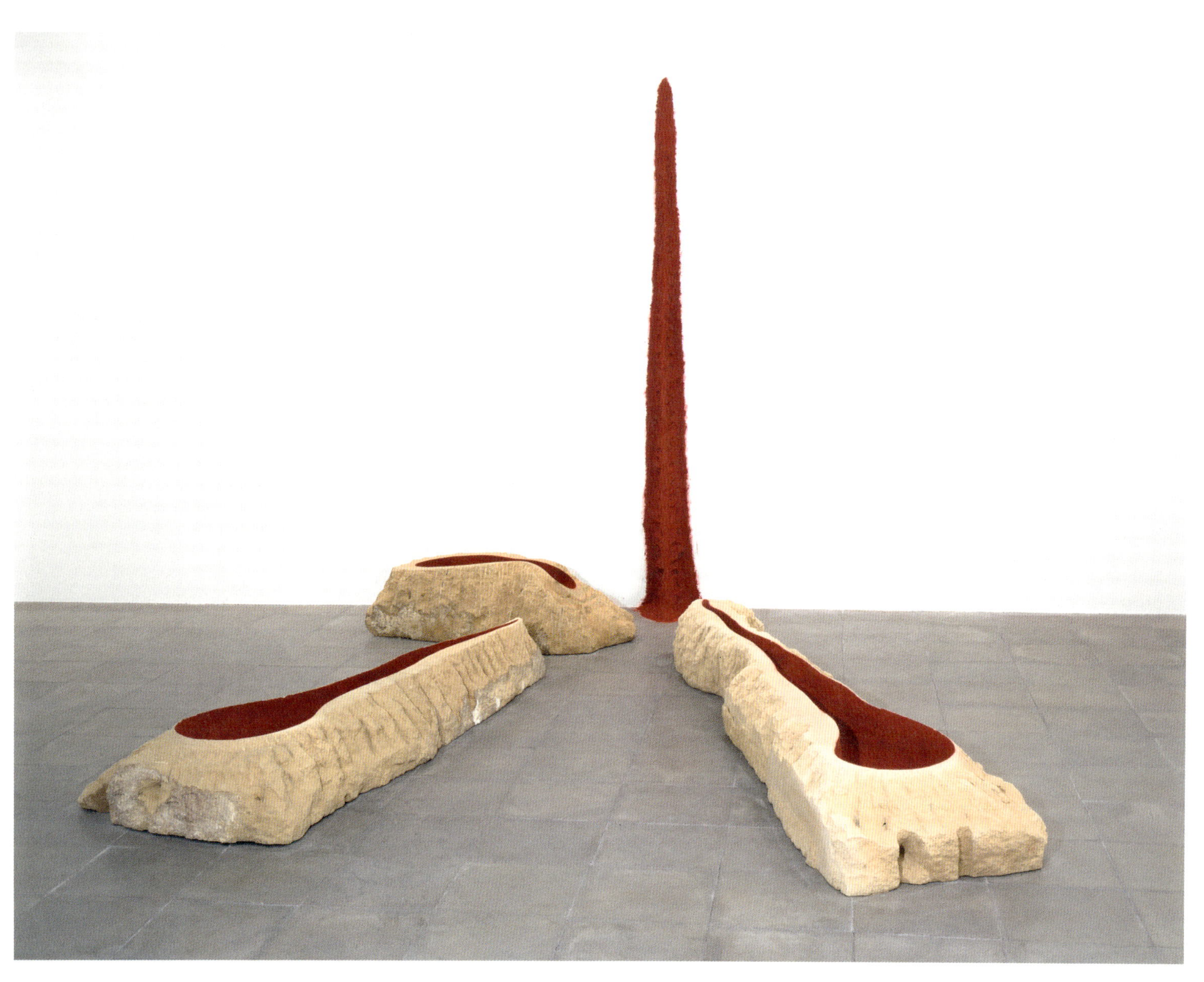

Wound, 1988
Limestone, pigment
310 × 475 × 394 cm

It Is Man, 1989-90
Sandstone, pigment
241 × 127 × 114 cm

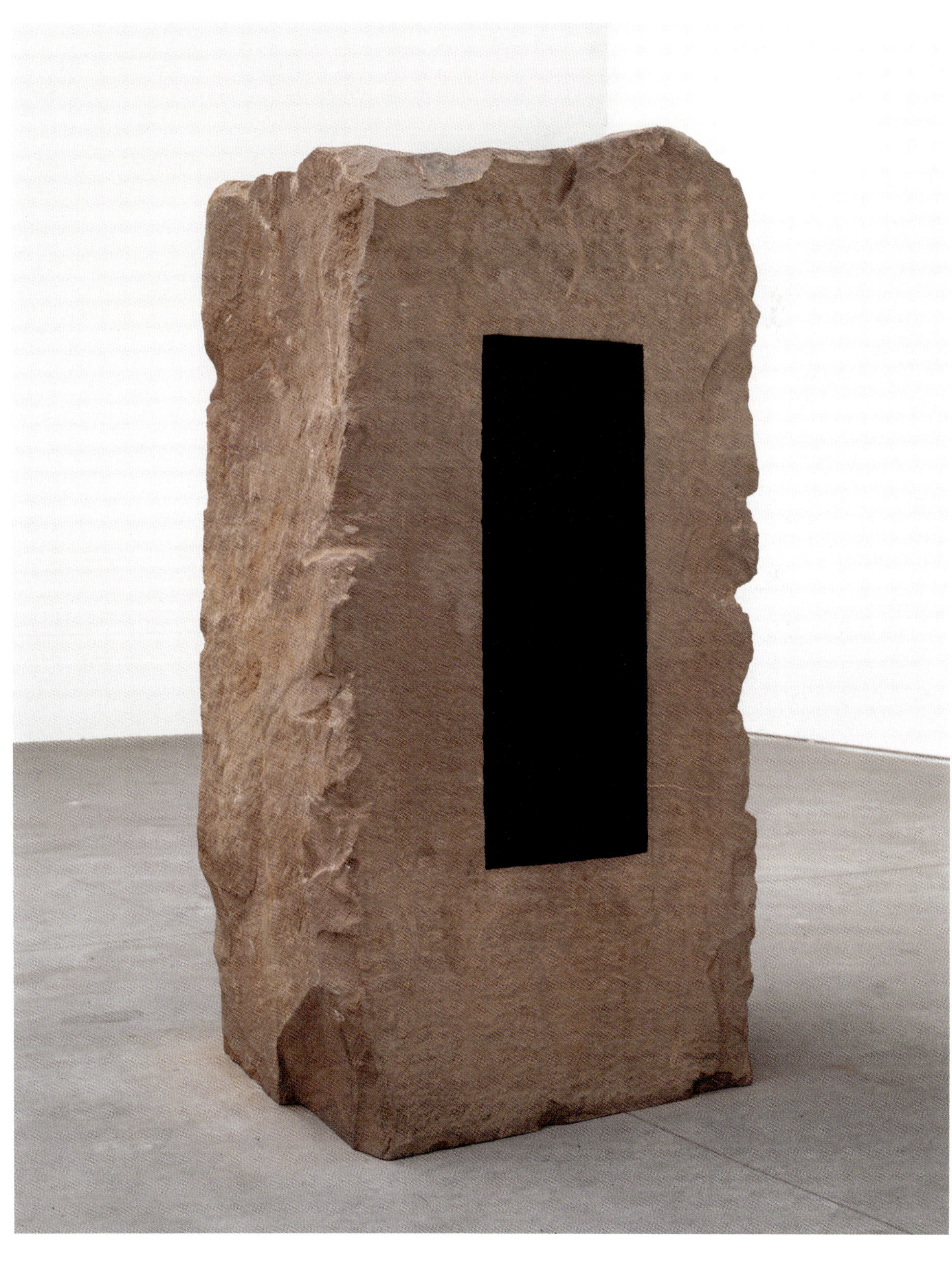

Grave, 2019
Resin, earth, pigment
270 × 250 × 247 cm
ARKEN Museum of Contemporary Art, Ishøj

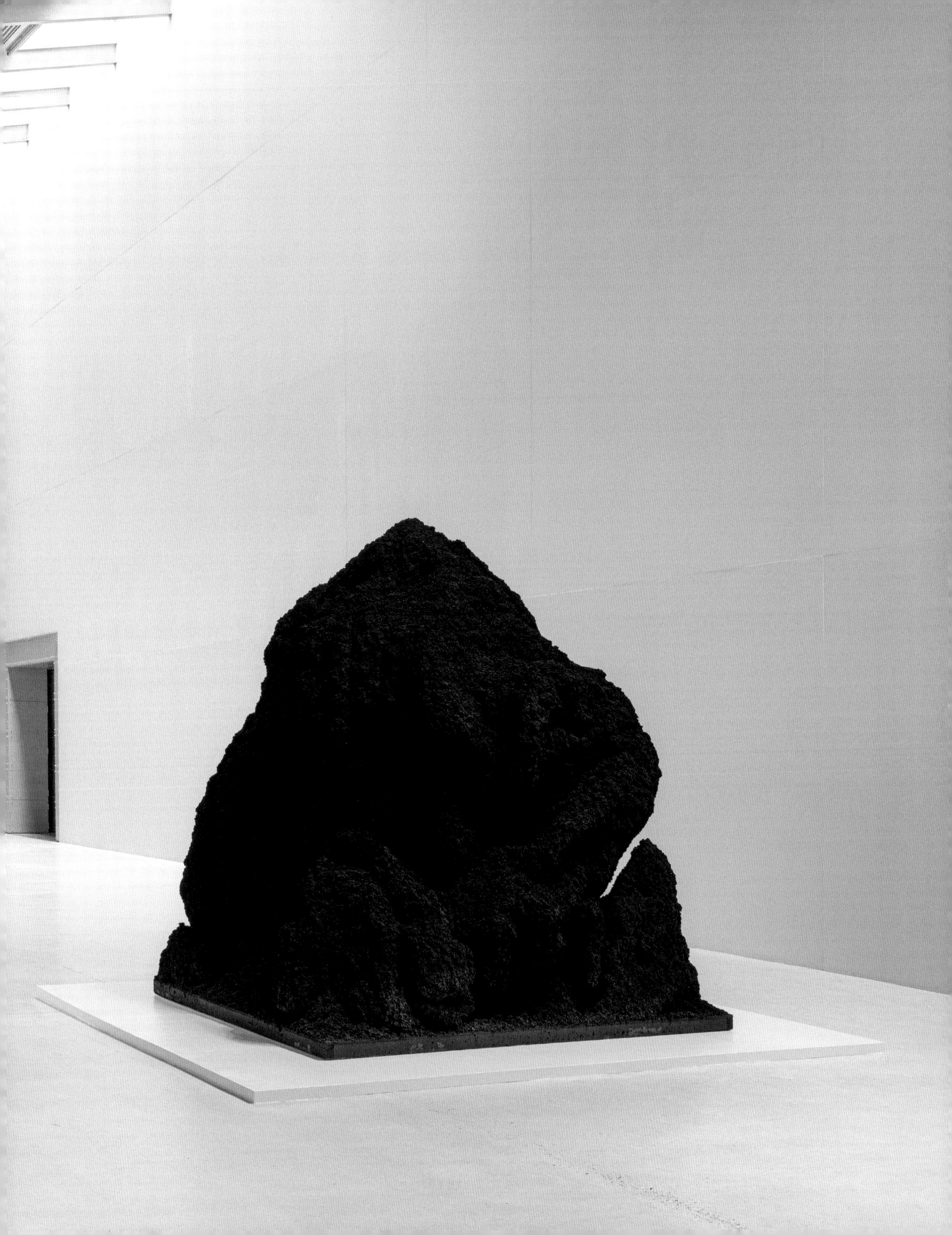

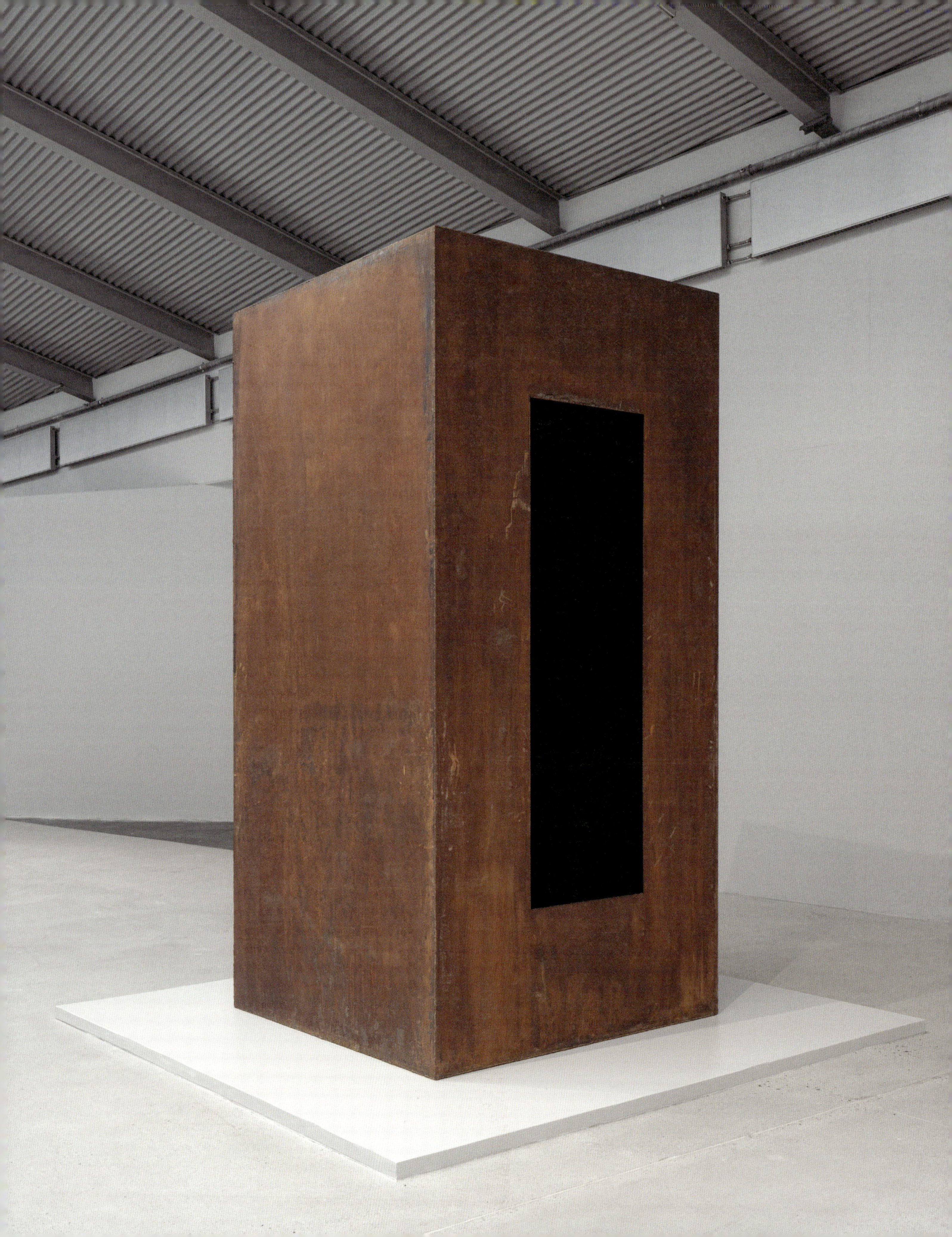

Untitled, 2022
Steel, lacquer, paint
300 × 150 × 150 cm
ARKEN Museum of Contemporary Art, Ishøj

Cave, 2012
Corten steel
551 × 800 × 805 cm

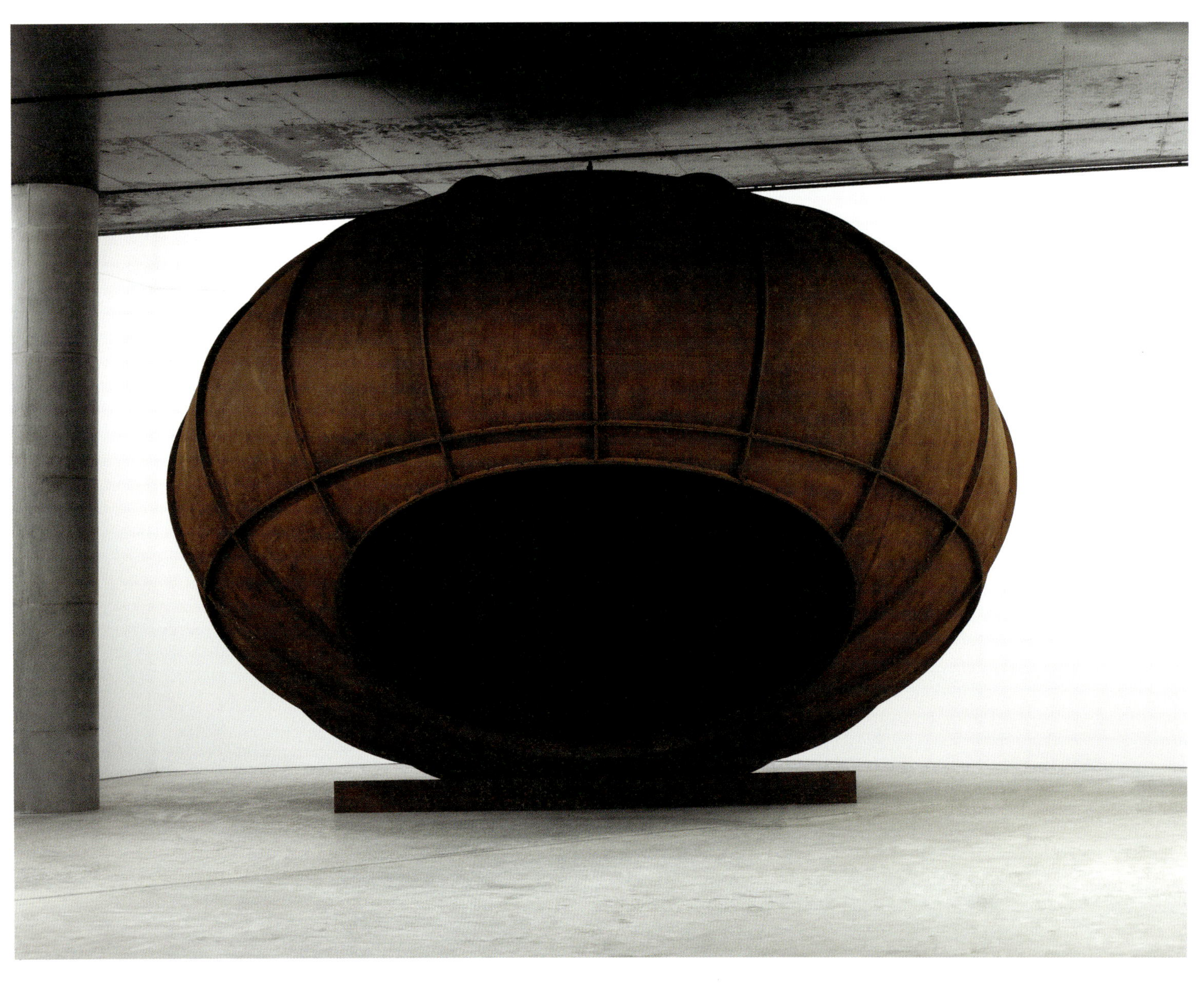

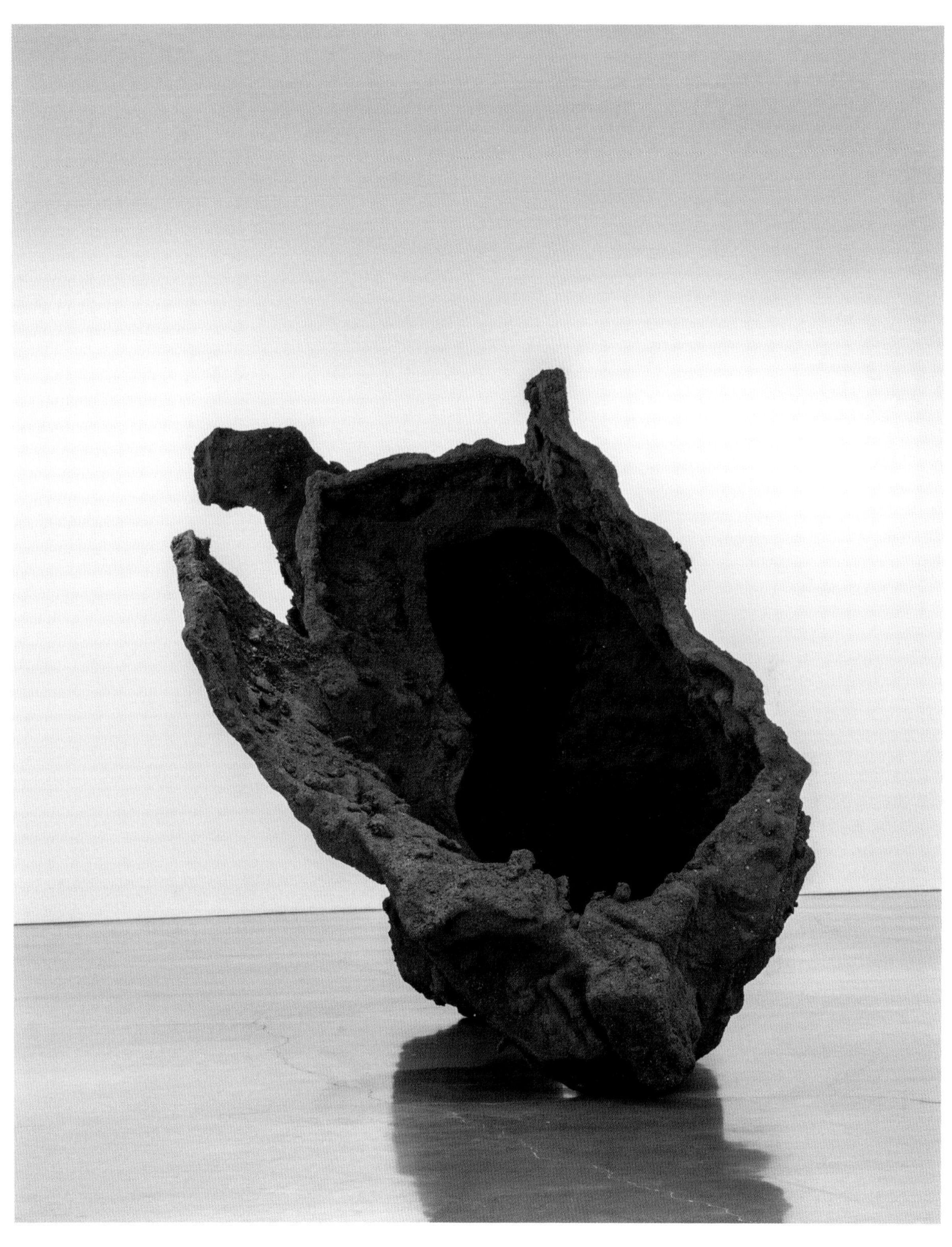

Gabriel, the Angel, stops and listens to the silence of the cave, 2014
Resin, earth
295 × 463 × 240 cm

Yellow, 1999
Fibreglass, pigment
600 × 600 × 300 cm

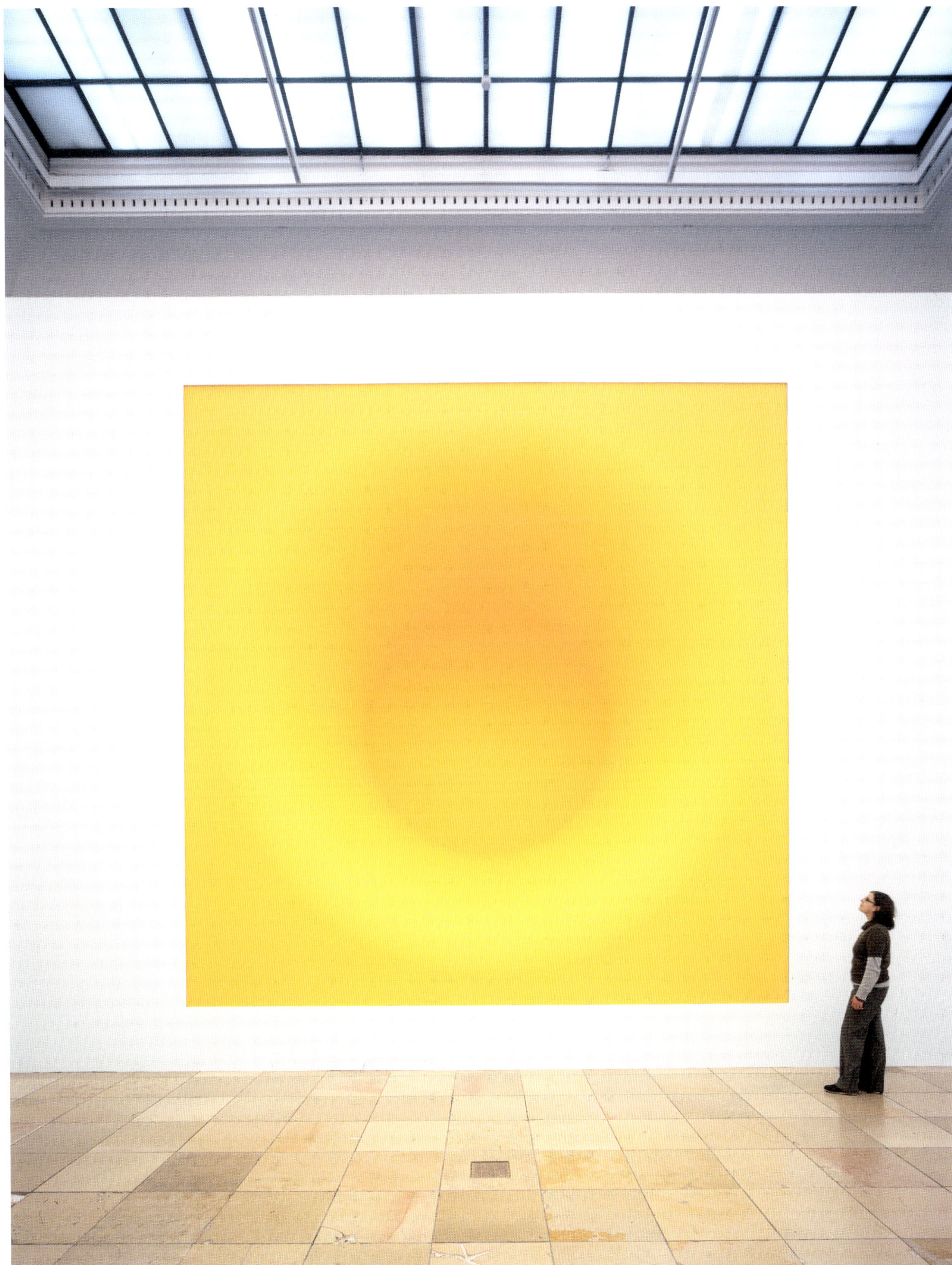

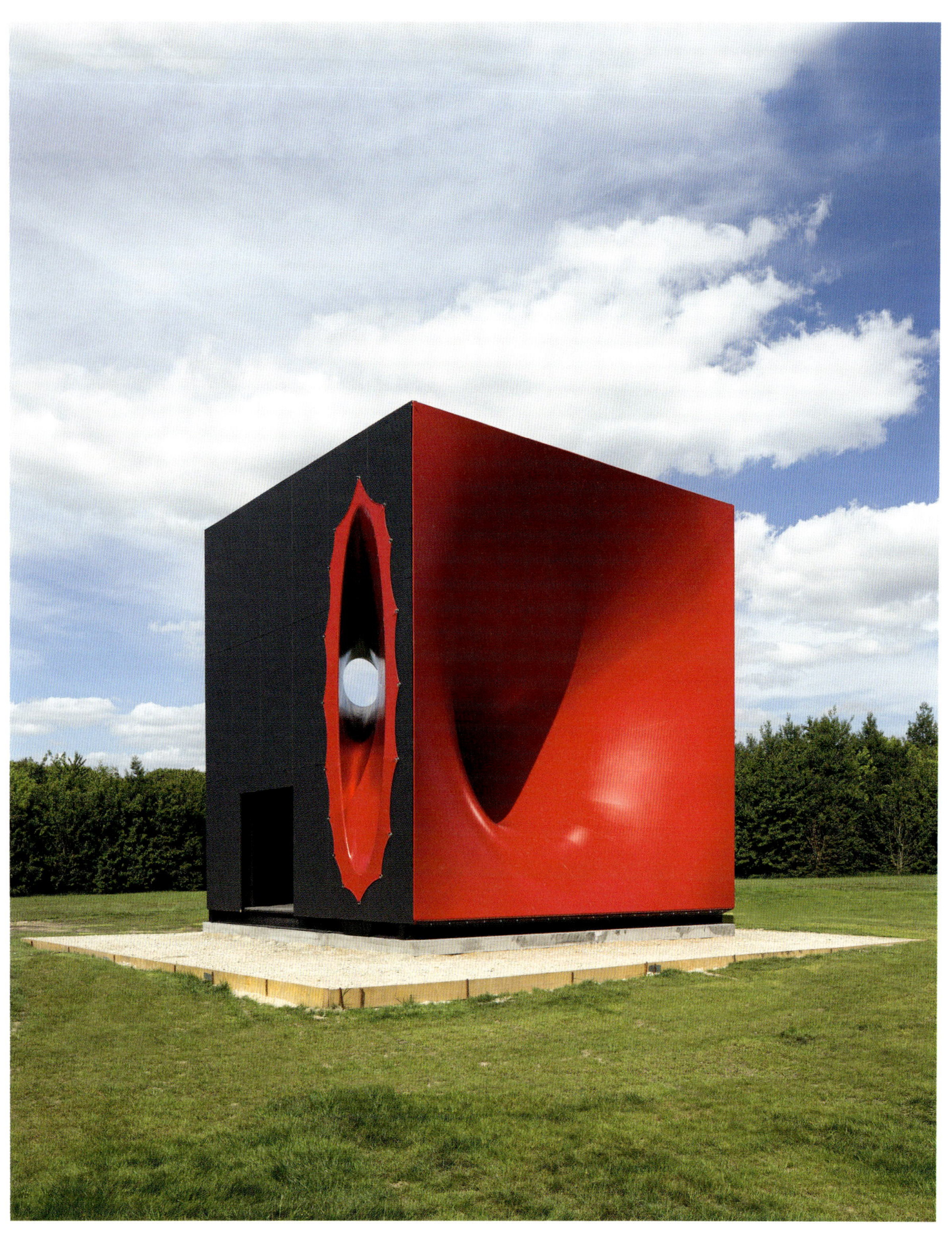

This spread
Sectional Body preparing for Monadic Singularity, 2015
PVC, steel
732 × 732 × 732 cm

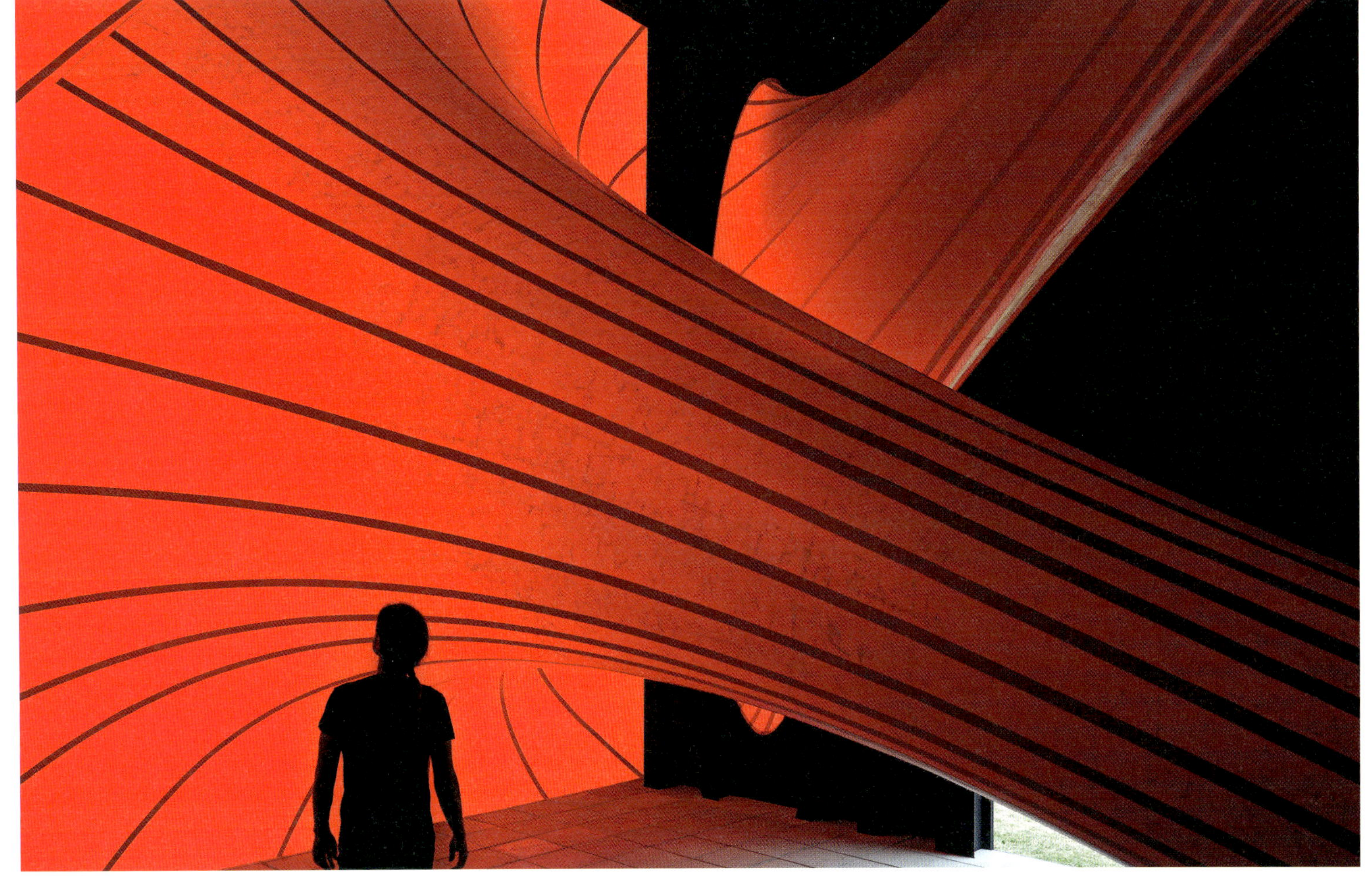

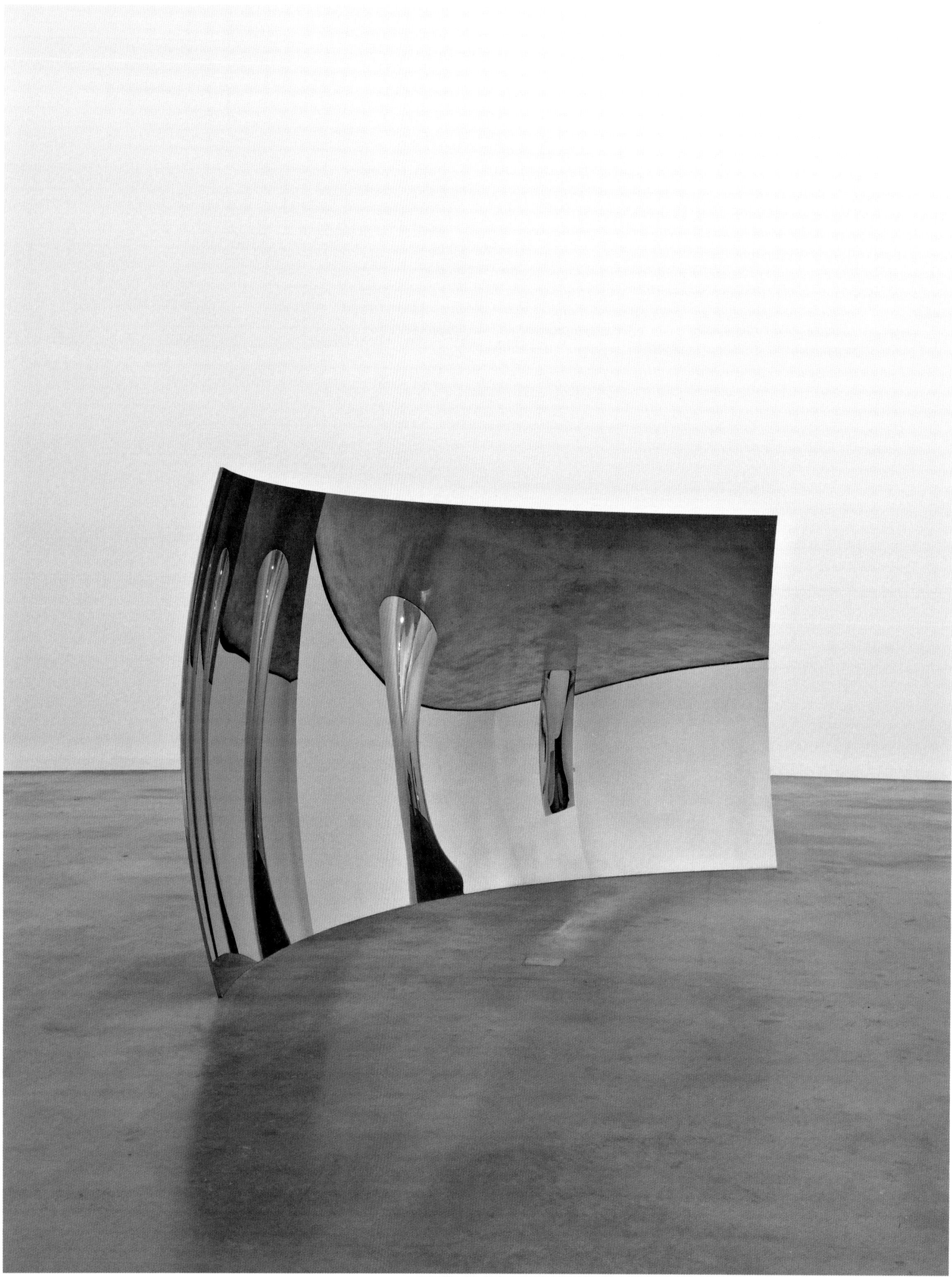

Vertigo, 2006
Stainless steel
225 × 480 × 60 cm

S-Curve, 2006
Stainless steel
216.5 × 975.4 × 121.9 cm
ARKEN Museum of Contemporary Art, Ishøj

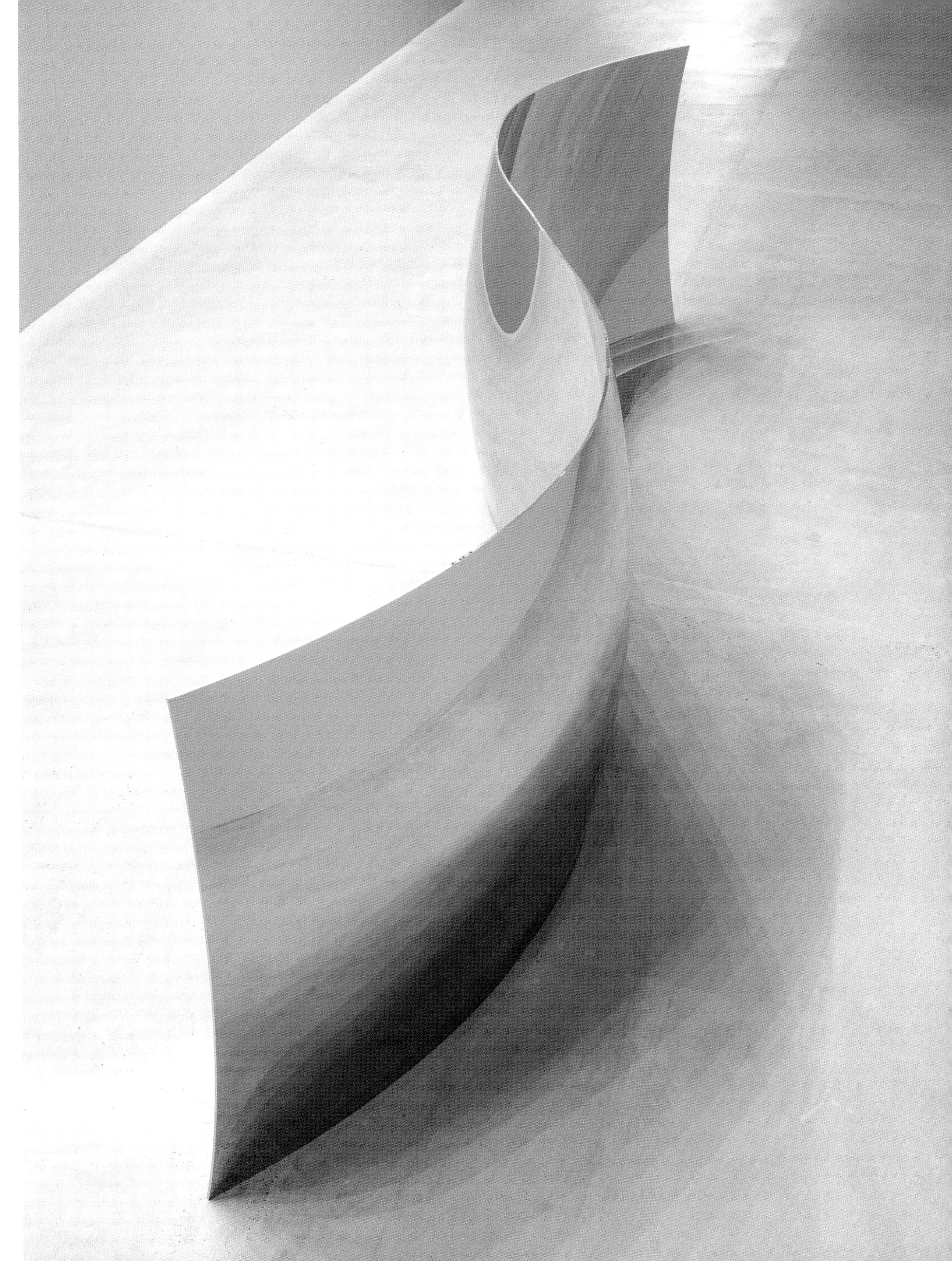

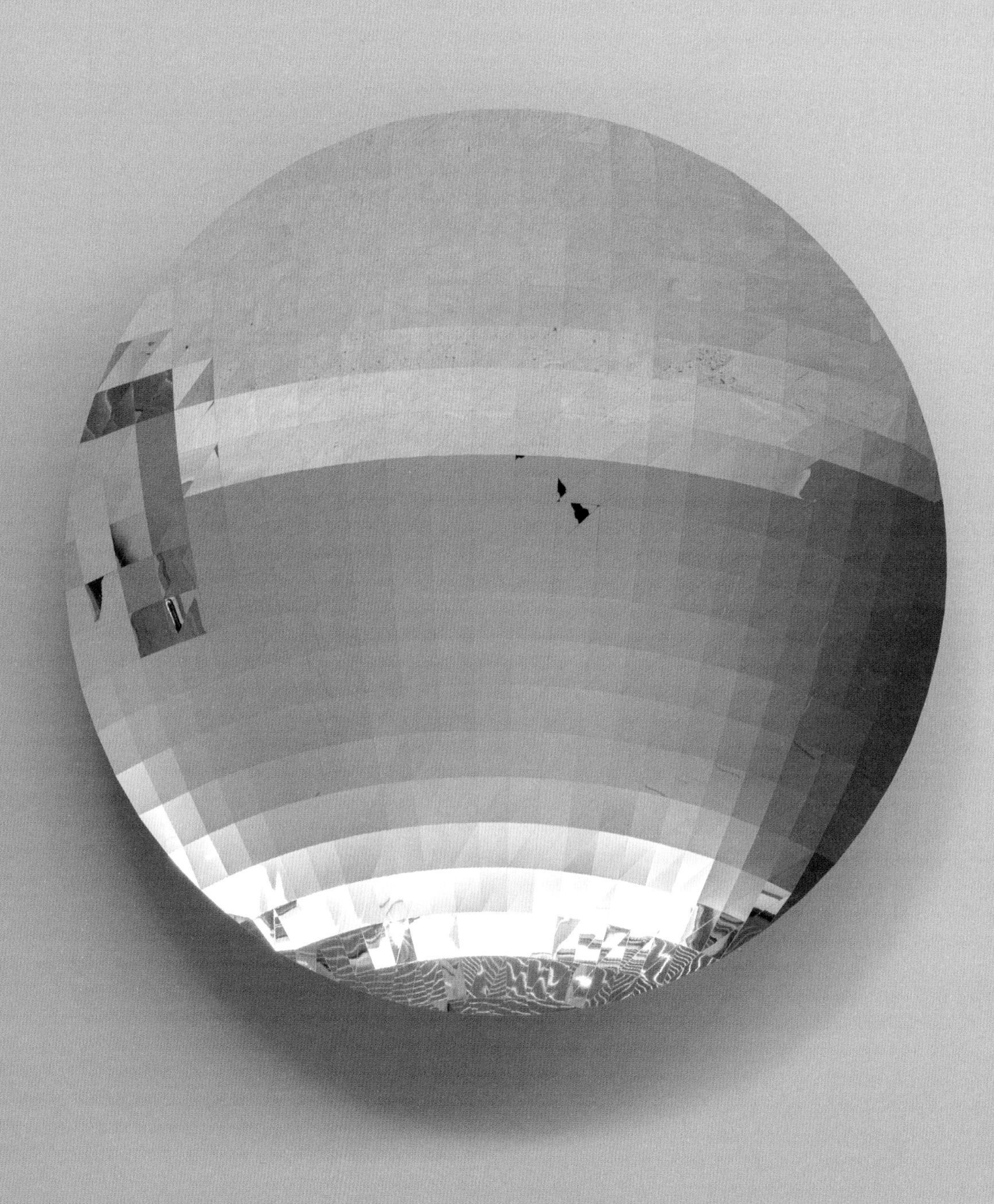

Random Triangle Mirror, 2017
Stainless steel, resin
199 × 199 × 35 cm
ARKEN Museum of Contemporary Art, Ishøj

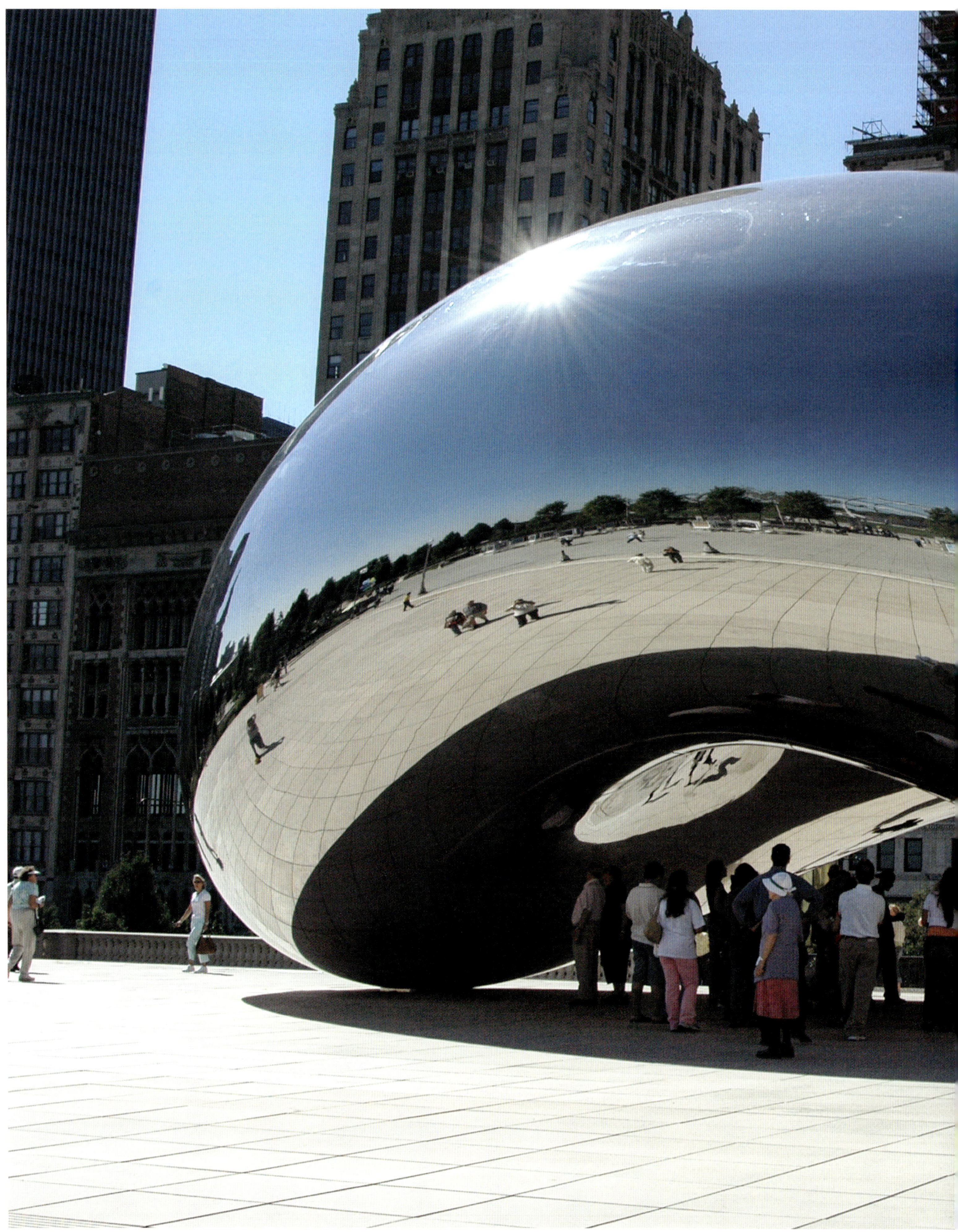

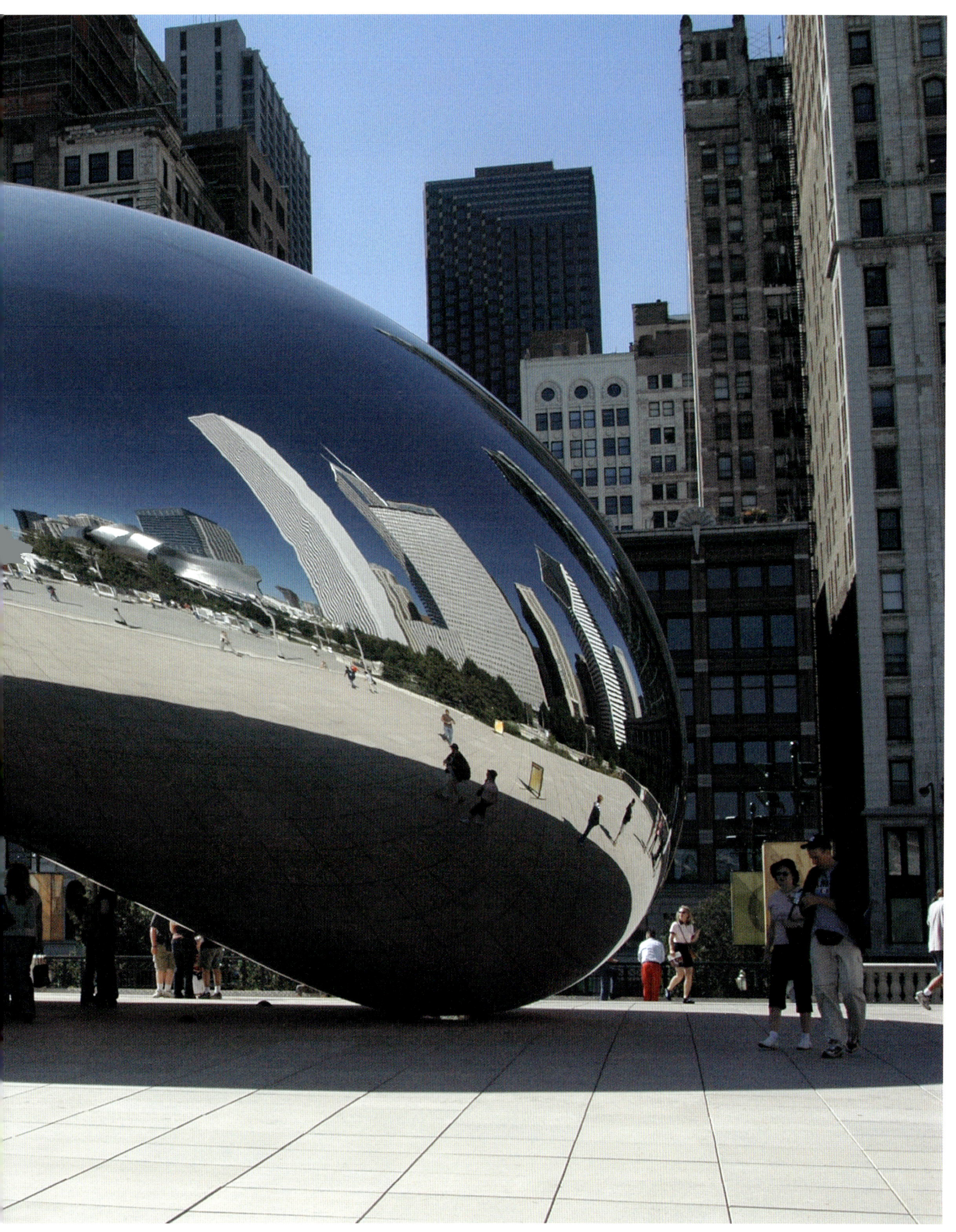

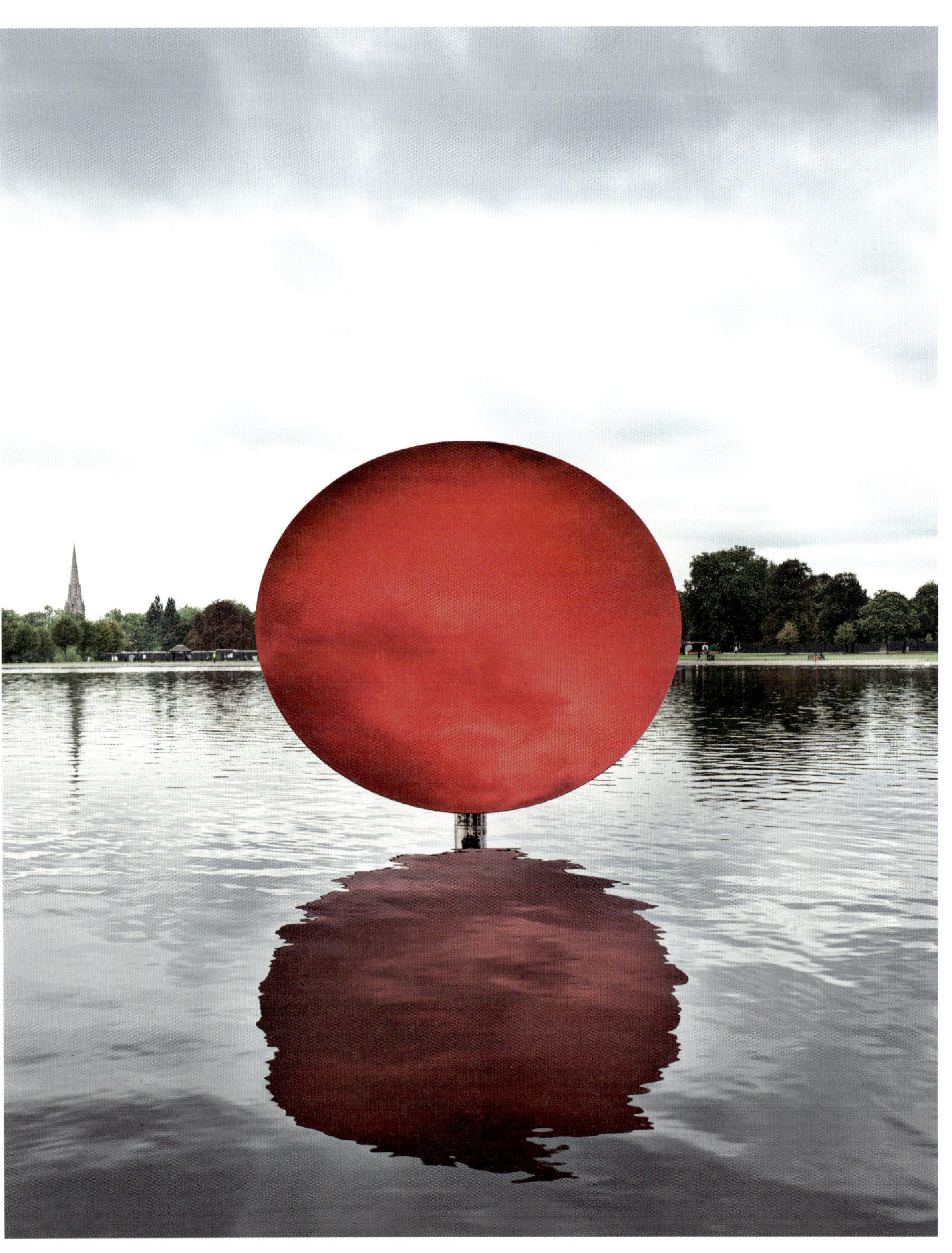

pp. 94-95
Cloud Gate, 2004
Stainless steel
10 × 20 × 12.8 m
Millennium Park, Chicago

Sky Mirror, Red, 2009
Stainless steel, lacquer
274 × 290 × 146 cm

Non-Object [Spire], 2007
Stainless steel
302.2 × 300 × 300 cm

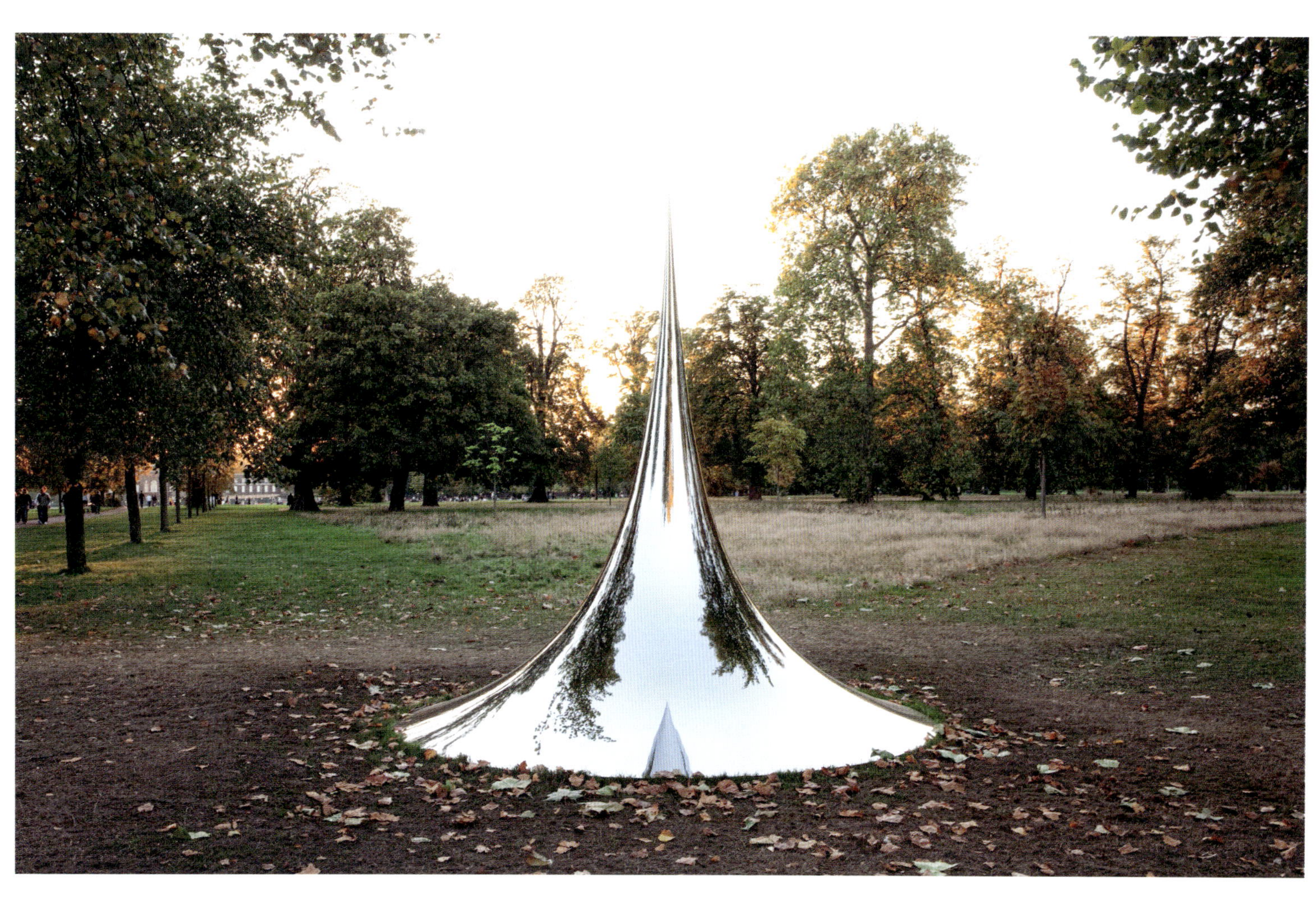

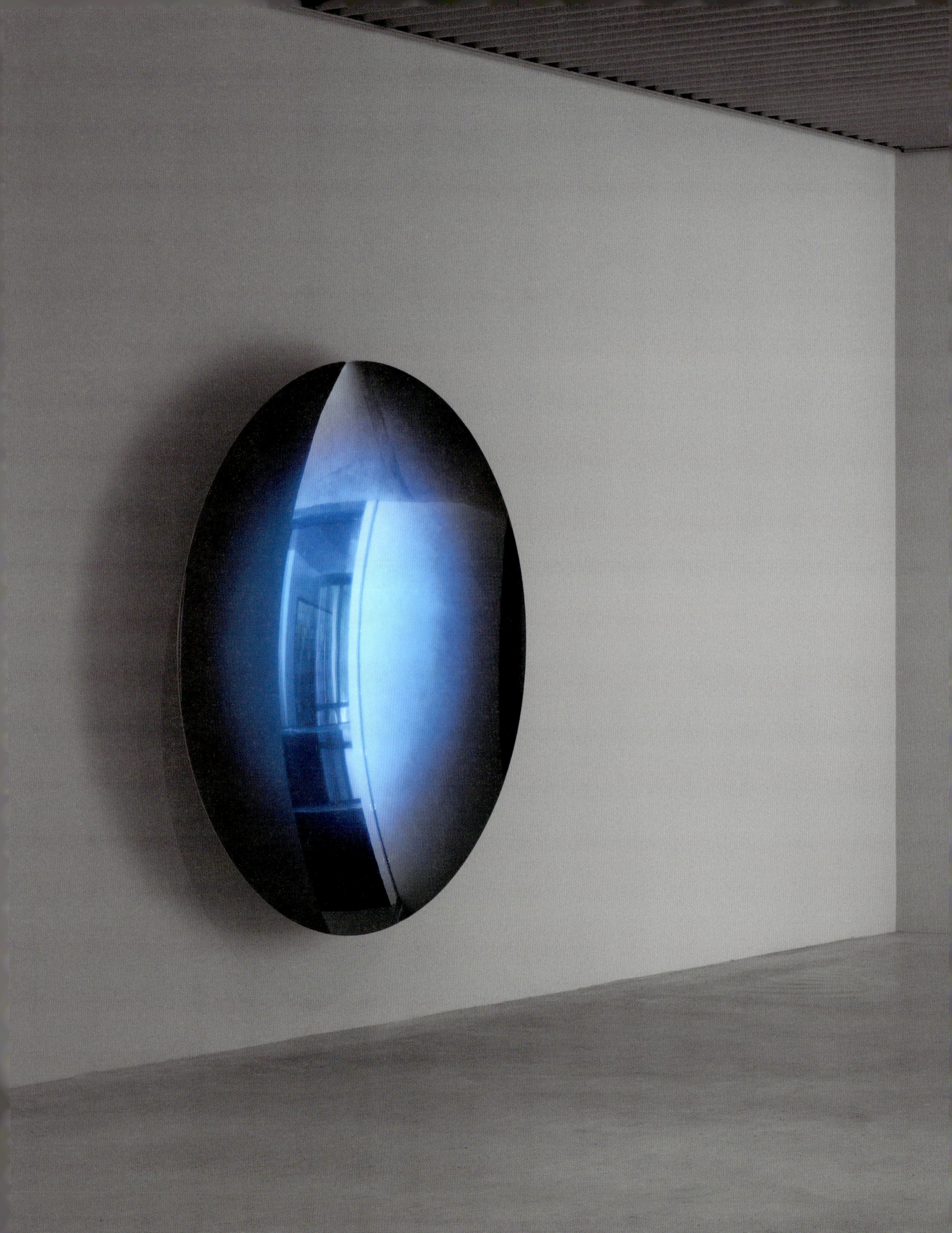

This and the following spread
Mipa Blue no.5 to Cobalt Blue and Black, 2021
Aluminium, paint
214 × 214 × 25 cm
 ARKEN Museum of Contemporary Art, Ishøj

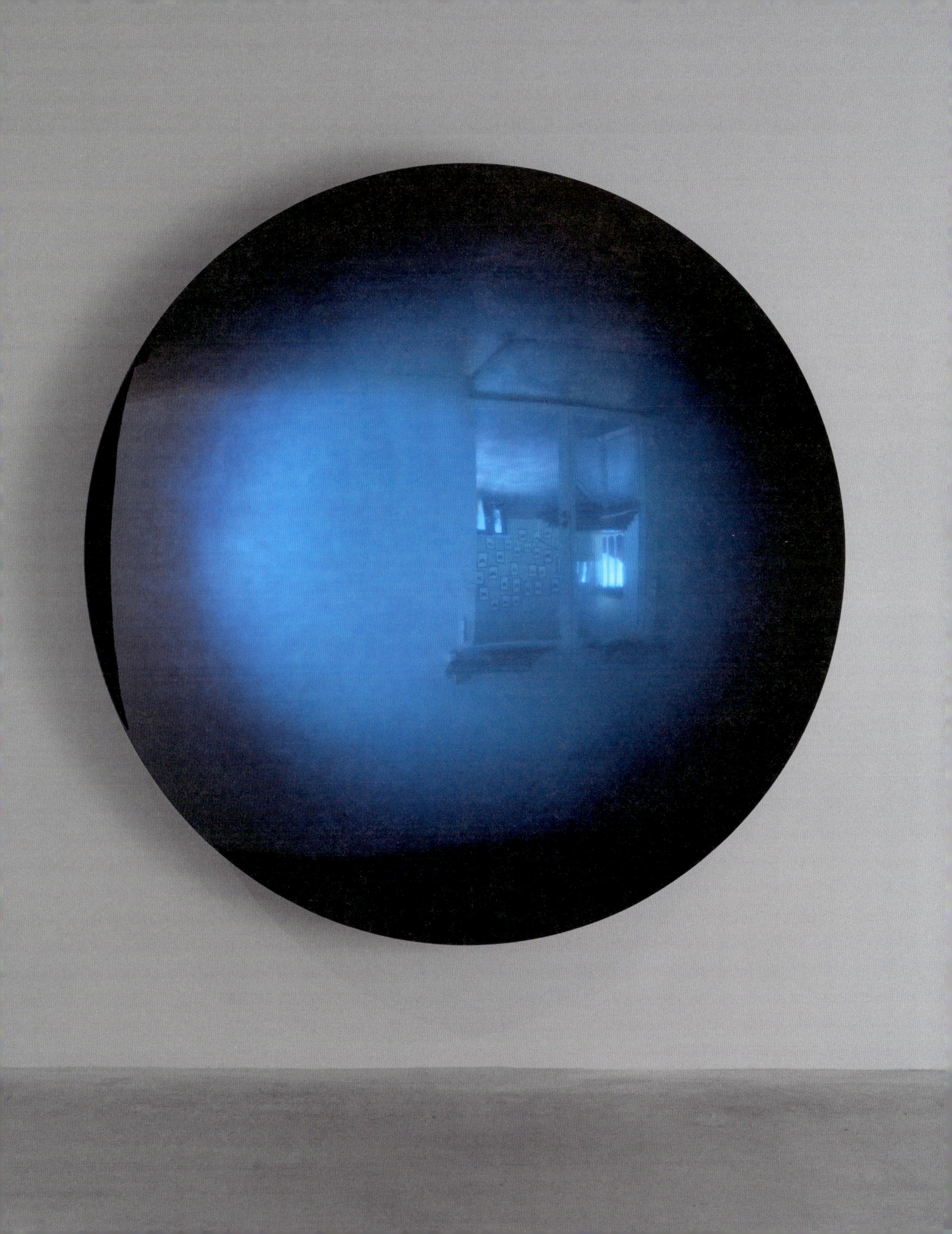

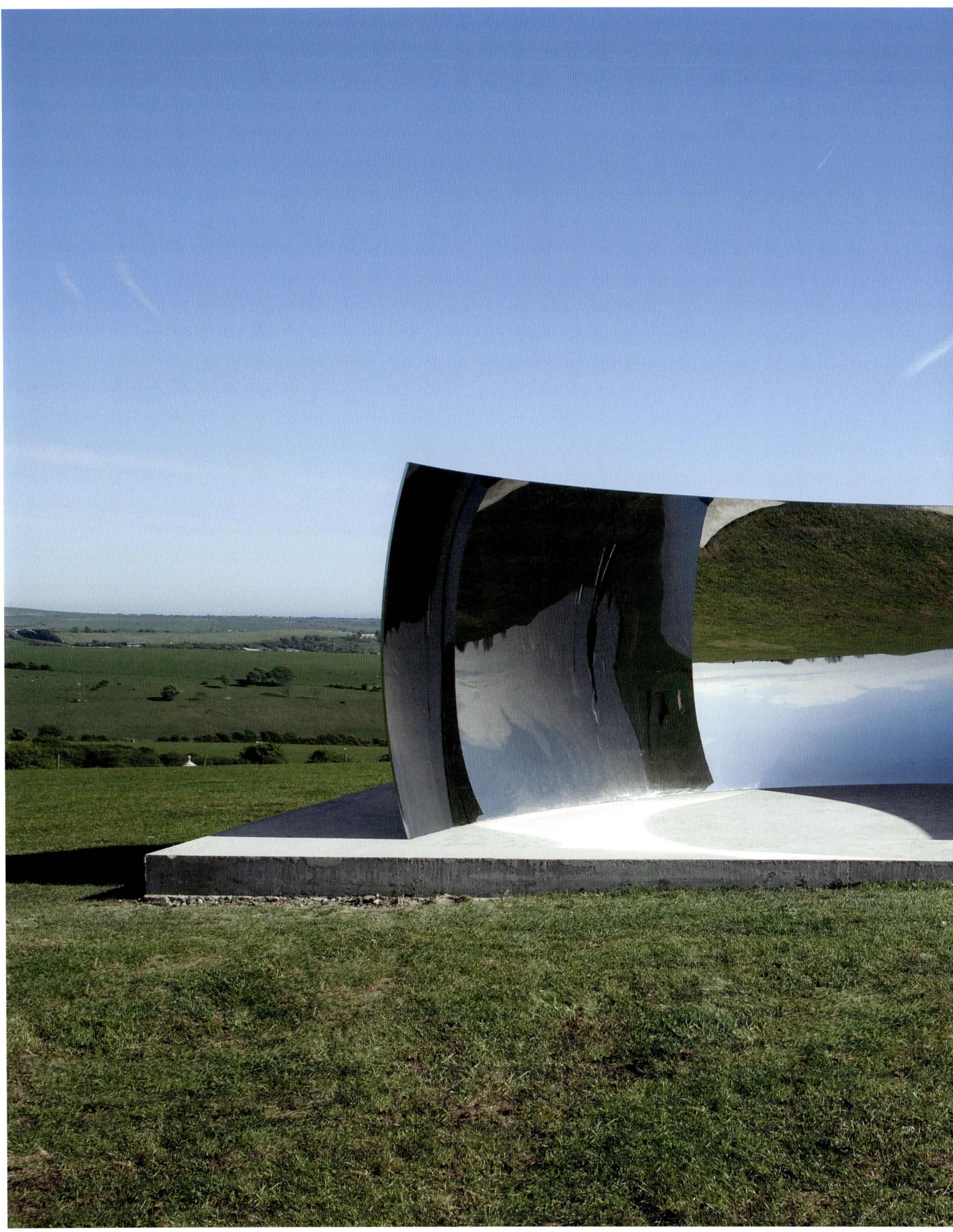

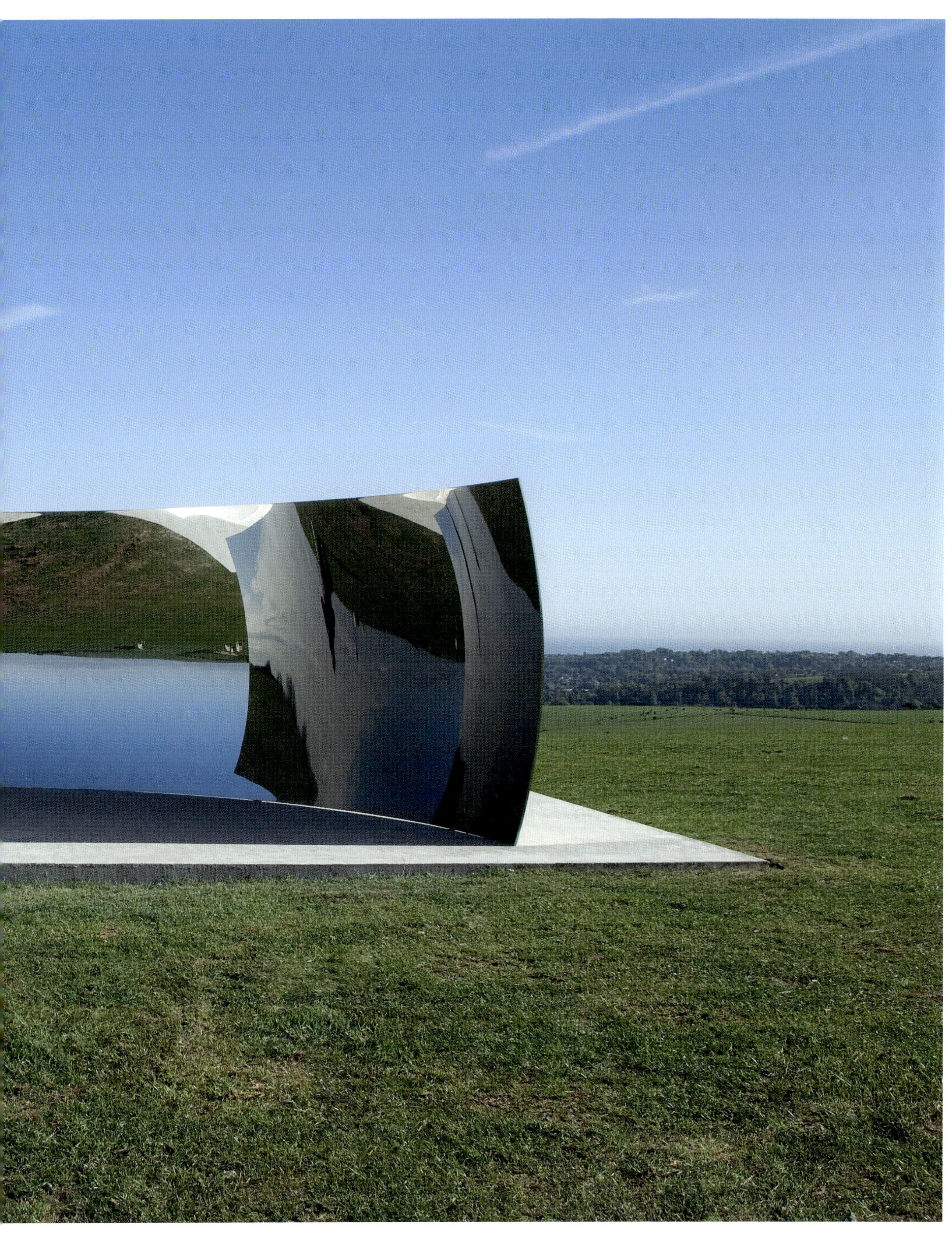

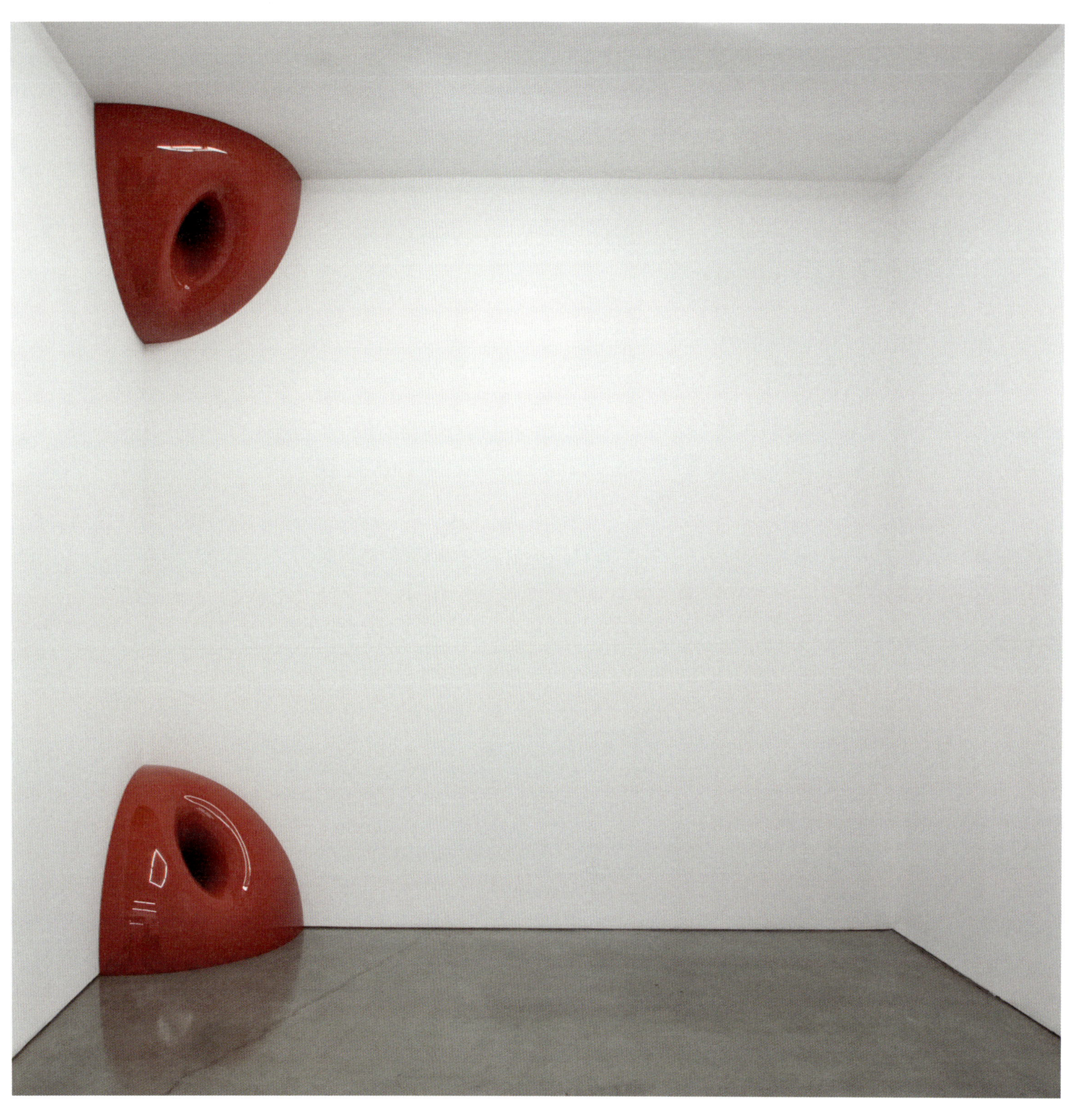

pp. 102-103
C-Curve, 2007
Stainless steel
220 × 770 × 300 cm

Double Corner, 2008
Resin, paint
Dimensions variable

Newborn, 2019
Stainless steel
300 × 300 × 300 cm

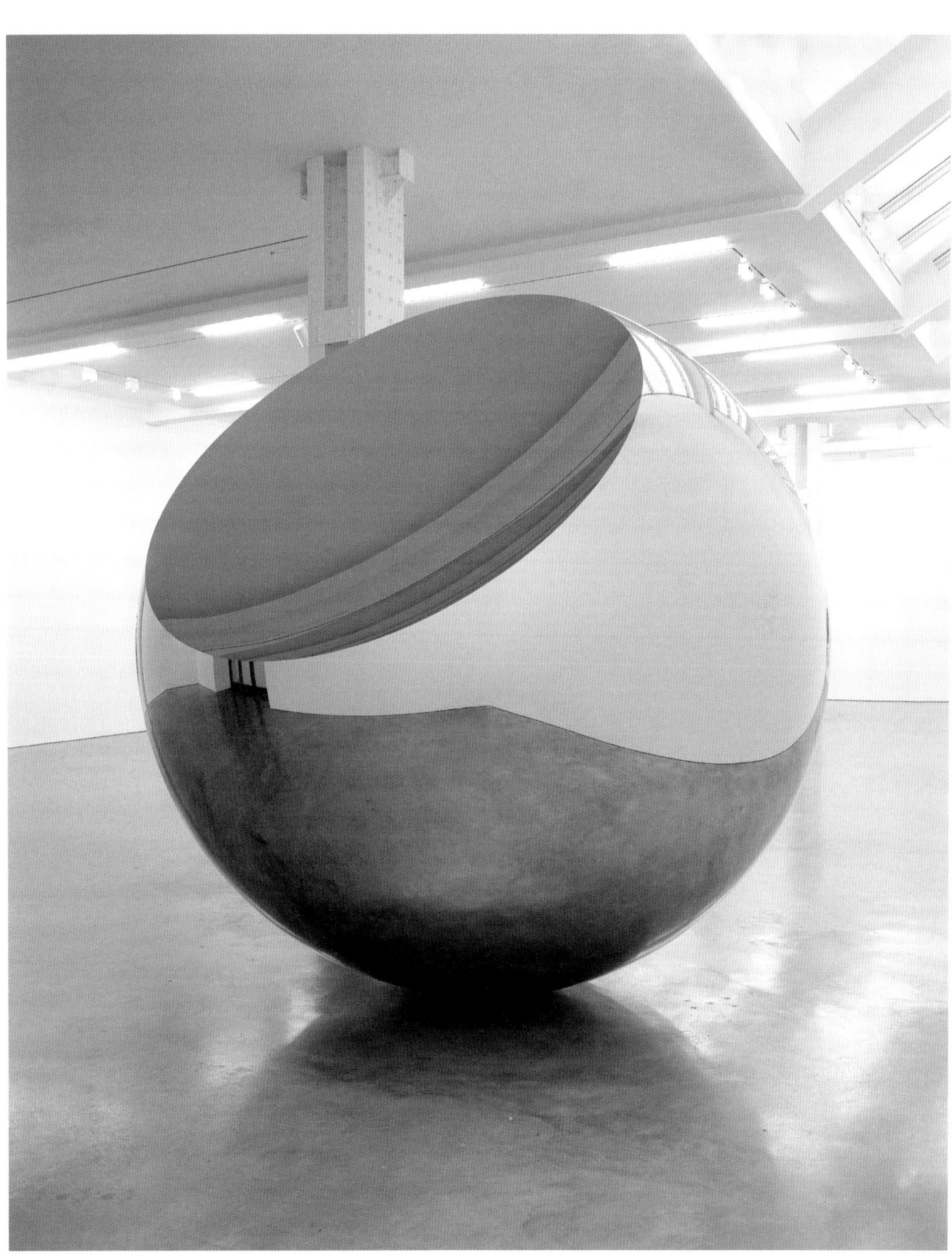

This and the following spread
Descent into Limbo, 1992
Mixed media
Dimensions variable
ARKEN Museum of Contemporary Art, Ishøj

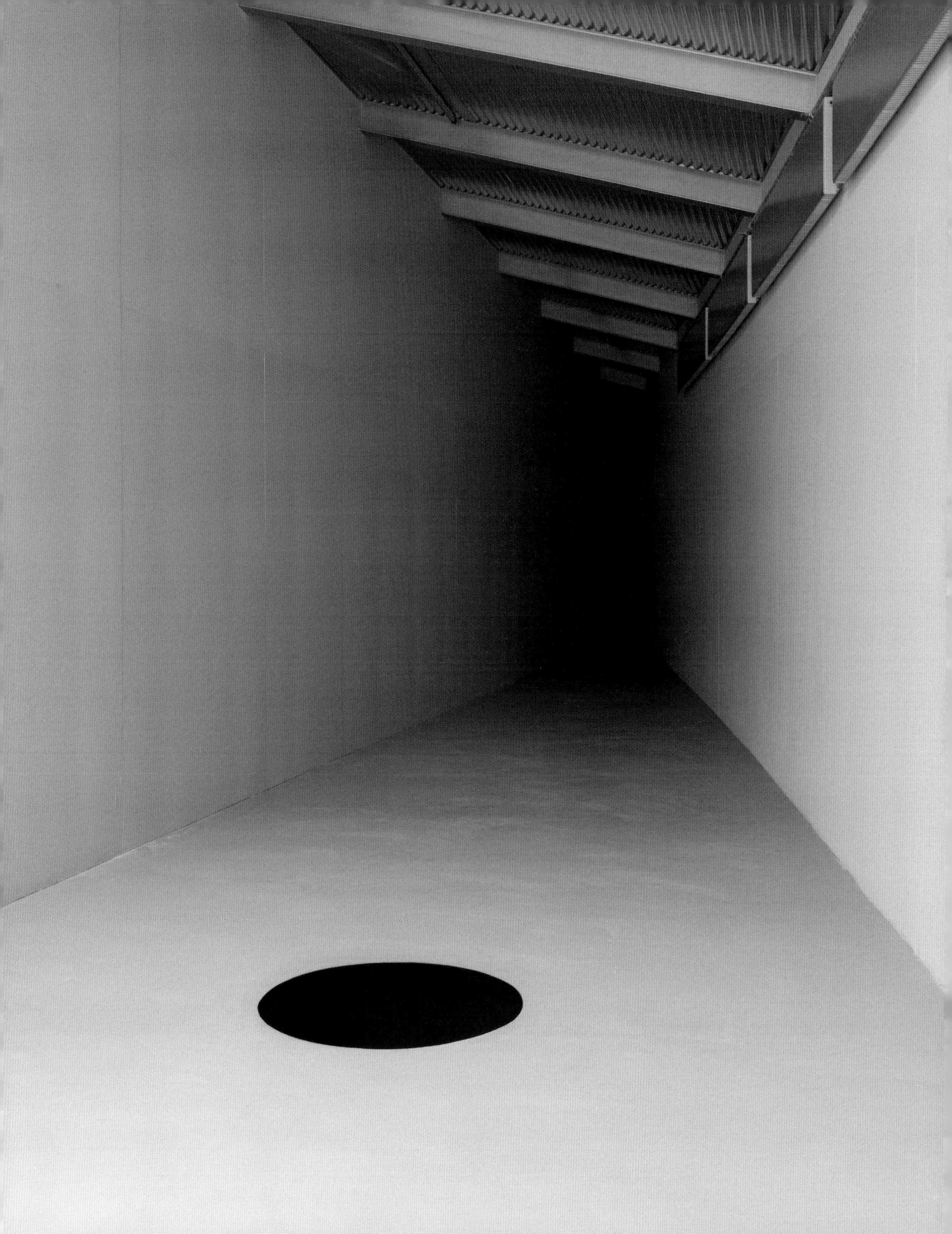

Untitled, 1996
Wood, pigment
Dimensions variable

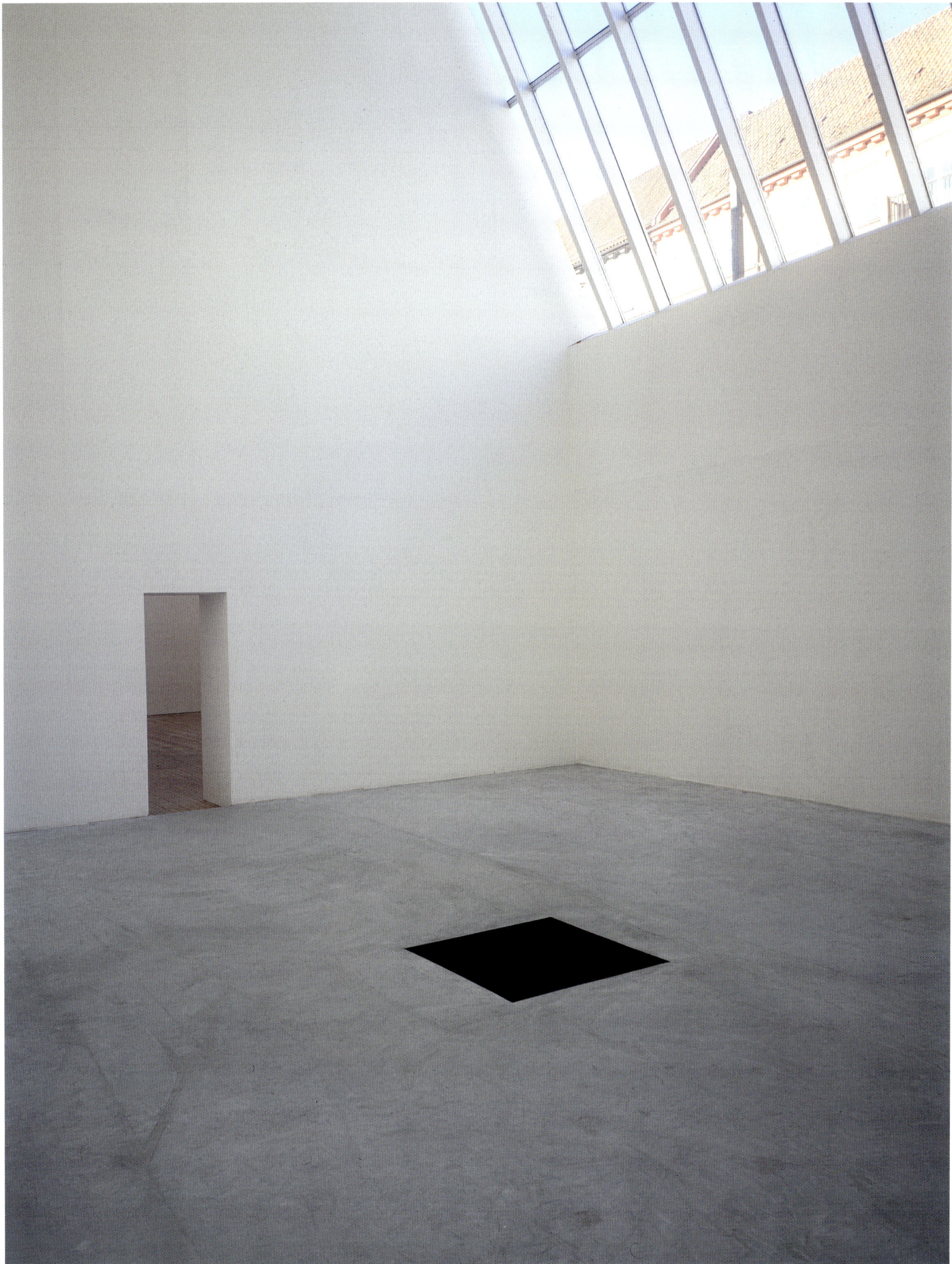

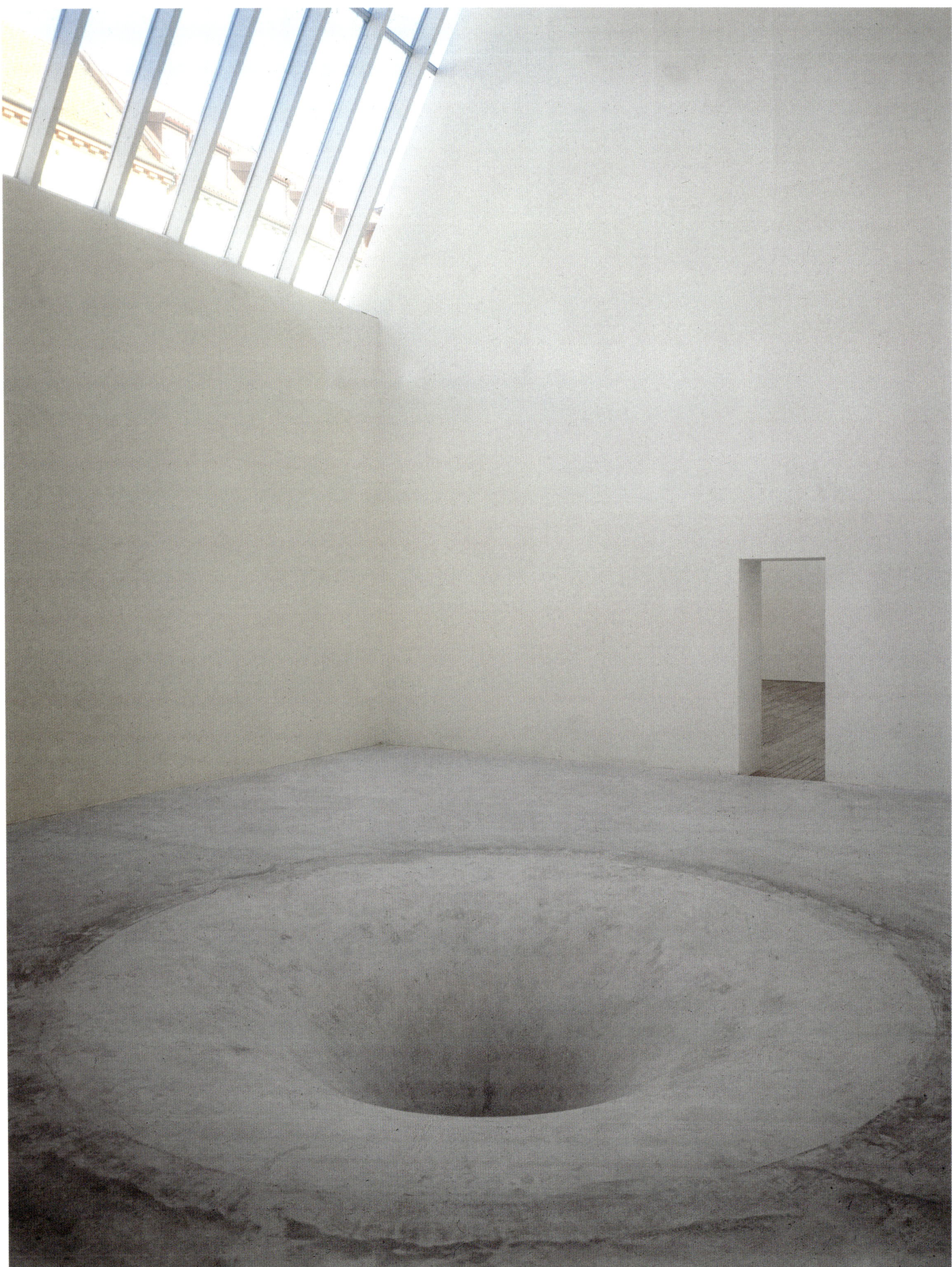

Untitled, 1996
Concrete
241 × 150 × 119 cm

p. 114
Ascension, 2011
Mixed media
Dimensions variable
Basilica di San Giorgio Maggiore, Venice

p. 115
Endless Column, 1992
Mixed media, pigment
Dimensions variable

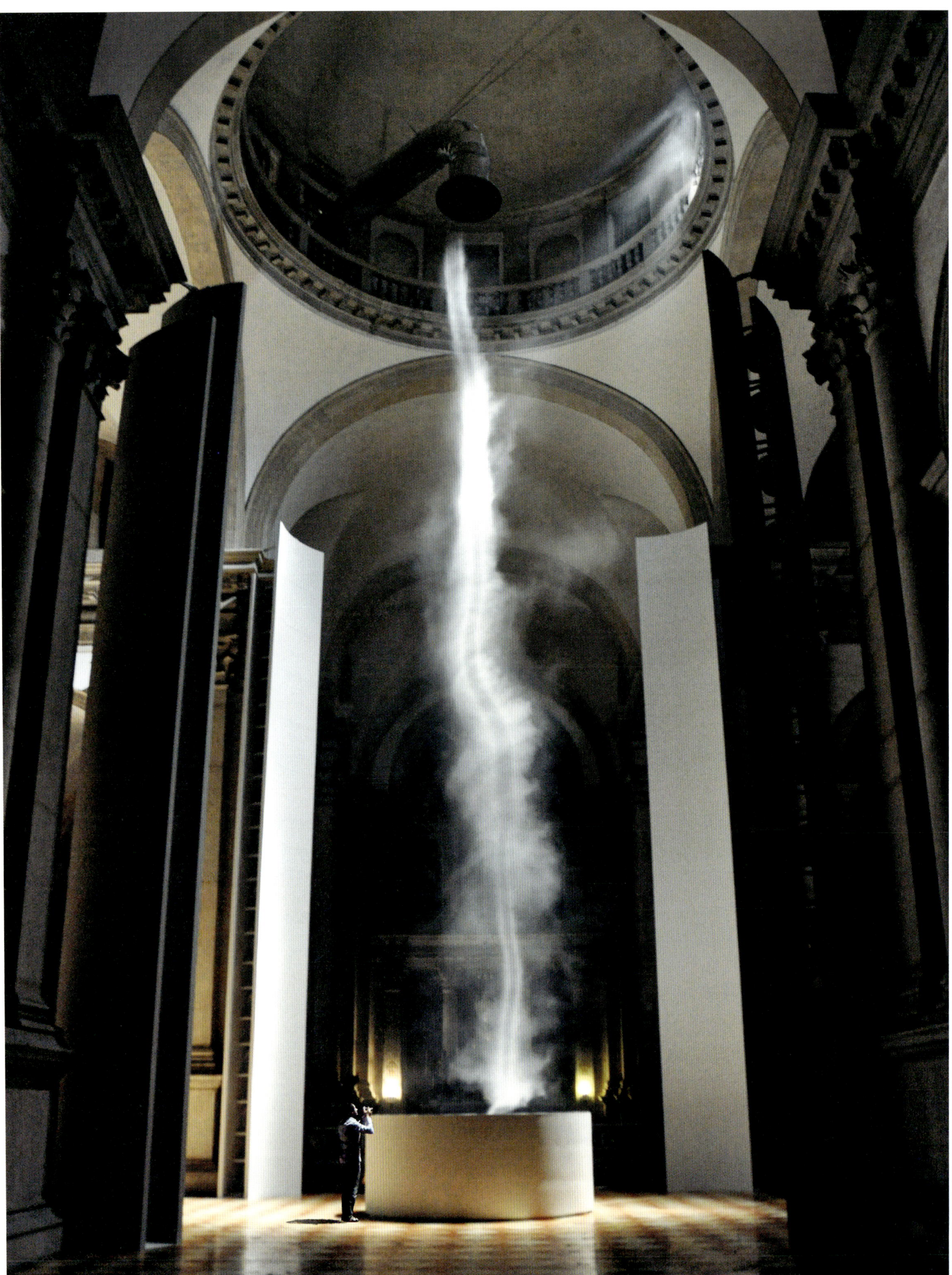

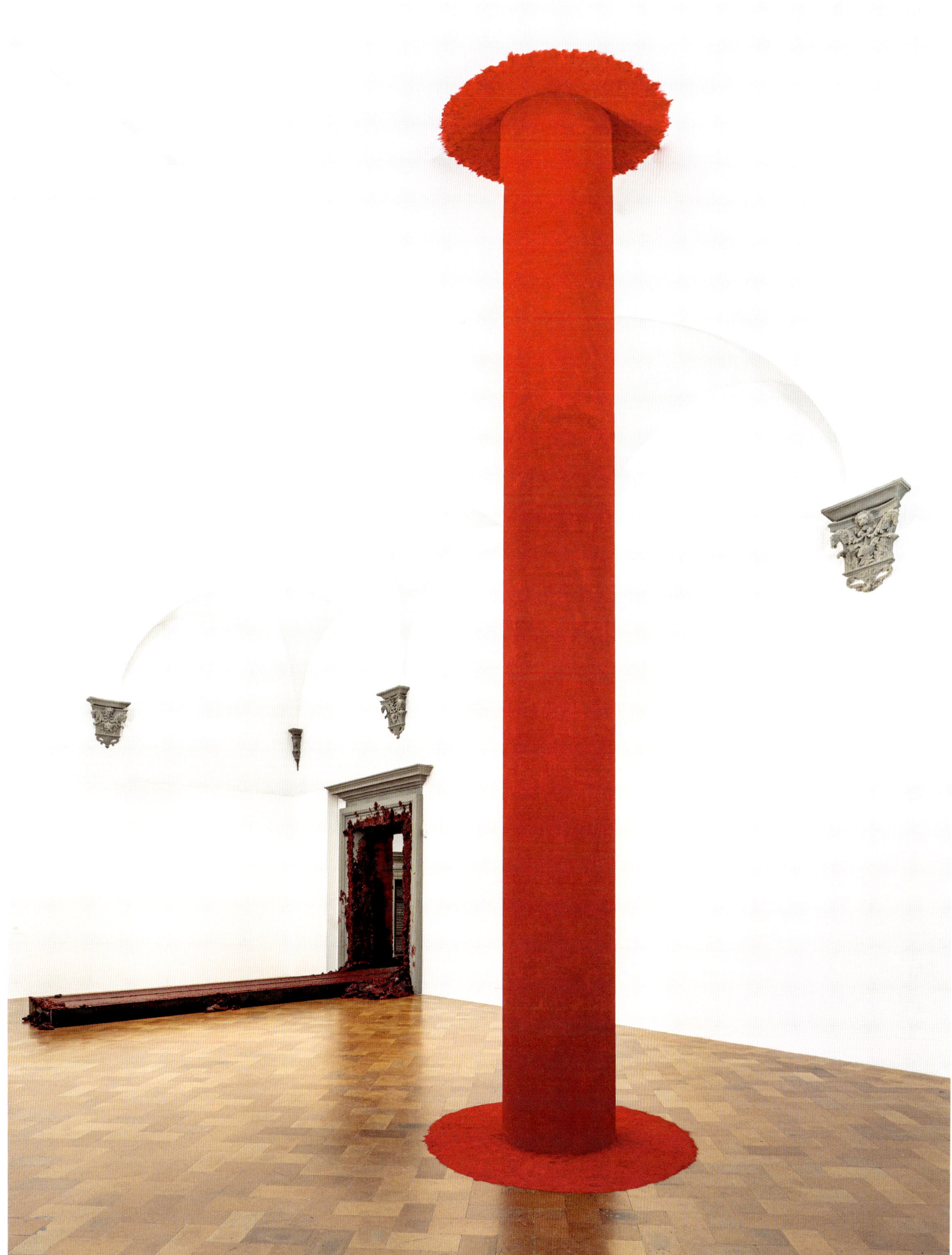

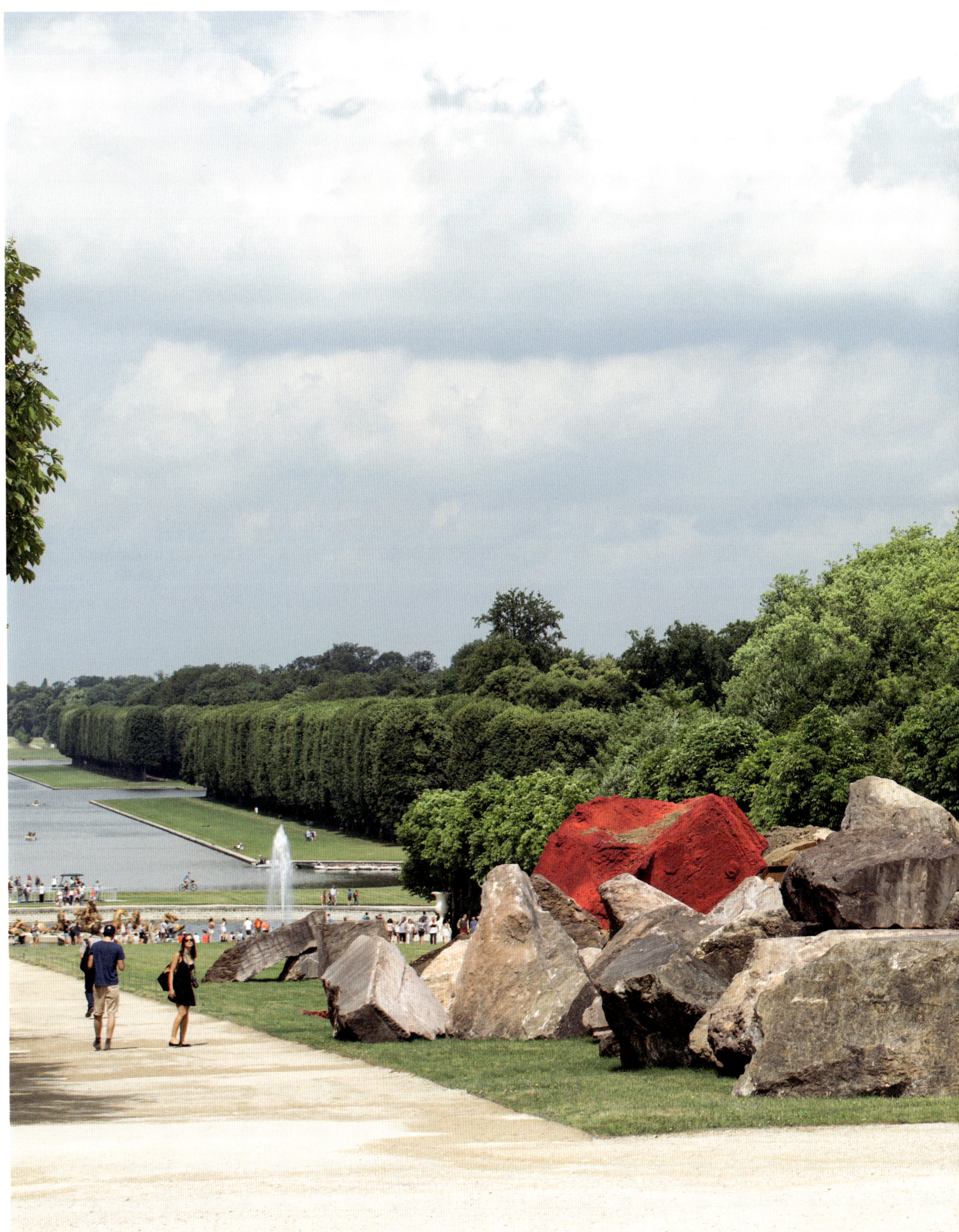

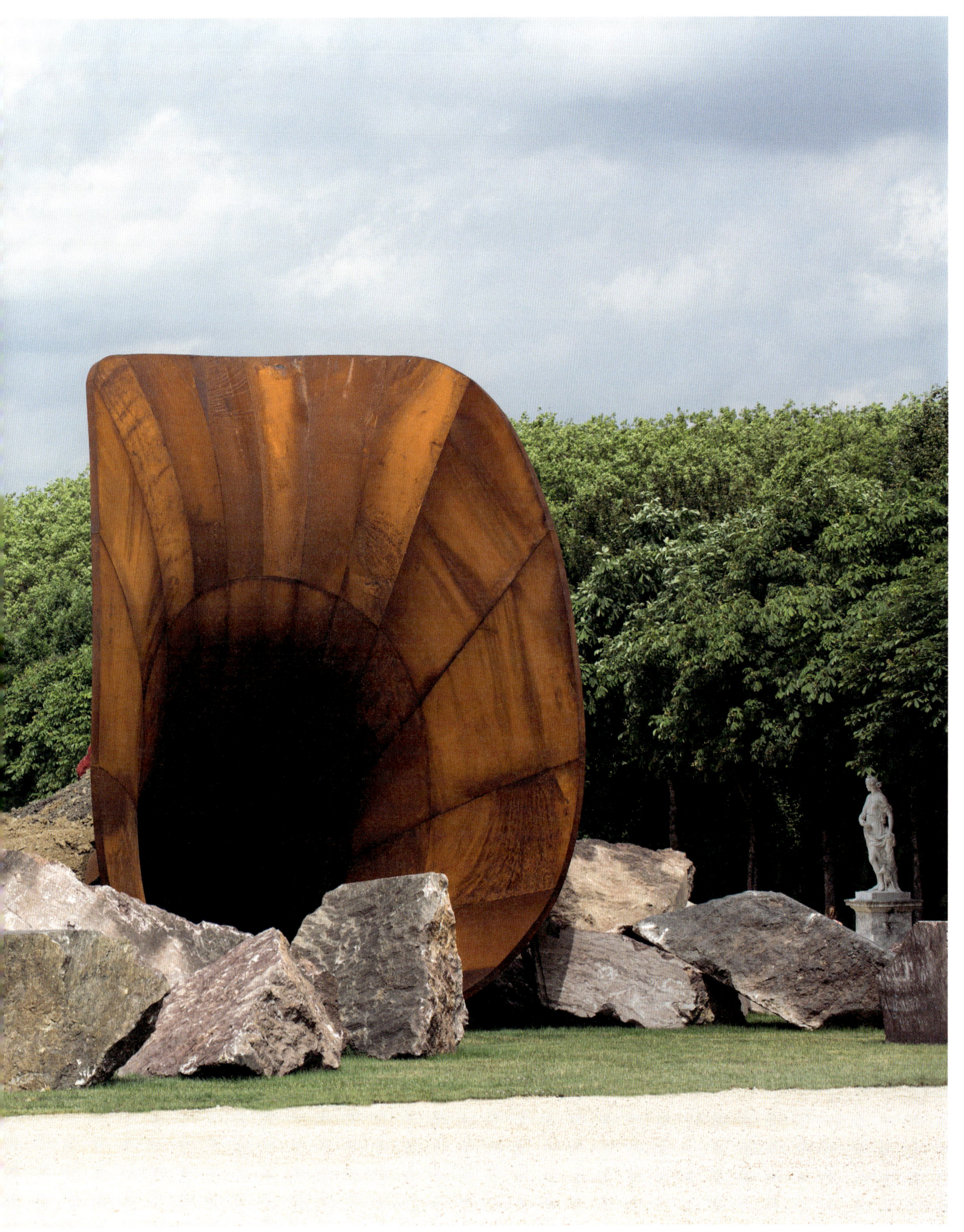

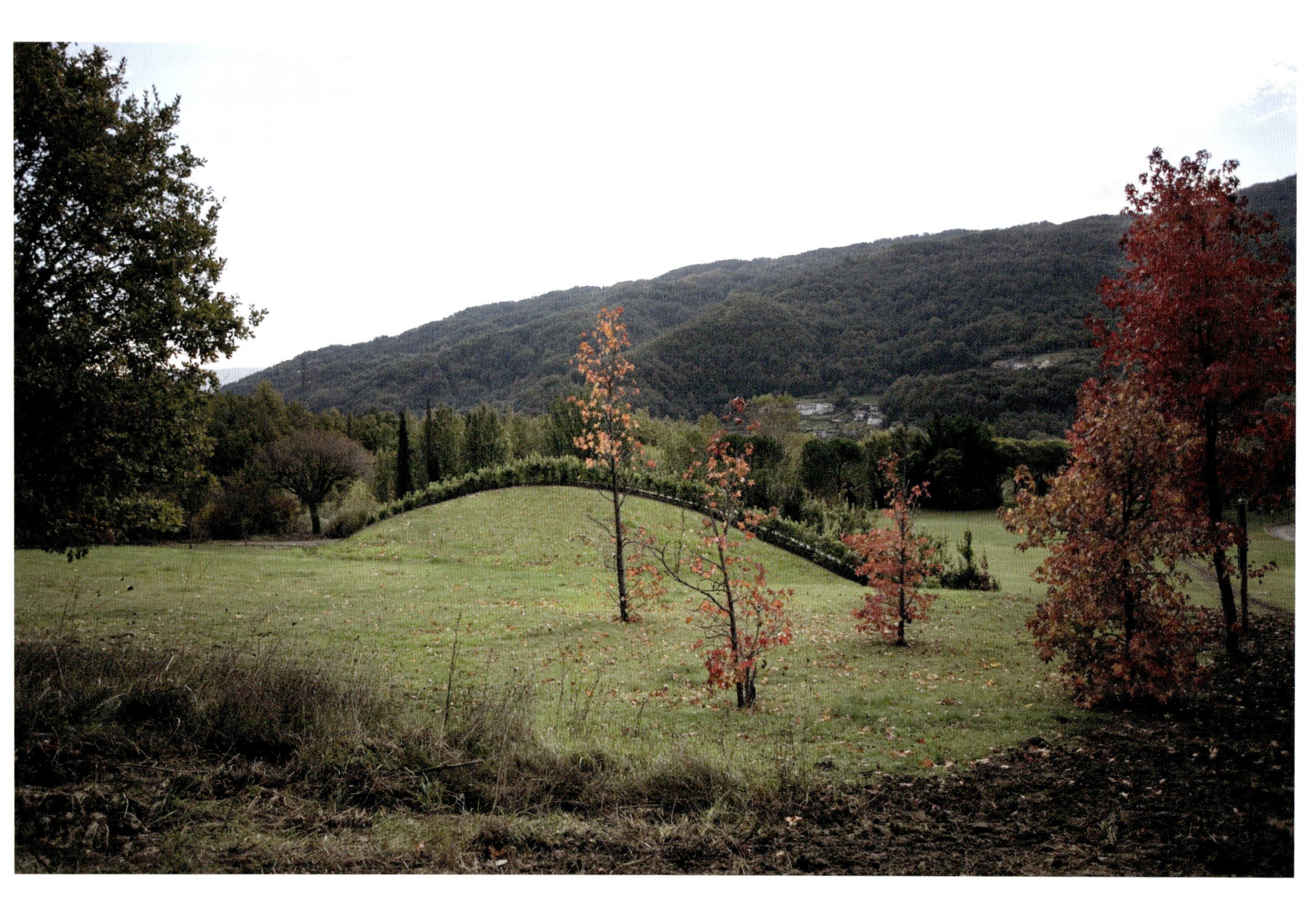

pp. 116-117
Dirty Corner, 2011-15
Corten steel, earth, mixed media
8.9 × 6.55 × 60 m
Château de Versailles

This spread
Earth Cinema, 1995
Mixed media
45 × 7 m
Arte Pollino, Basilicata, Potenza

pp. 120-121
San Gennaro, 2003
Steel, water, dye
Dimensions variable

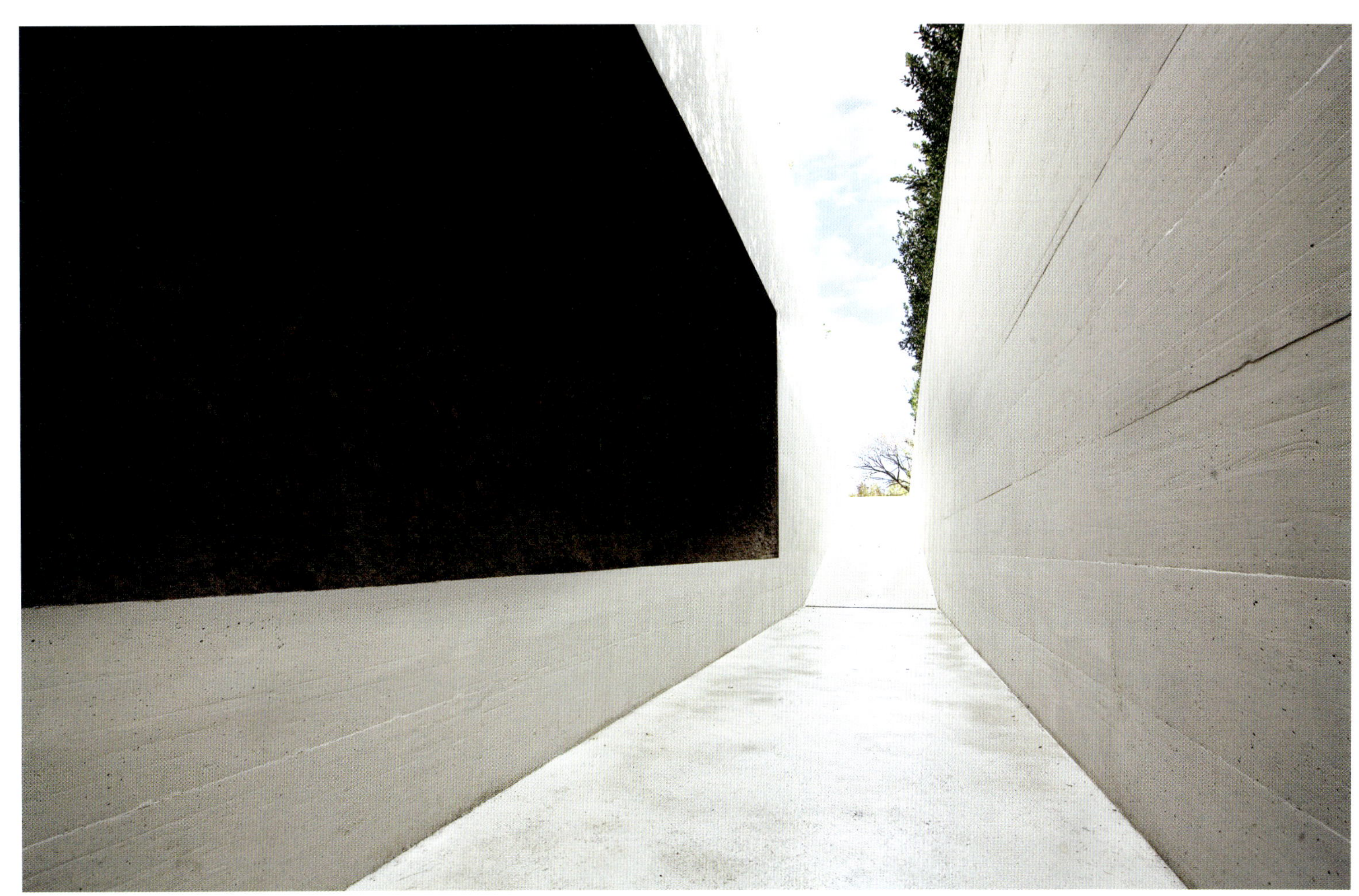

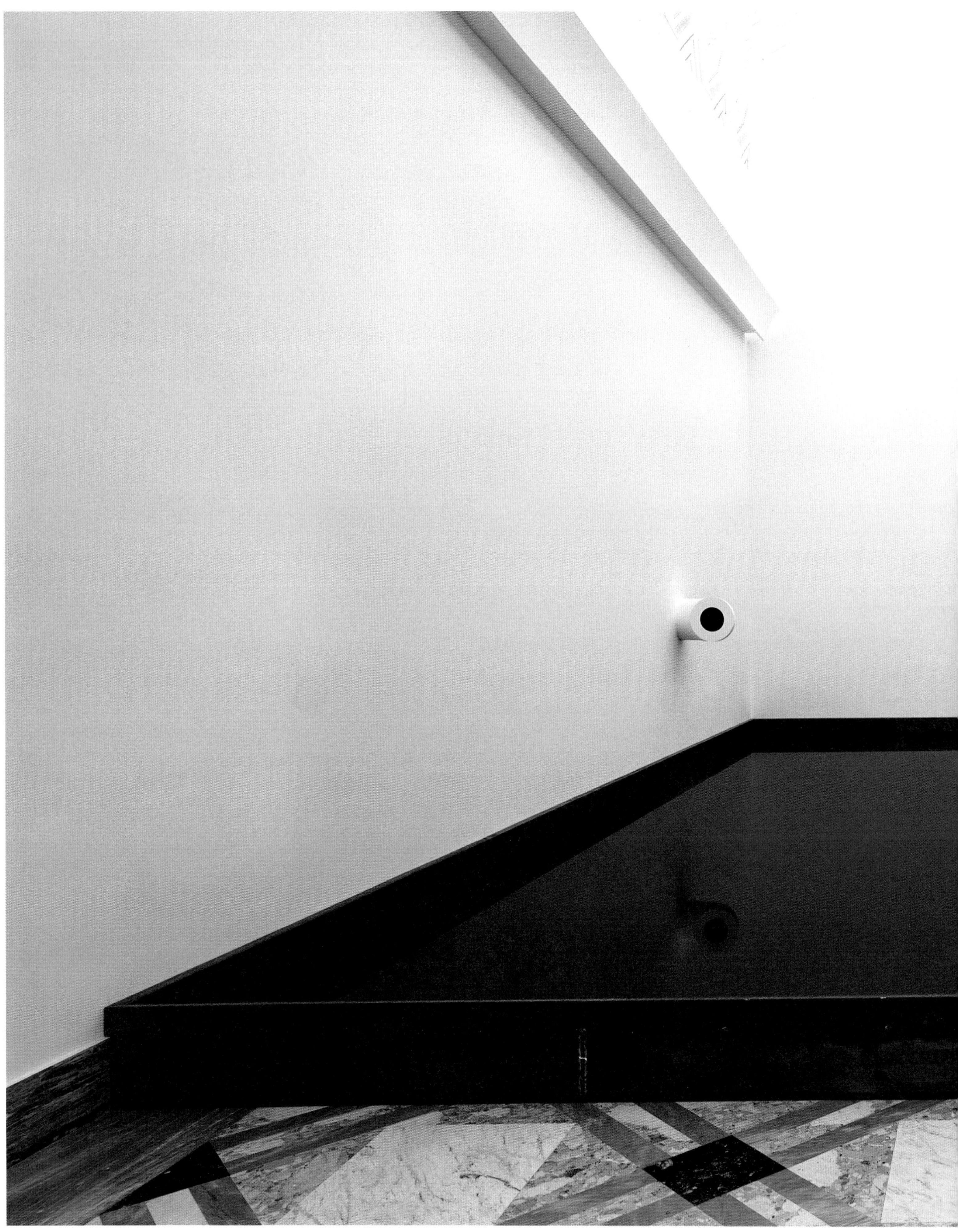

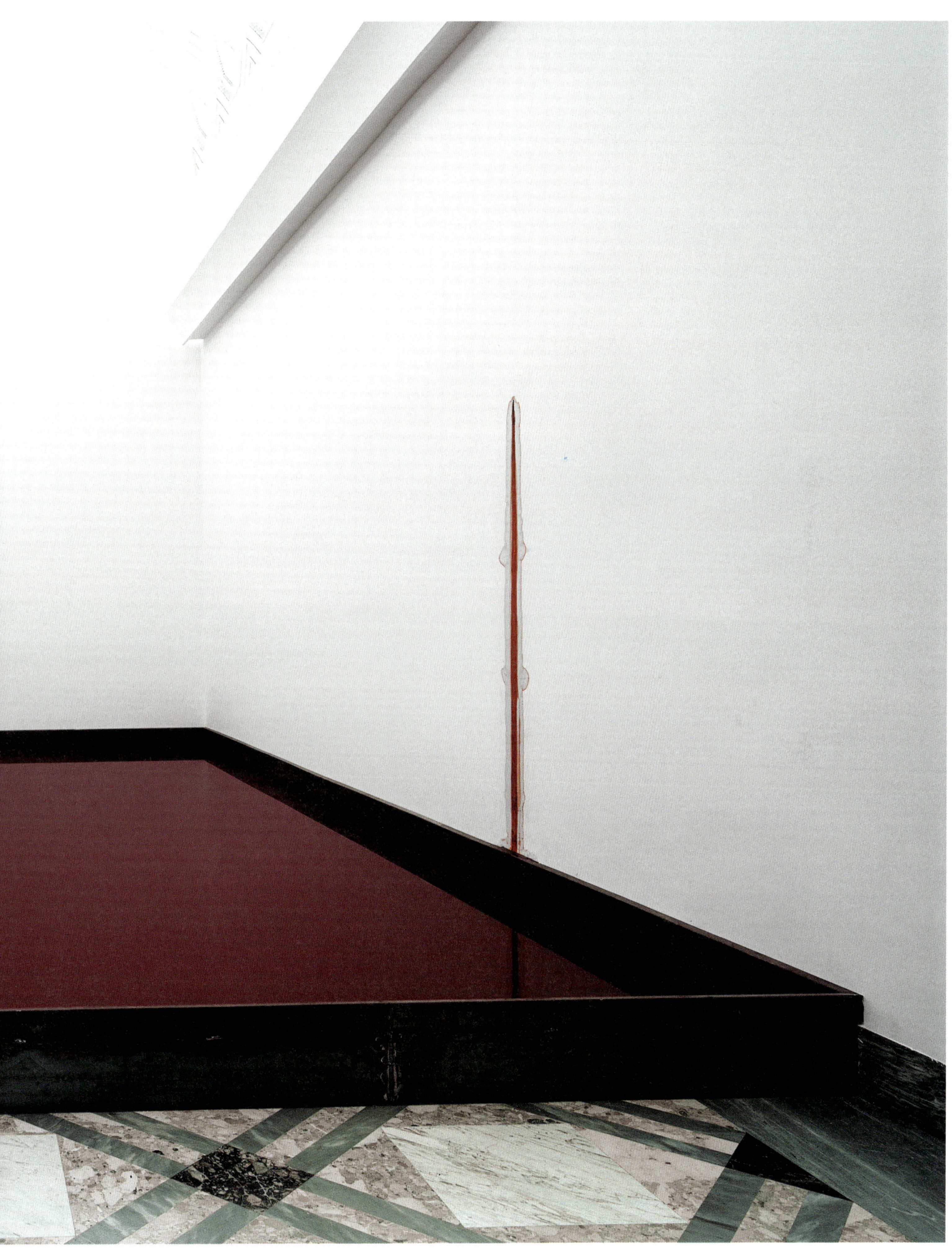

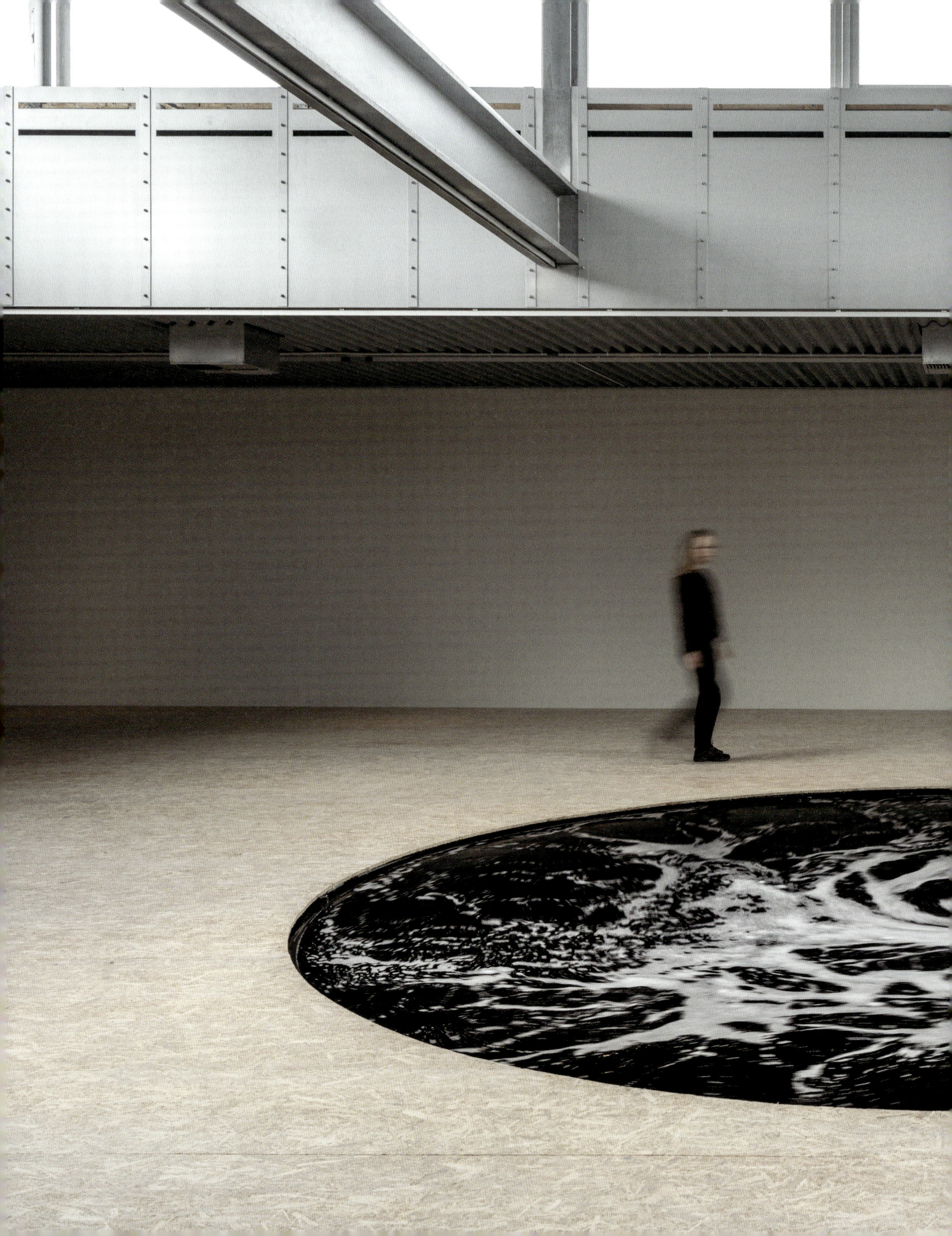

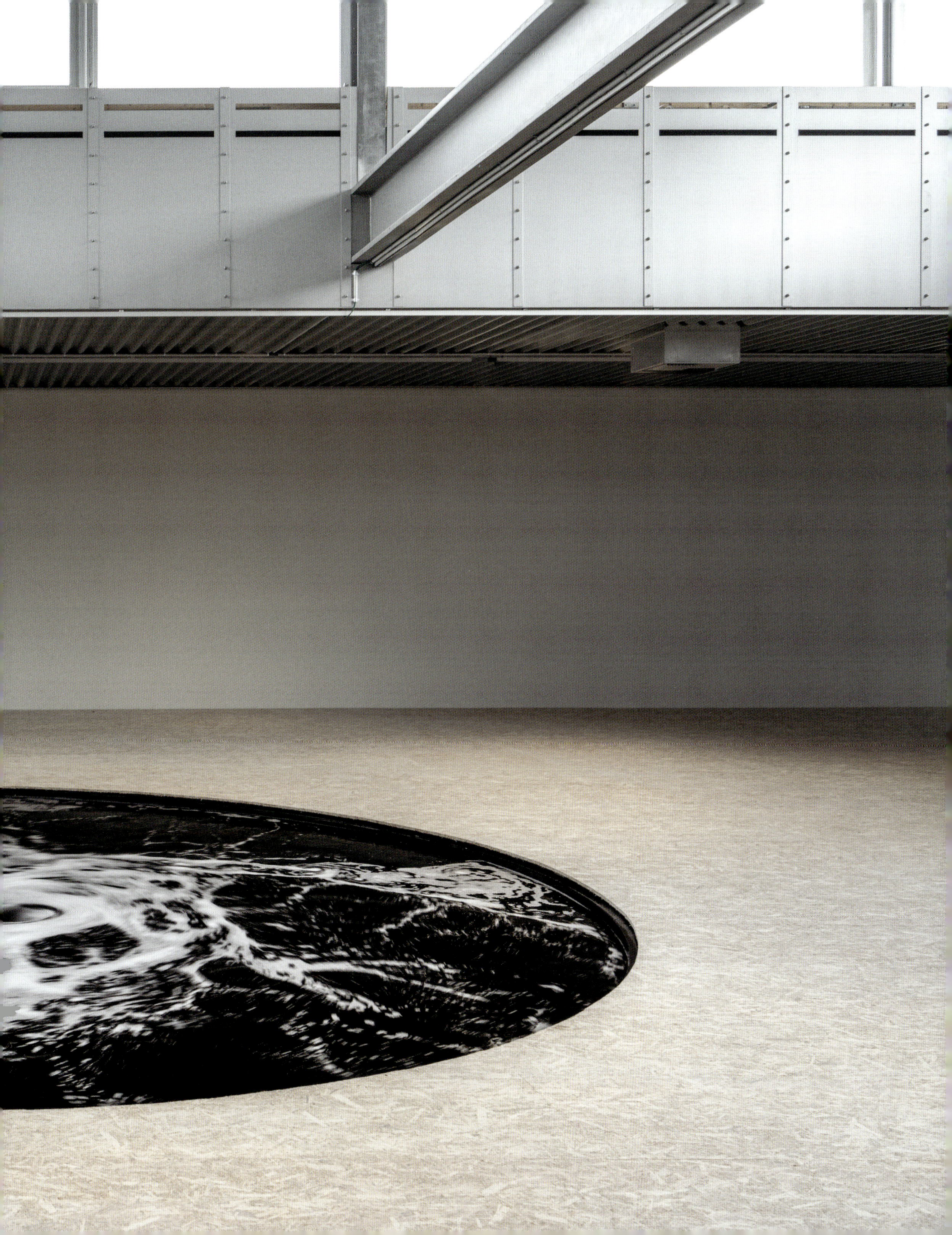

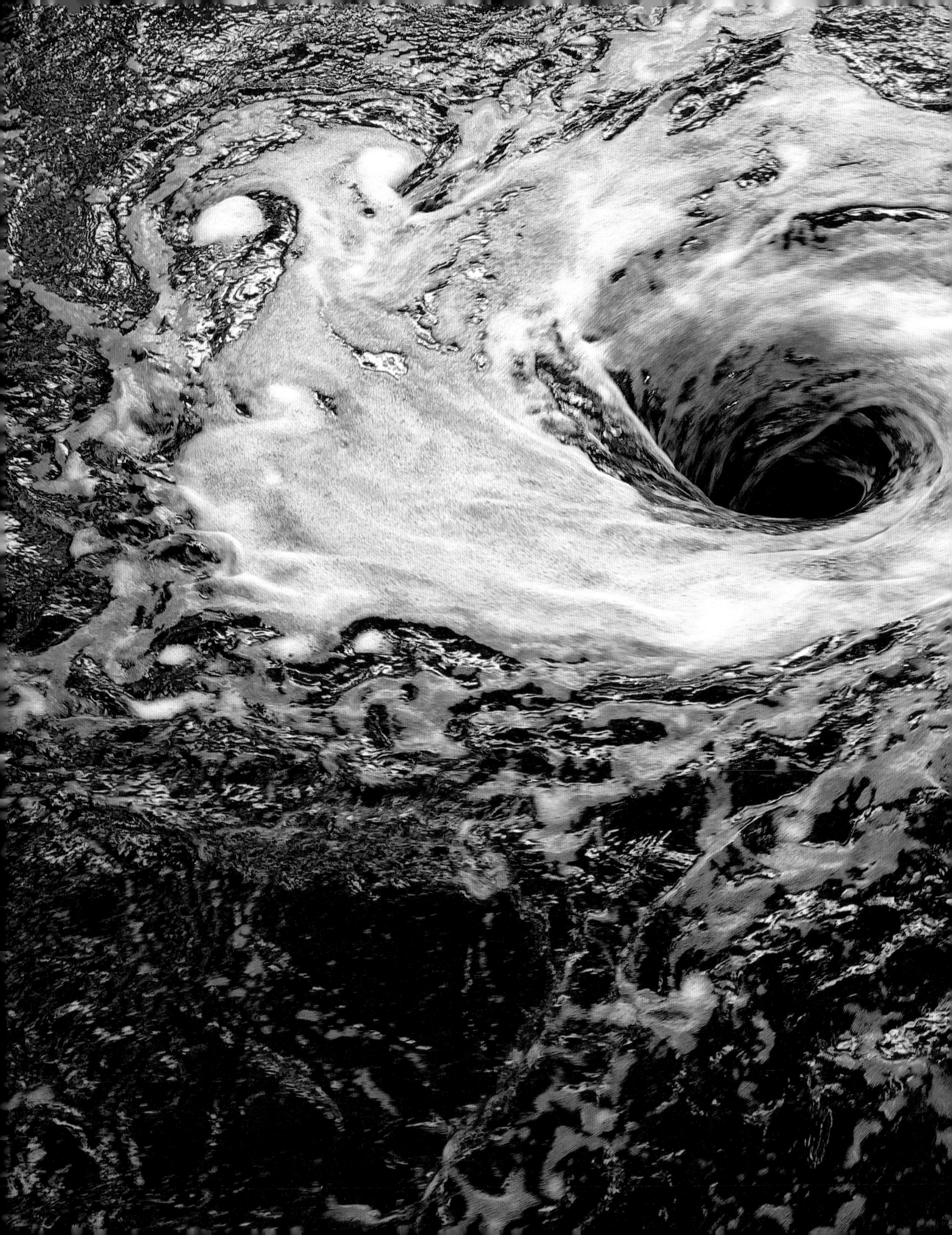

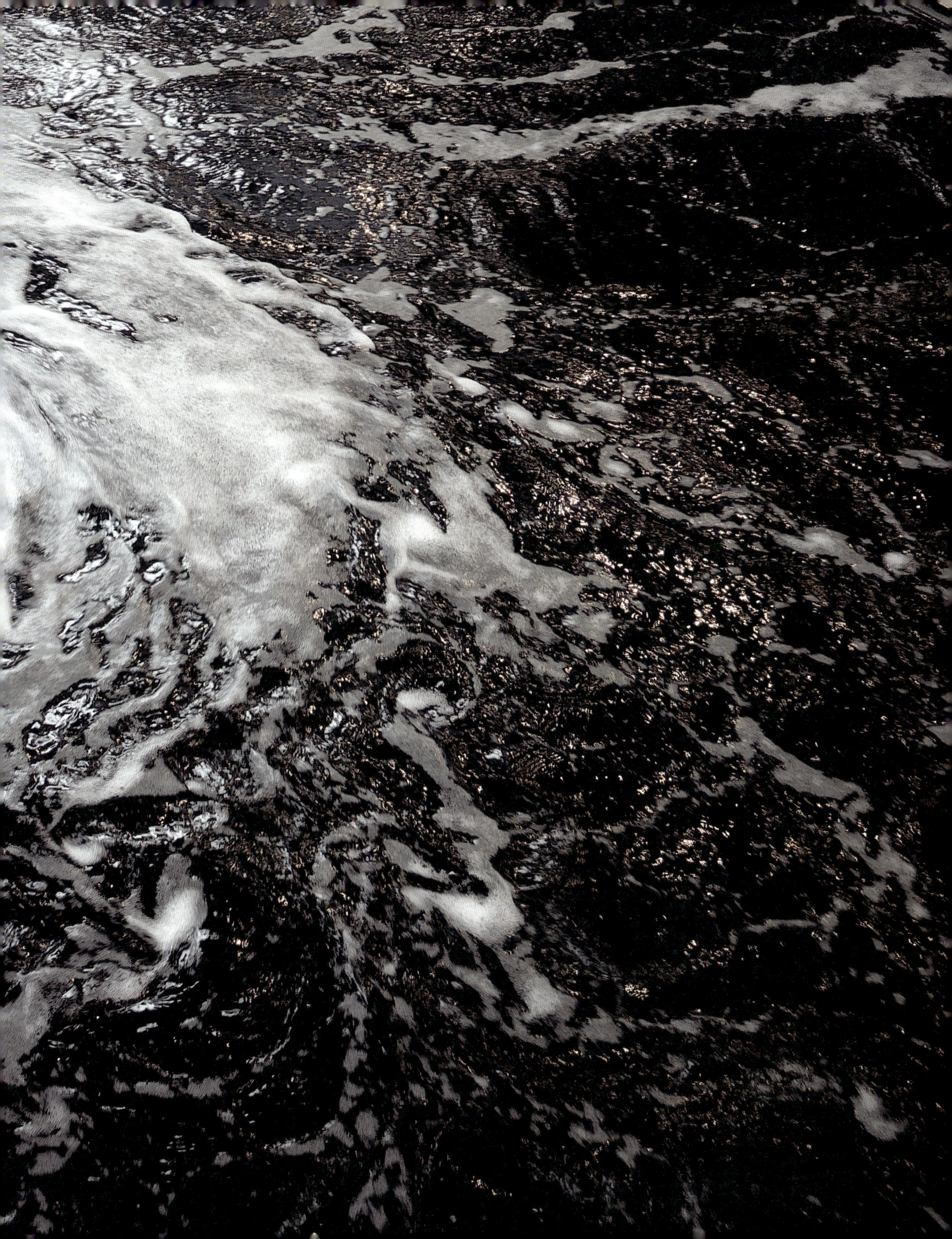

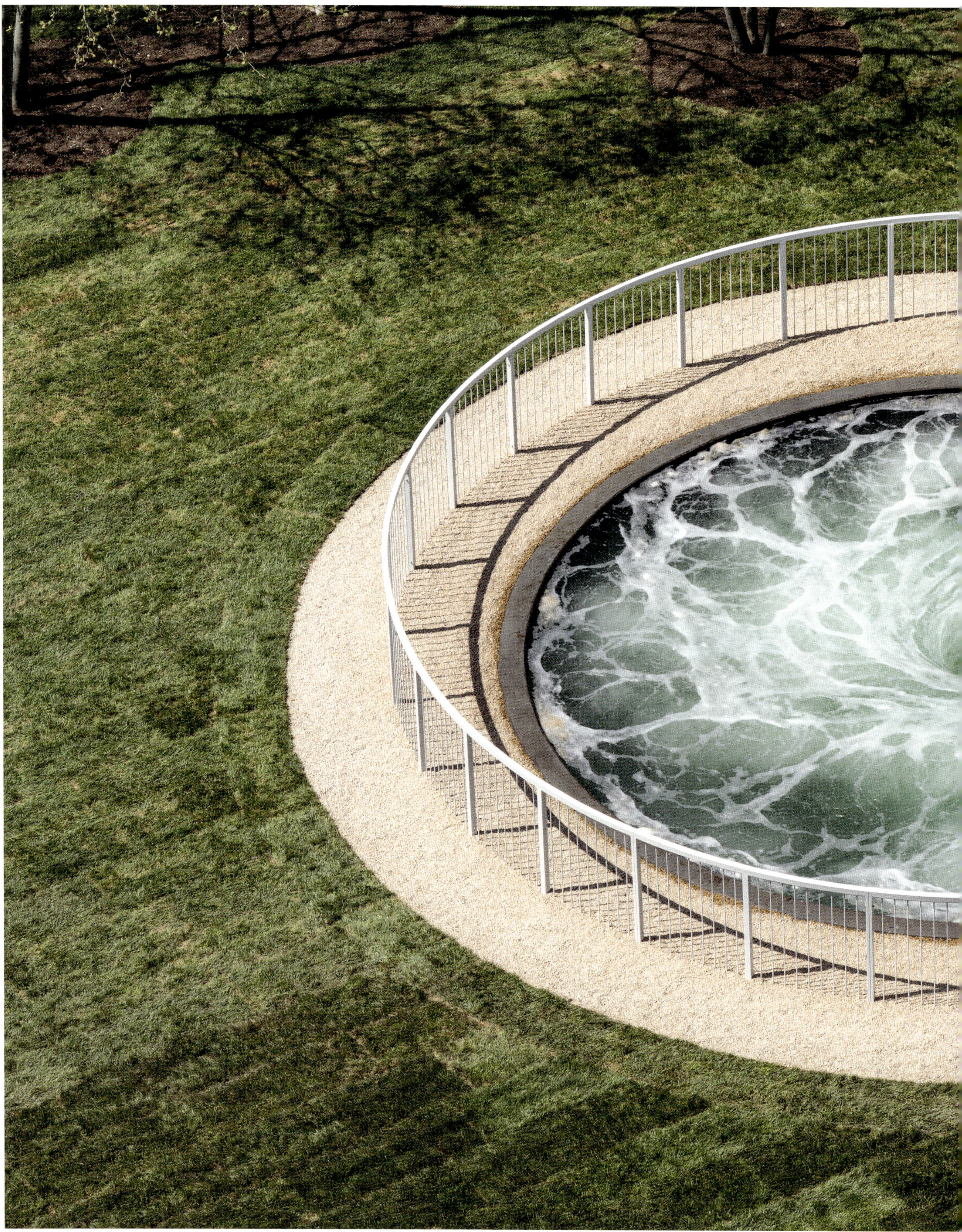

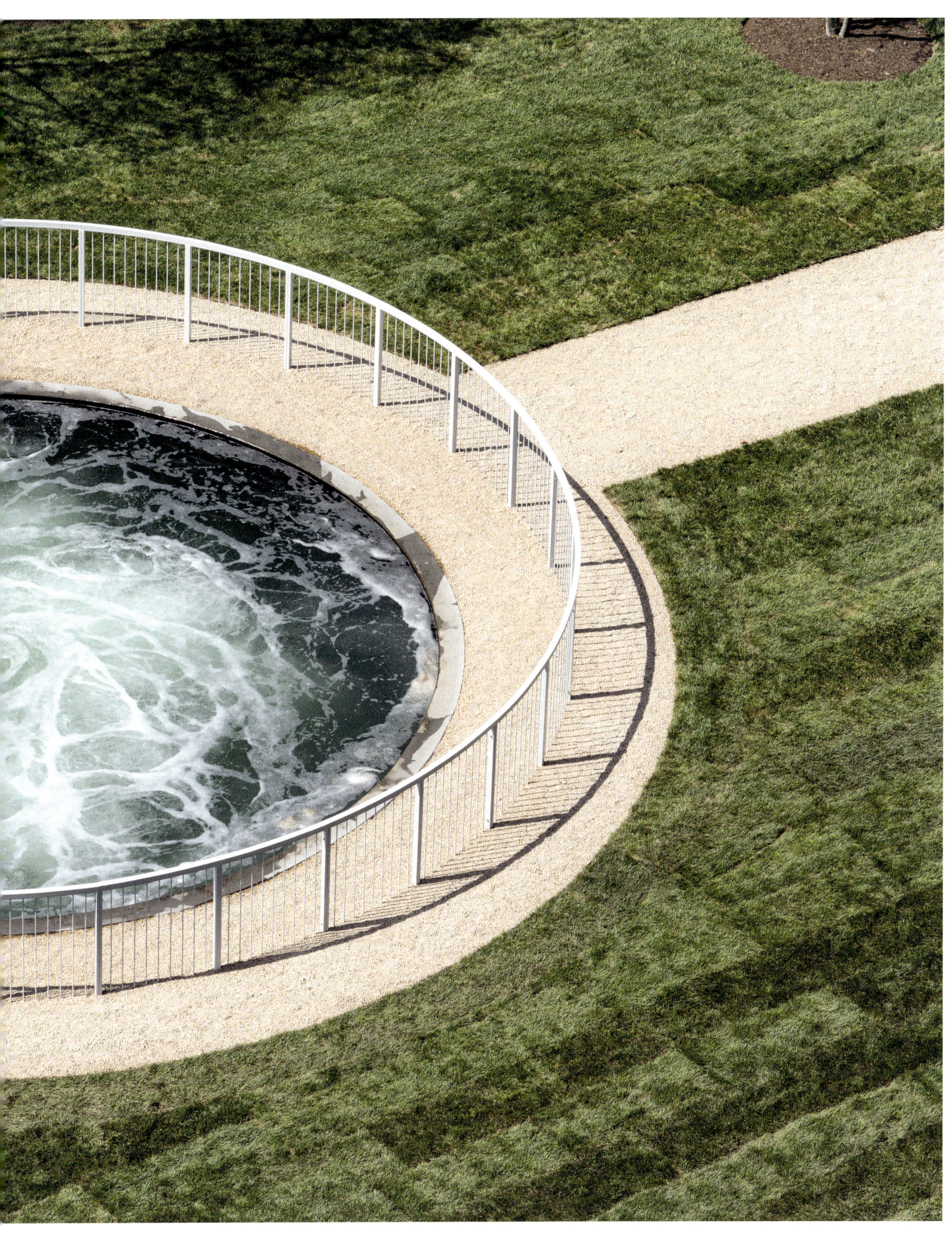

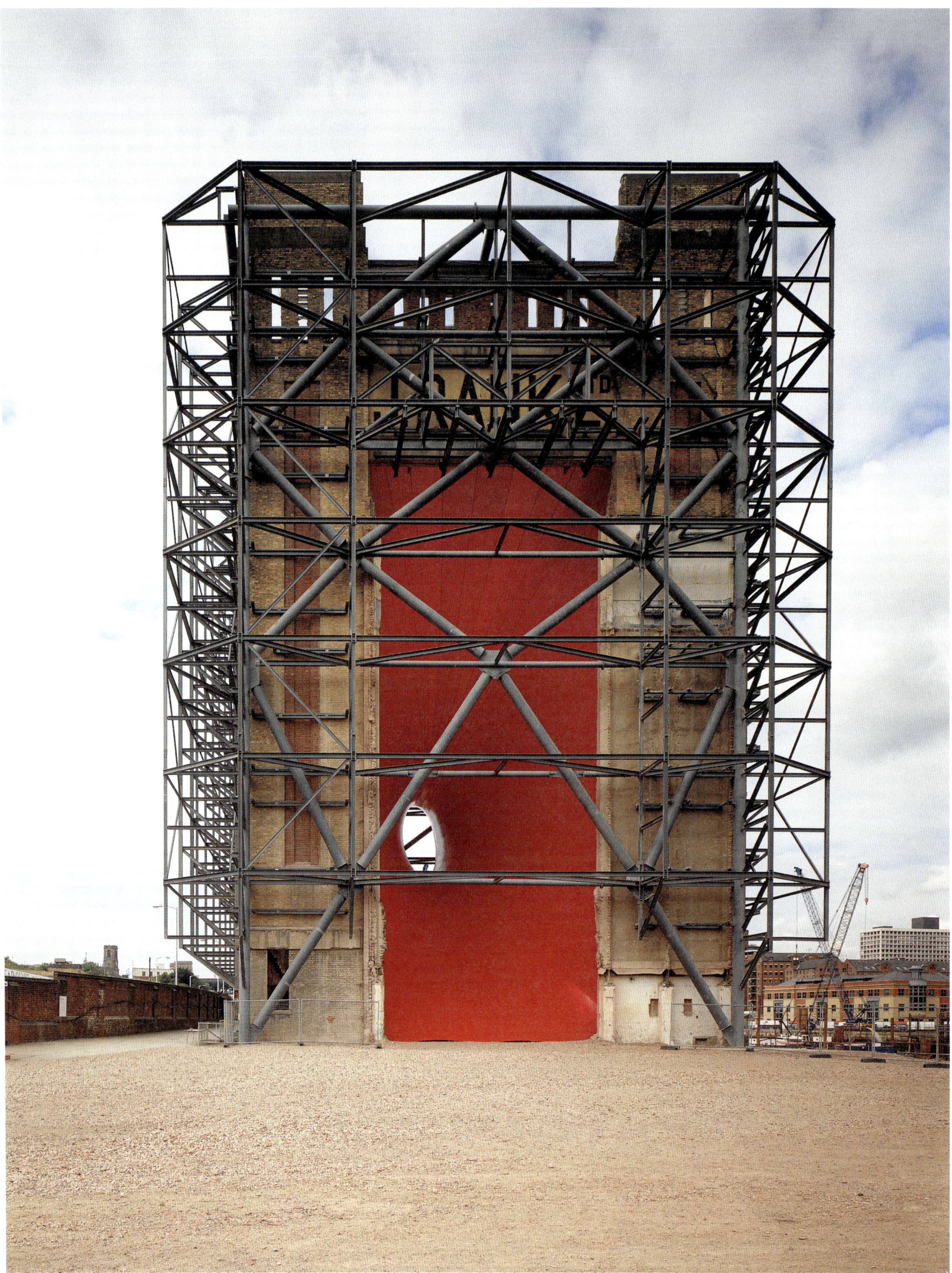

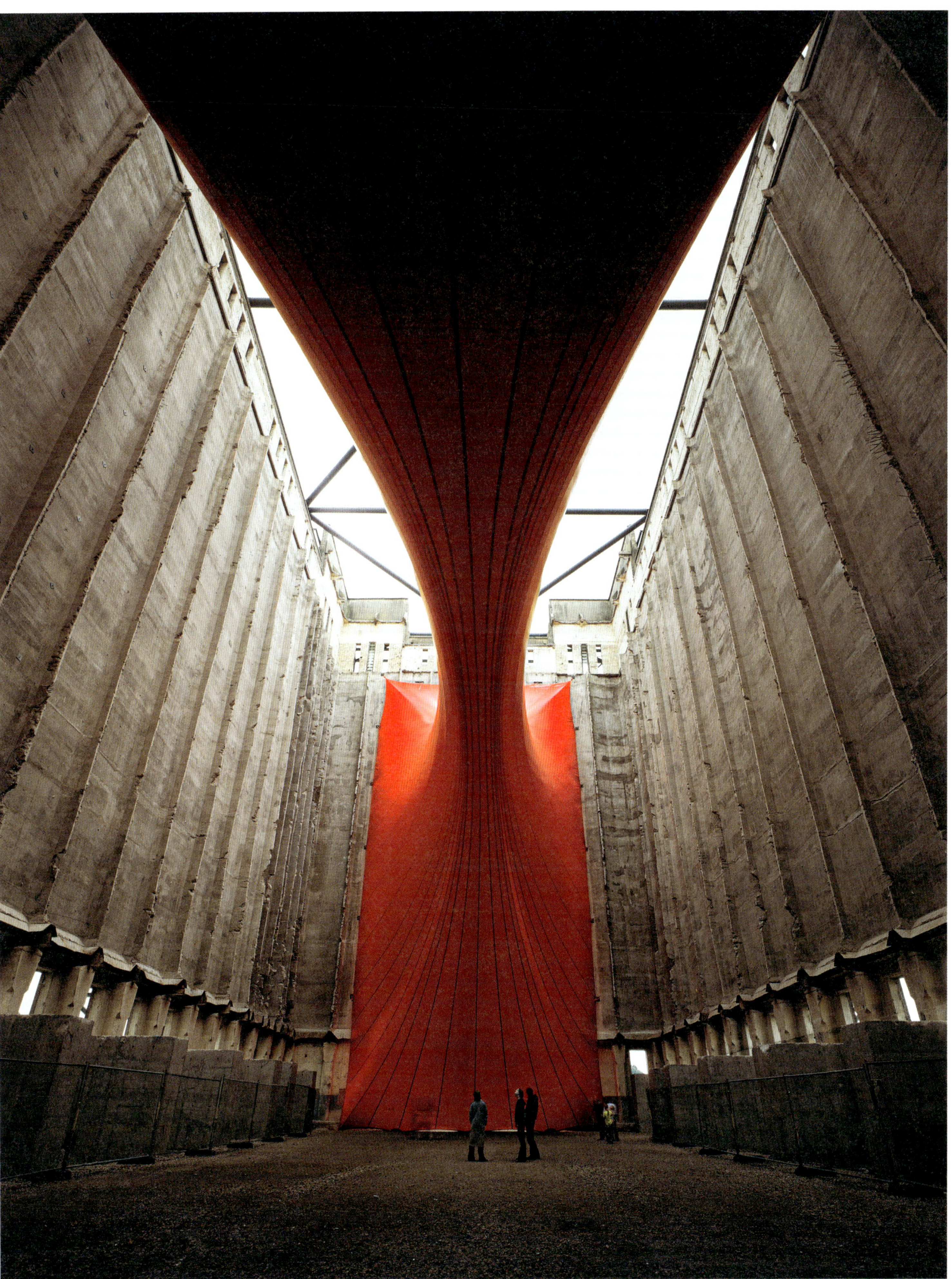

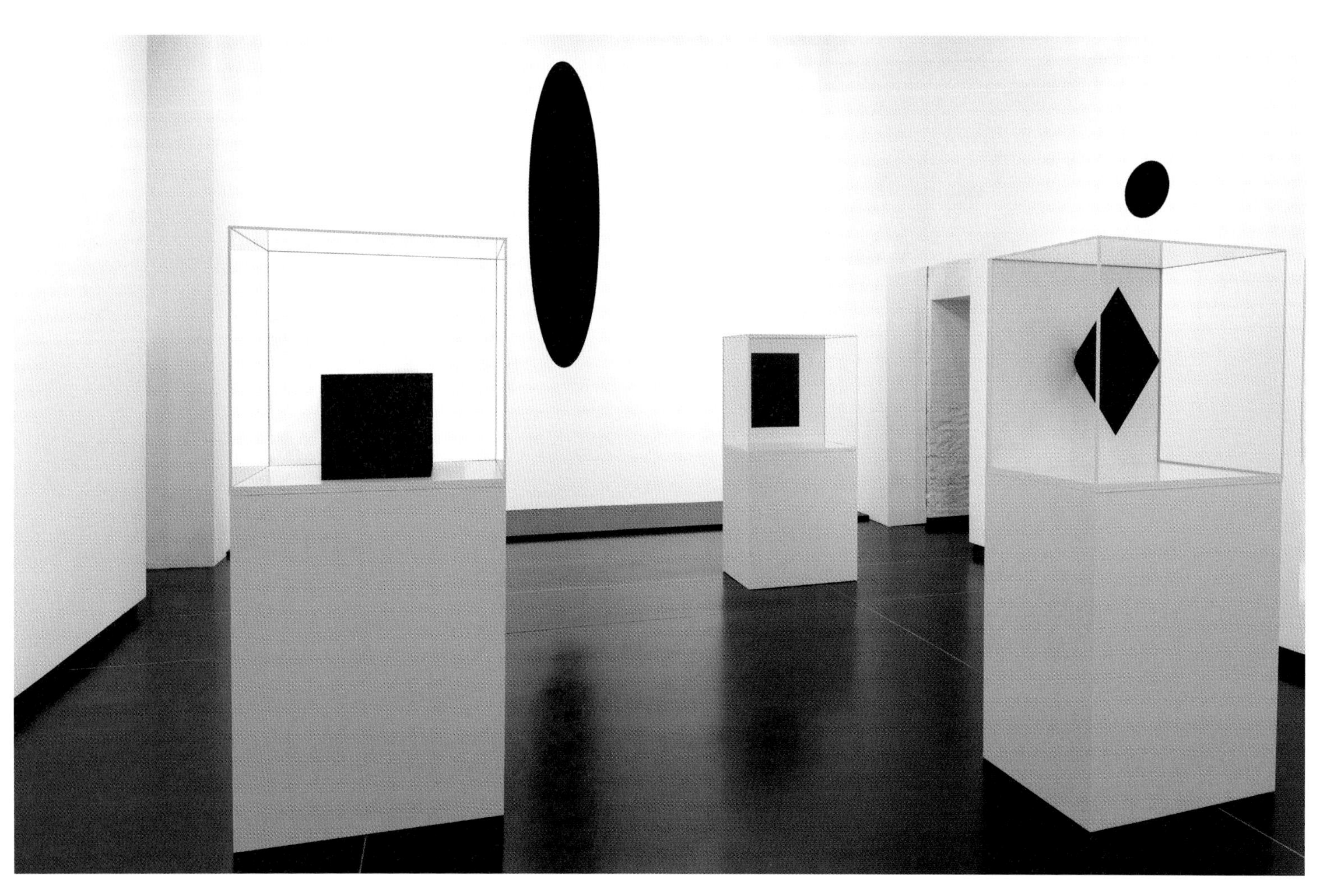

Foreground:
Non-Object Black, 2019; 2018; 2021
Background:
Vertical Abyss, 2022
Untitled, 2022

pp. 122-125
Descension, 2014
ARKEN Museum of Contemporary Art, Ishøj

pp. 126-127
Descension, 2014
Brooklyn Bridge Park, New York

pp. 128-129
Taratantara, 1999
PVC, steel
51.8 × 32.6 × 16 m

Untitled, 2023
Mixed media, paint
Dimensions variable

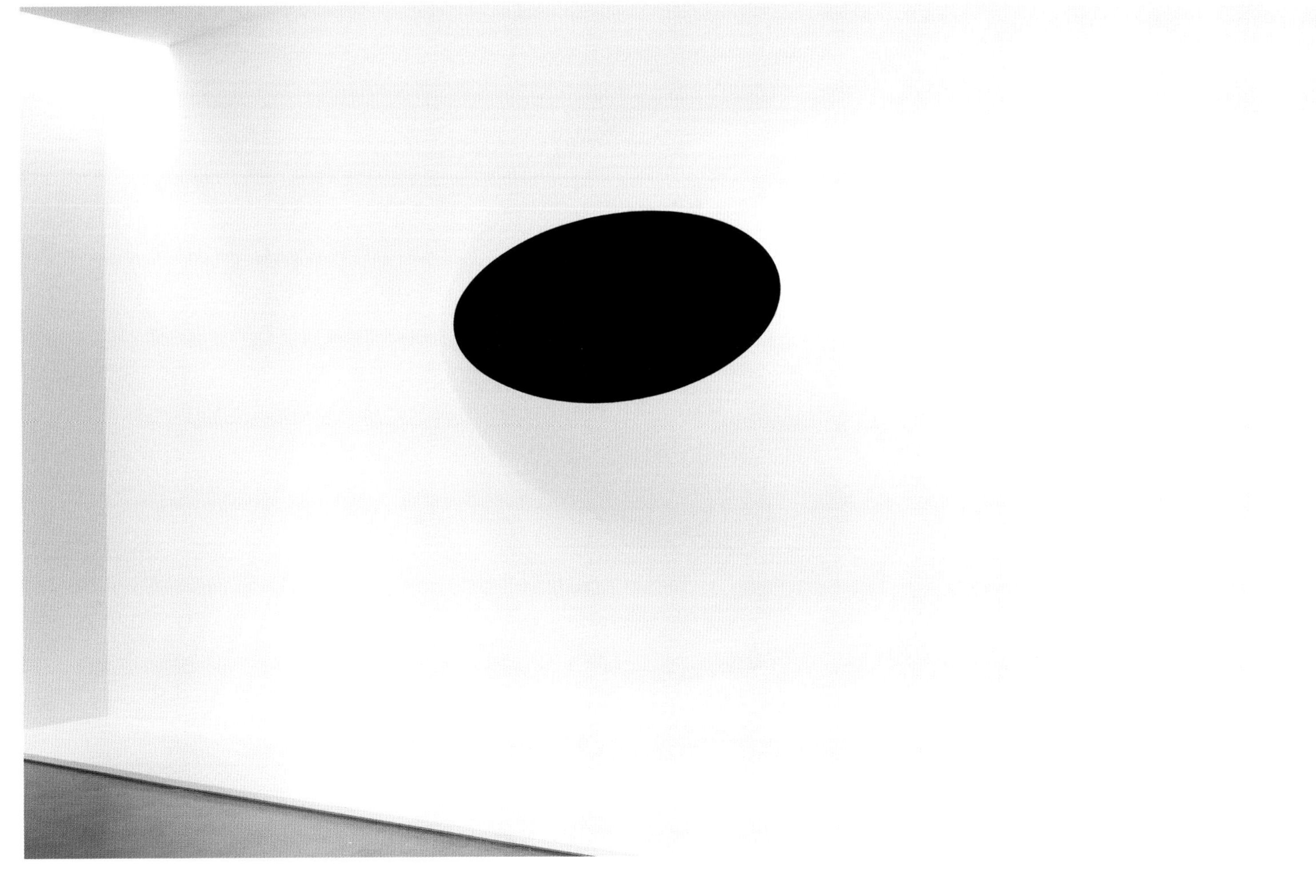

Ishi's Light, 2003
Fibreglass, paint
315 × 258 × 244 cm

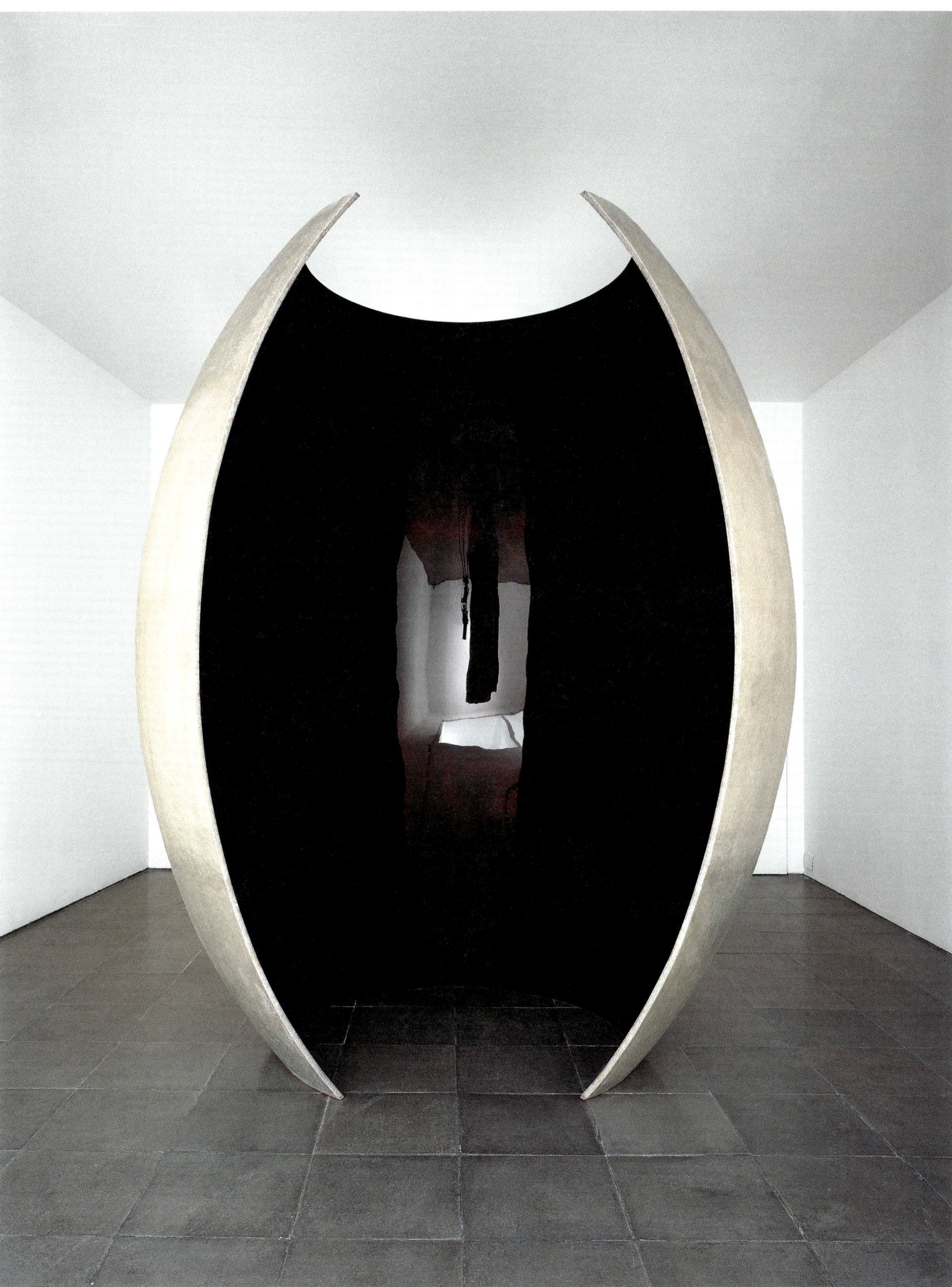

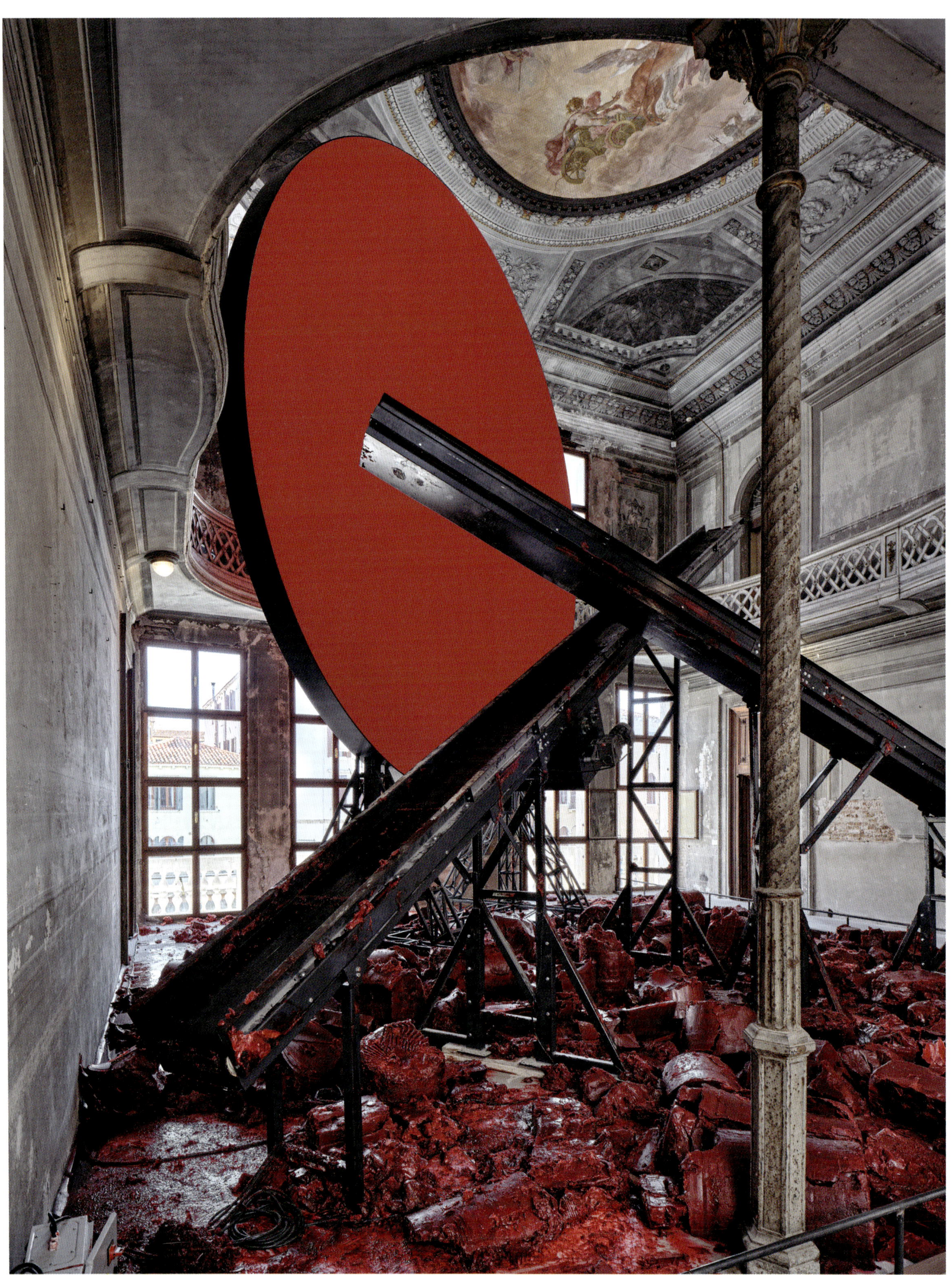

Symphony for a Beloved Sun, 2013
Wax, steel, canvas, paint
Dimensions variable

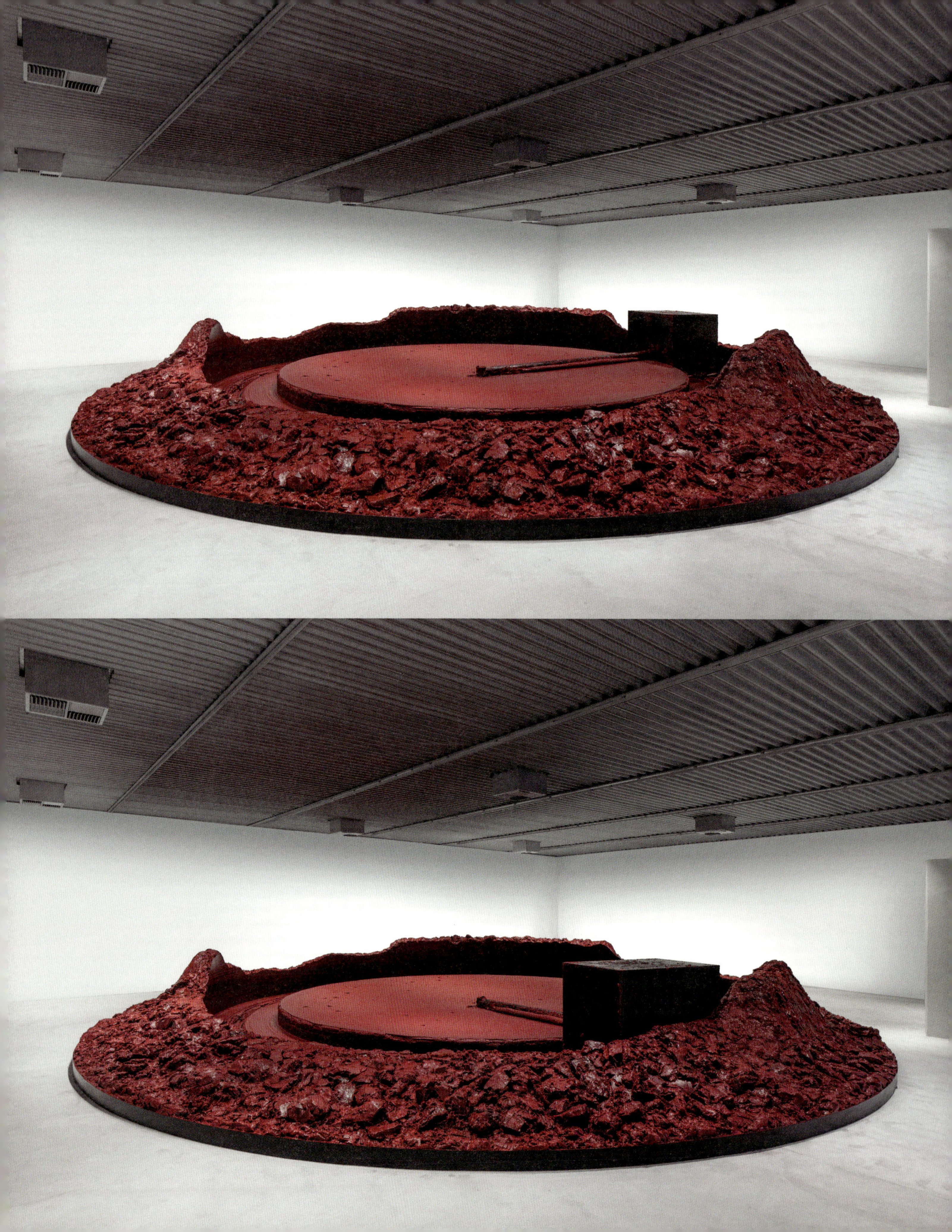

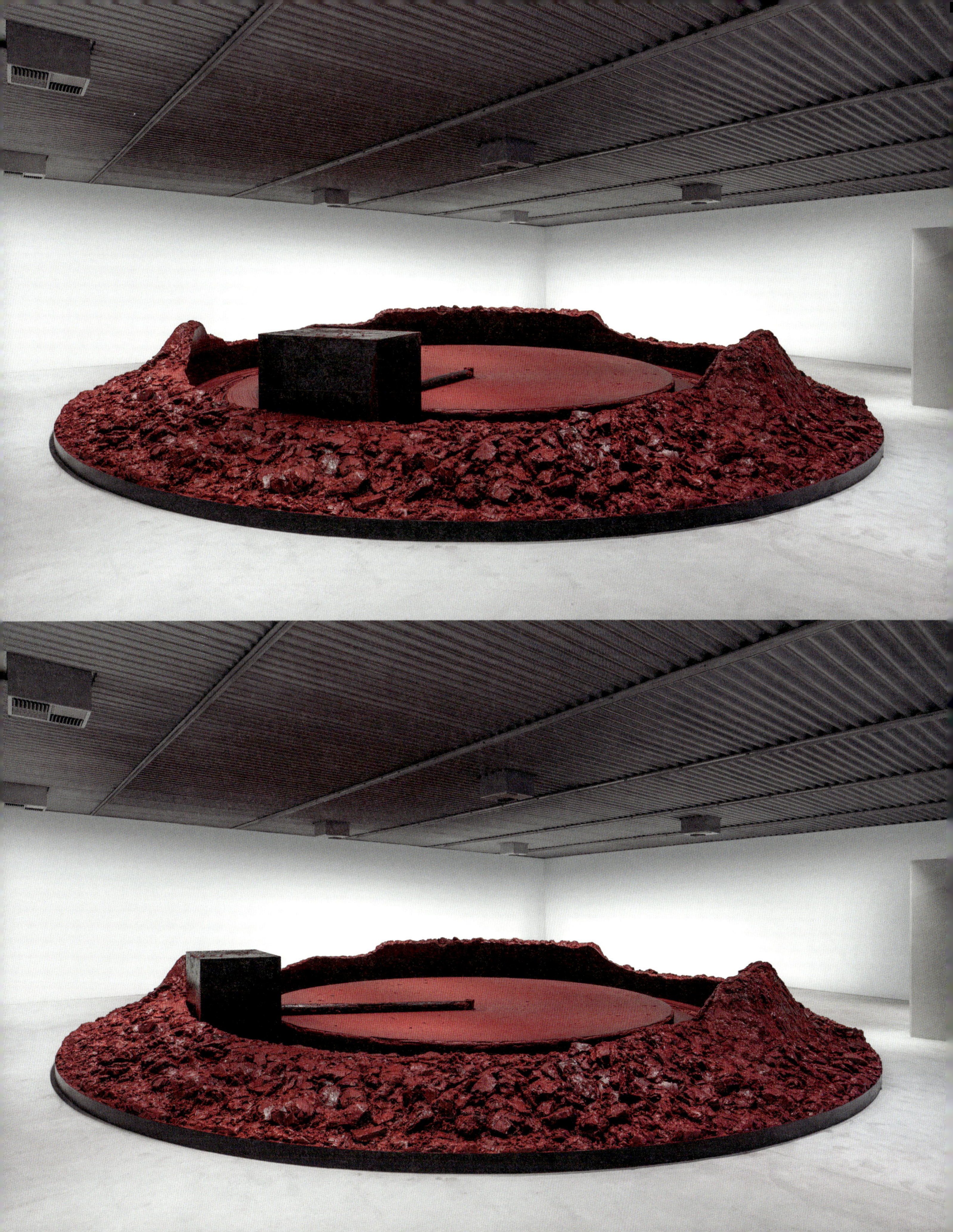

This and the preceding spread
My Red Homeland, 2003
Wax, oil-based paint, steel arm, motor
Diameter 12 m
 ARKEN Museum of Contemporary Art, Ishøj

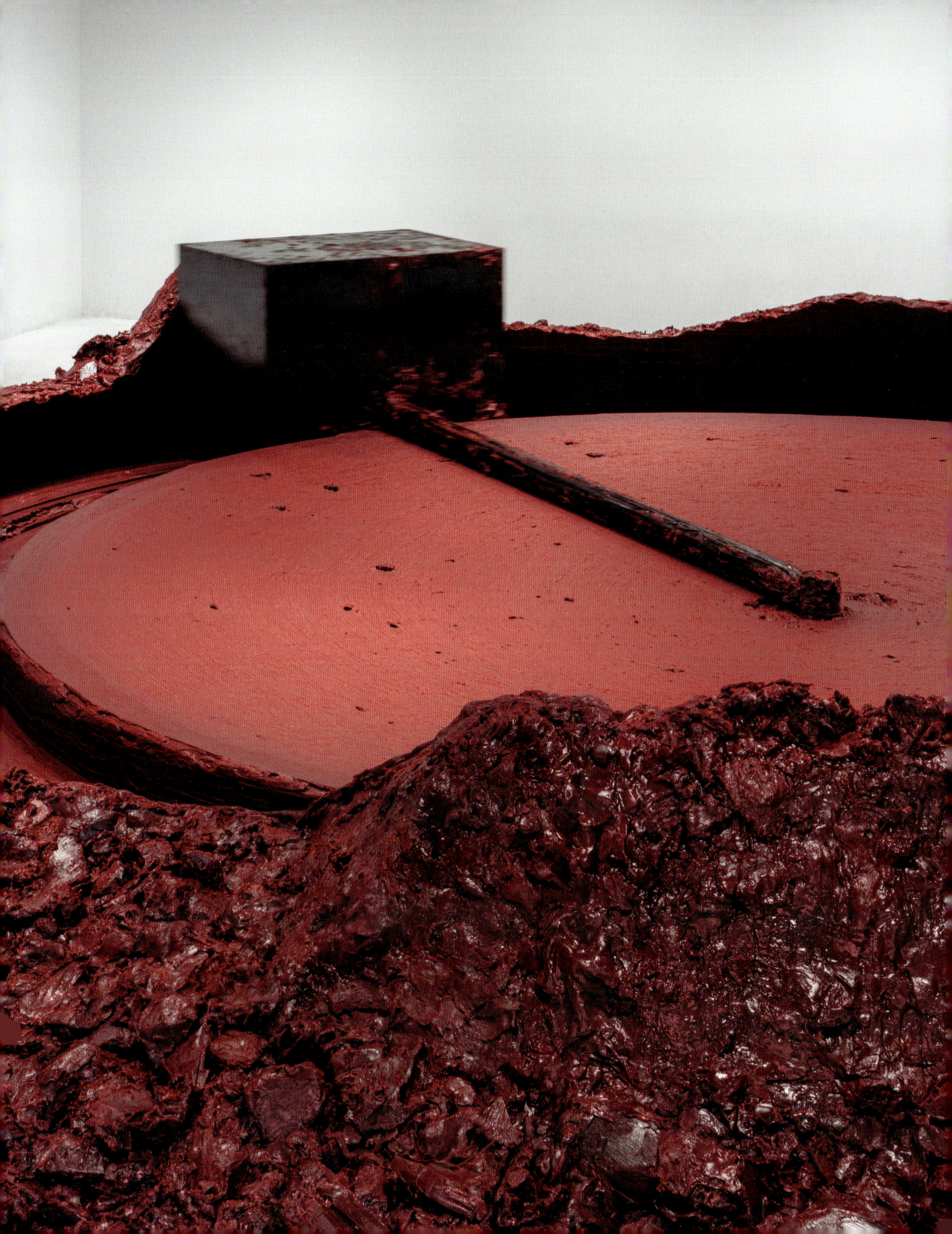

Shooting into the Corner, 2008-09
Mixed media
Dimensions variable

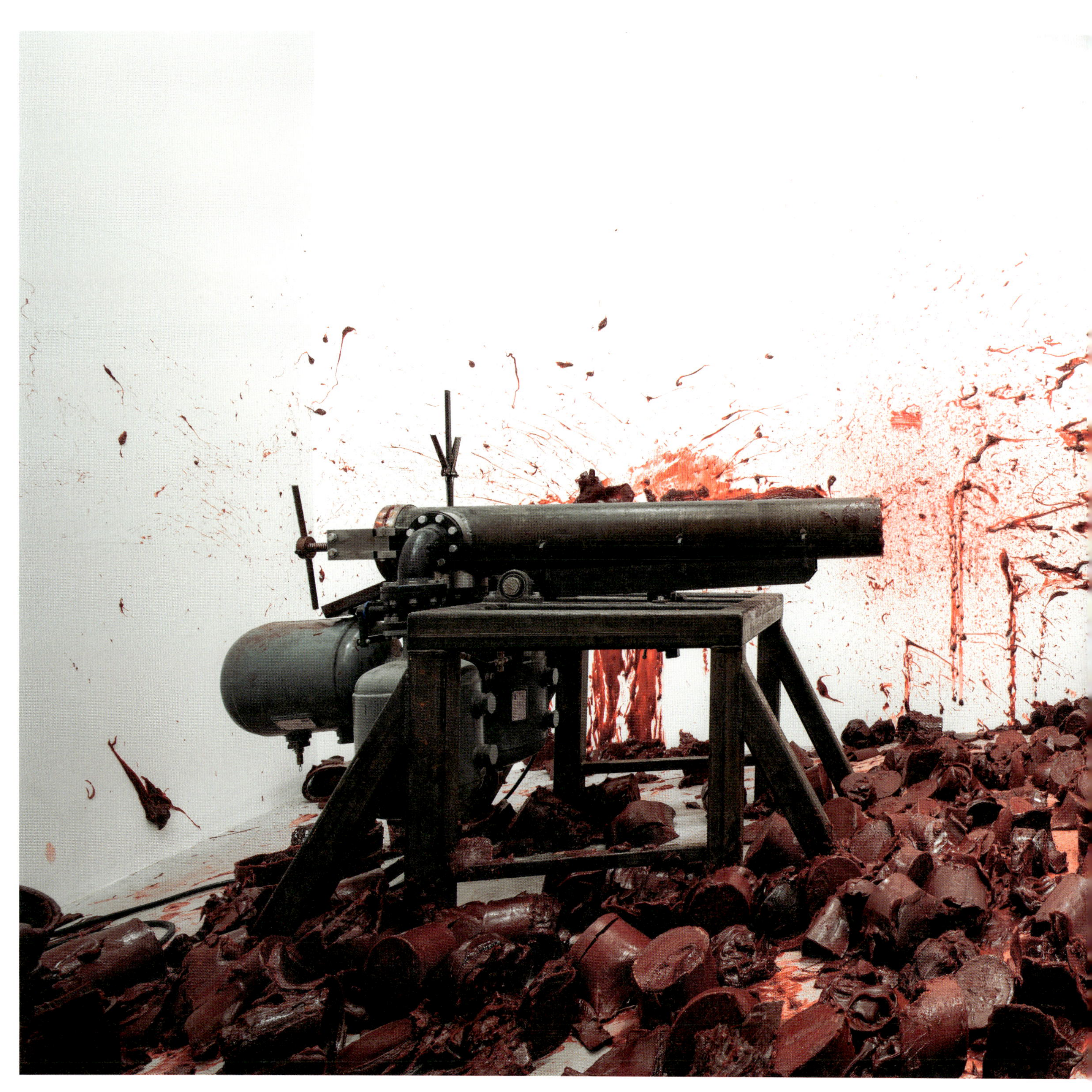

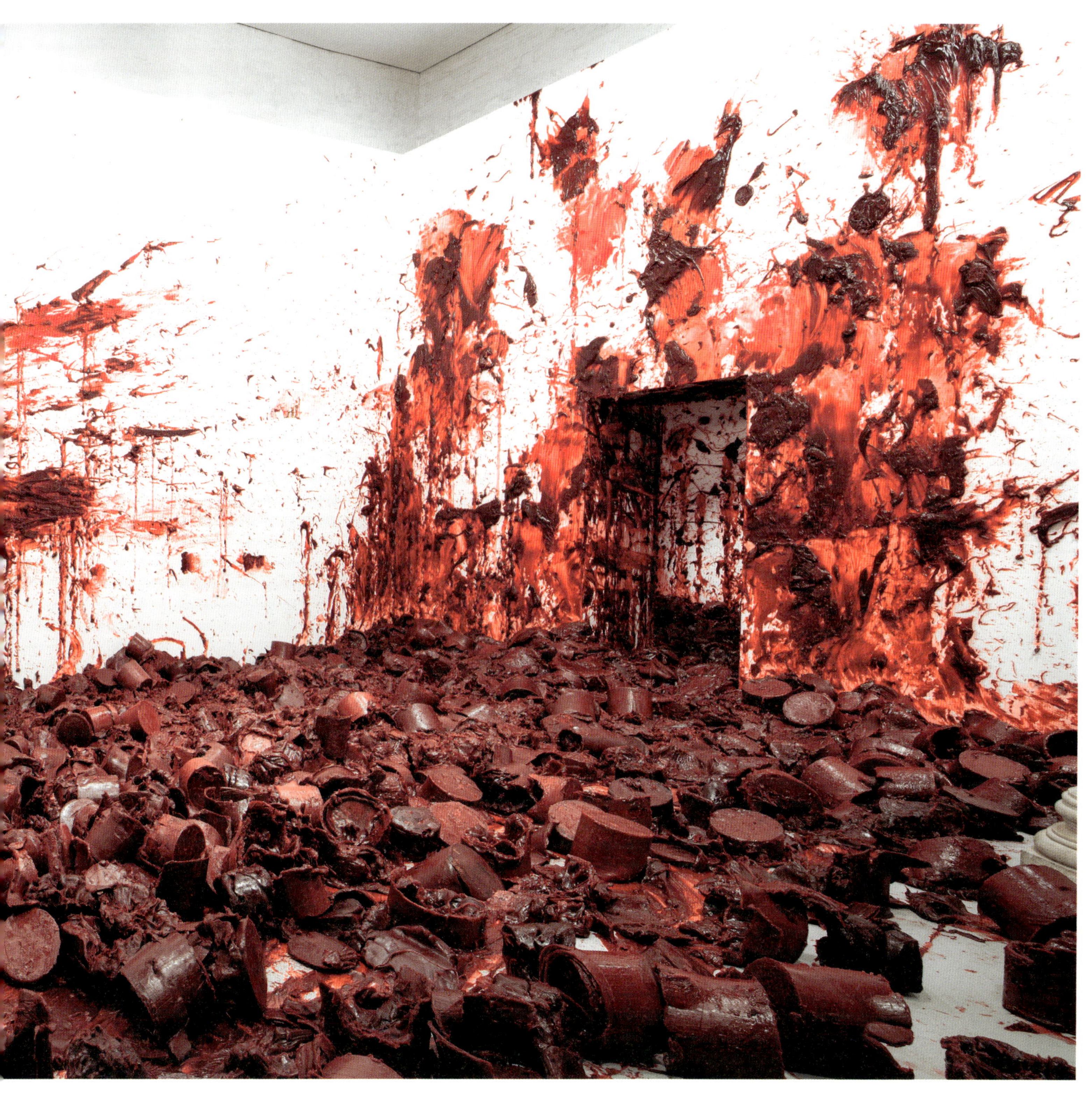

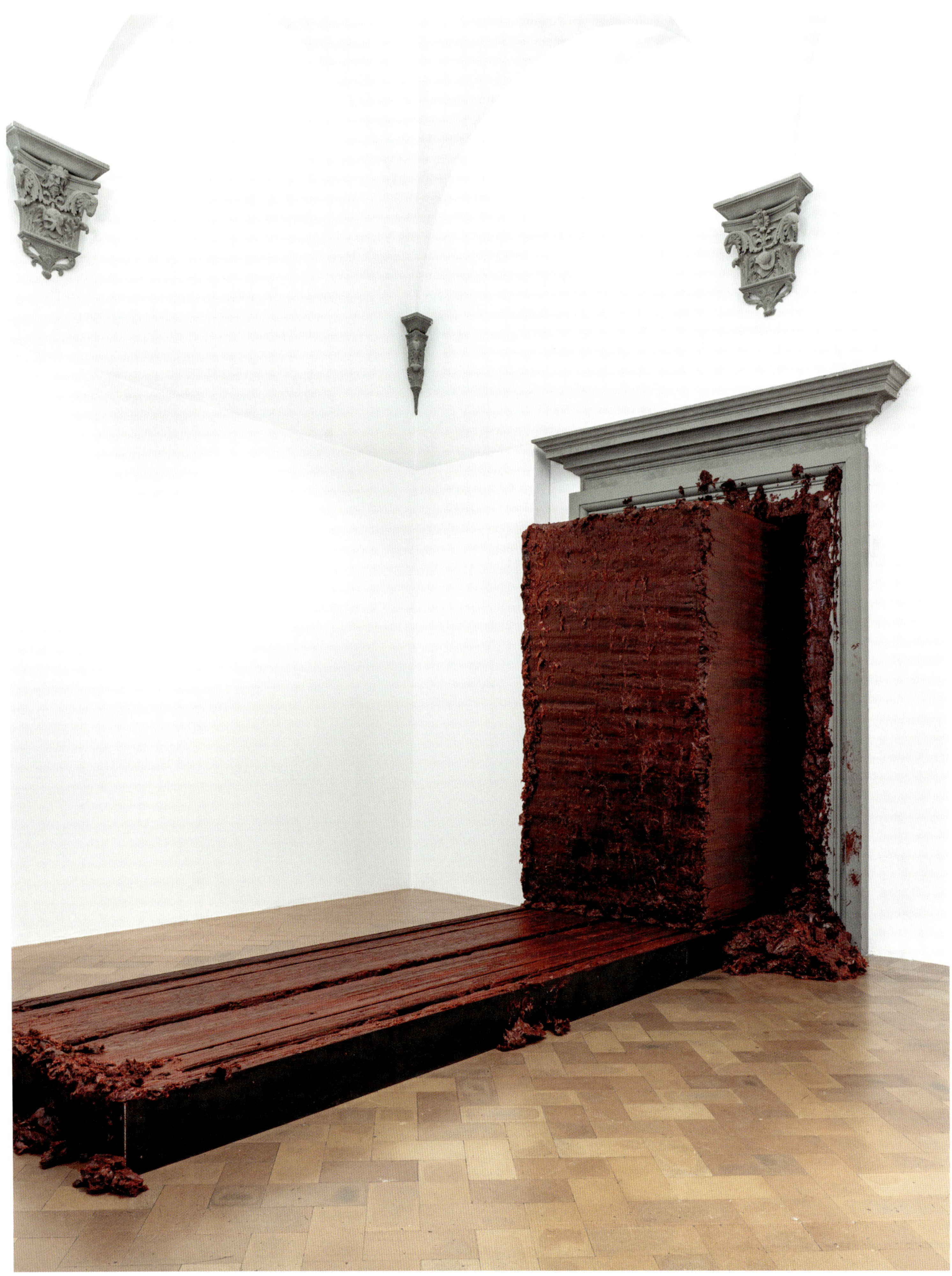

This spread
Svayambhu, 2007
Wax, oil-based paint
Dimensions variable

pp. 144-145
*Turning Water into Mirror,
Blood into Sky,* 2003
Steel, water, motor
150 × 300 × 300 cm

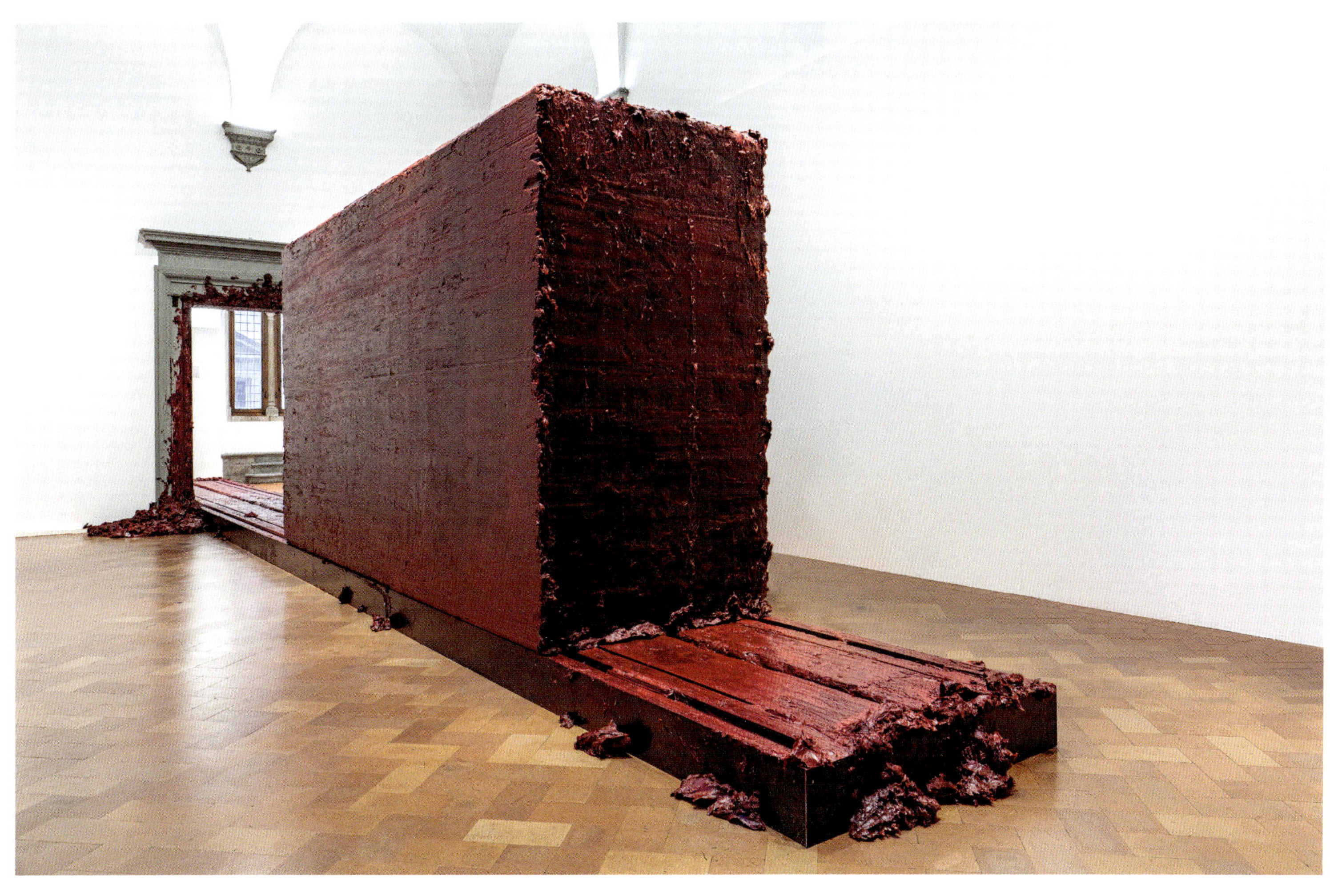

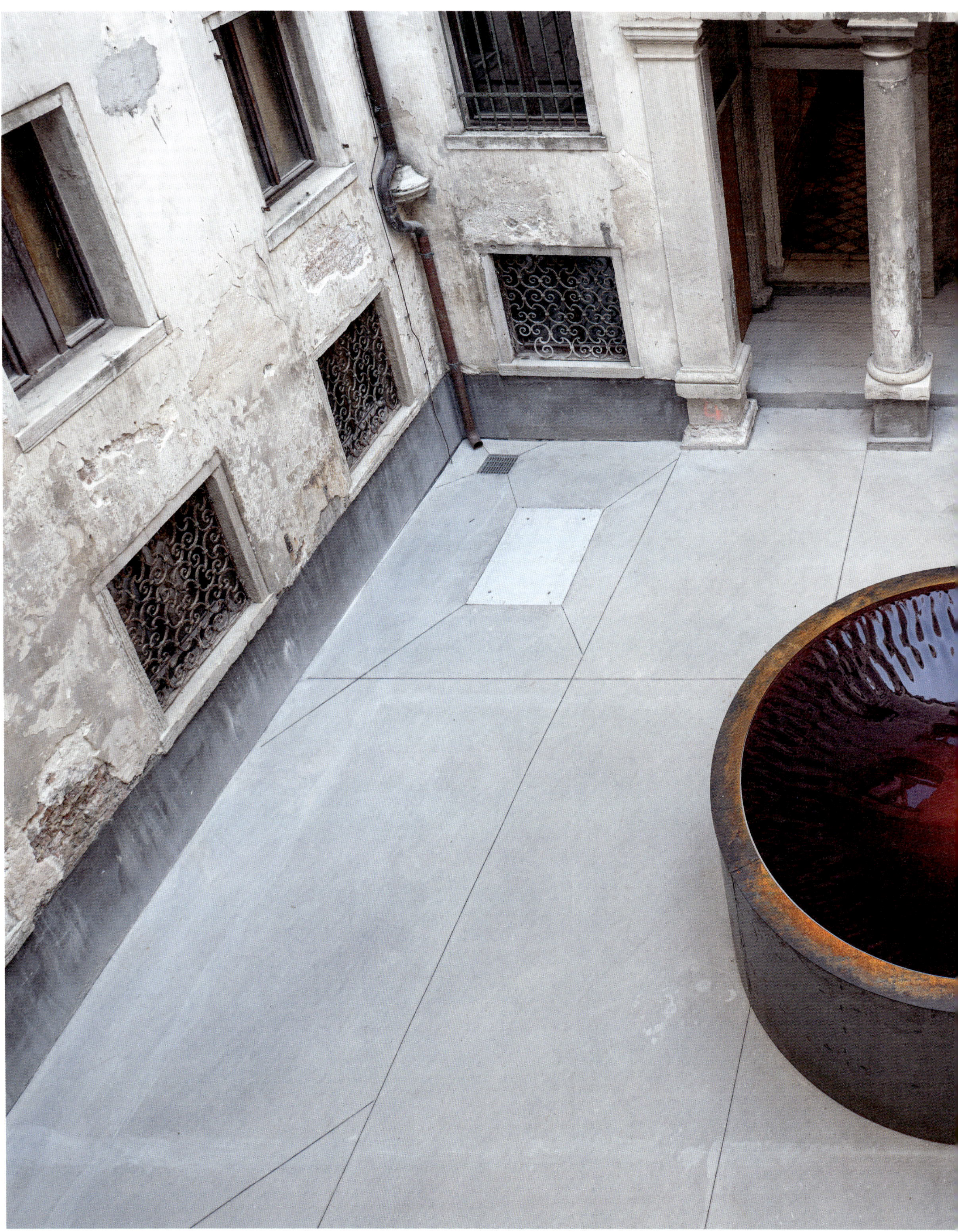

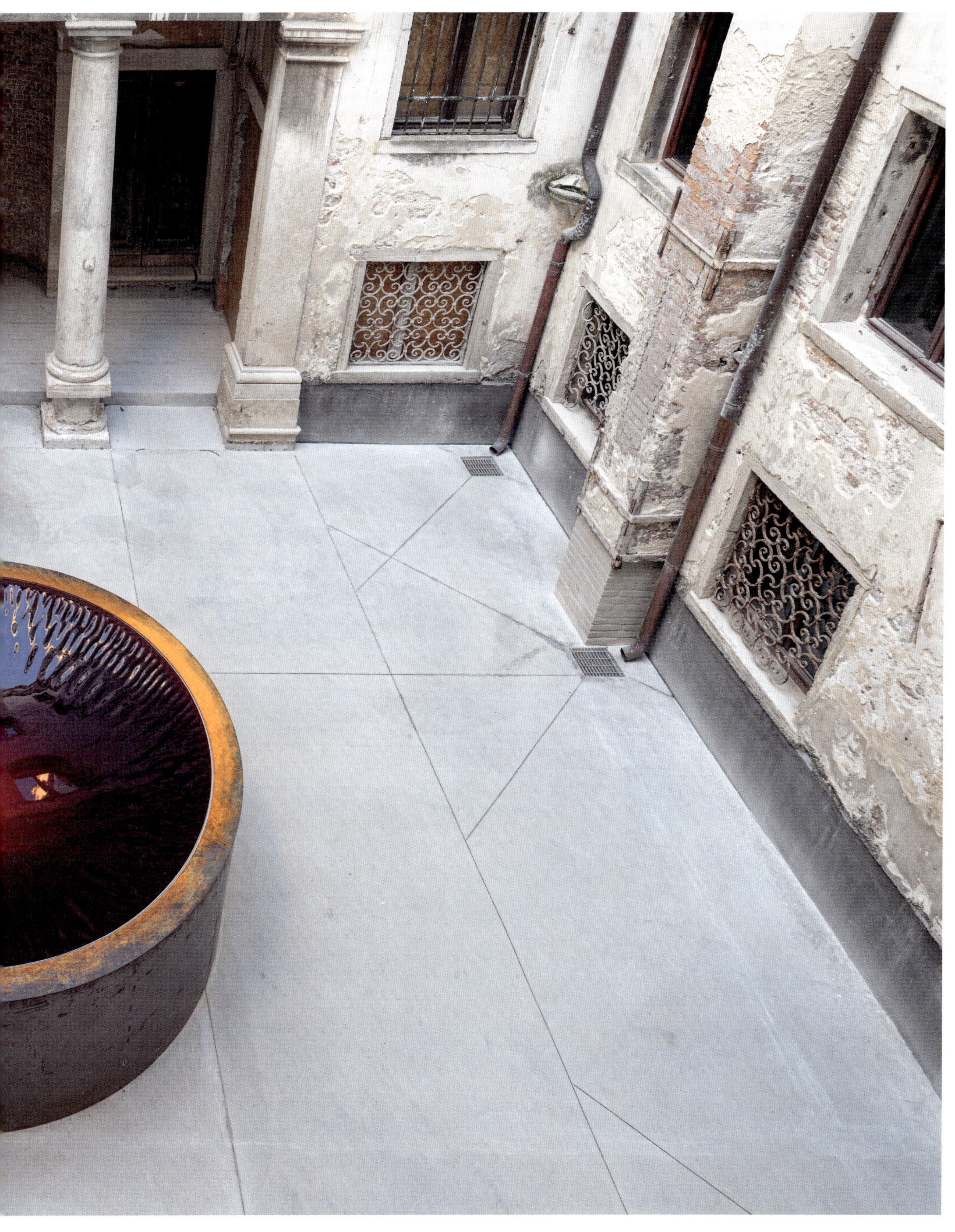

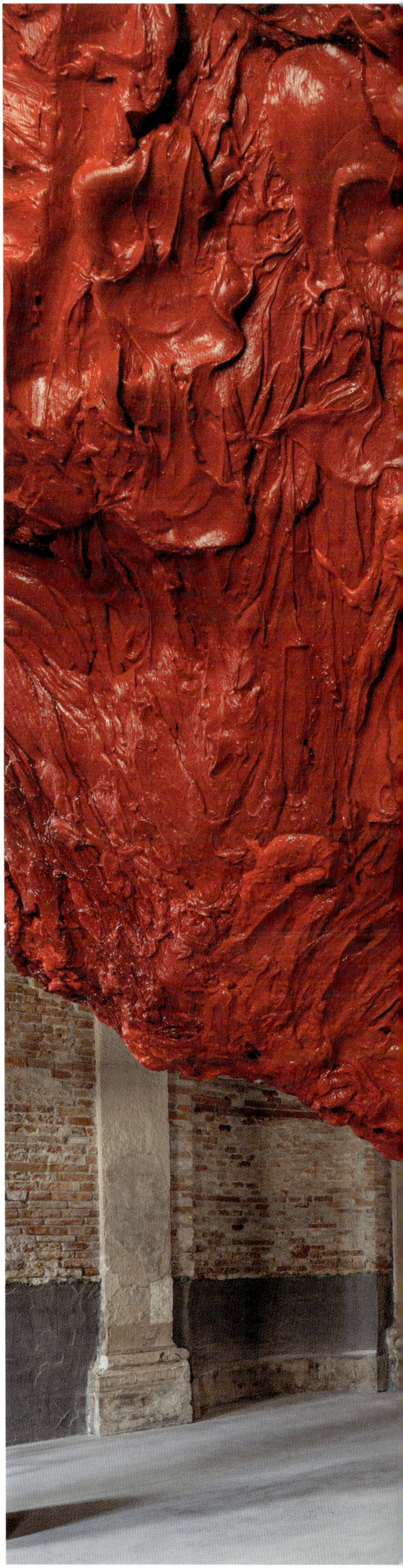

*Mount Moriah at the Gate
of the Ghetto,* 2022
Mixed media, paint
13.8 × 6.8 × 3.9 m

pp. 148-151
Destierro, 2017
Earth, pigment, mechanical digger
Dimensions variable
ARKEN Museum of Contemporary Art, Ishøj

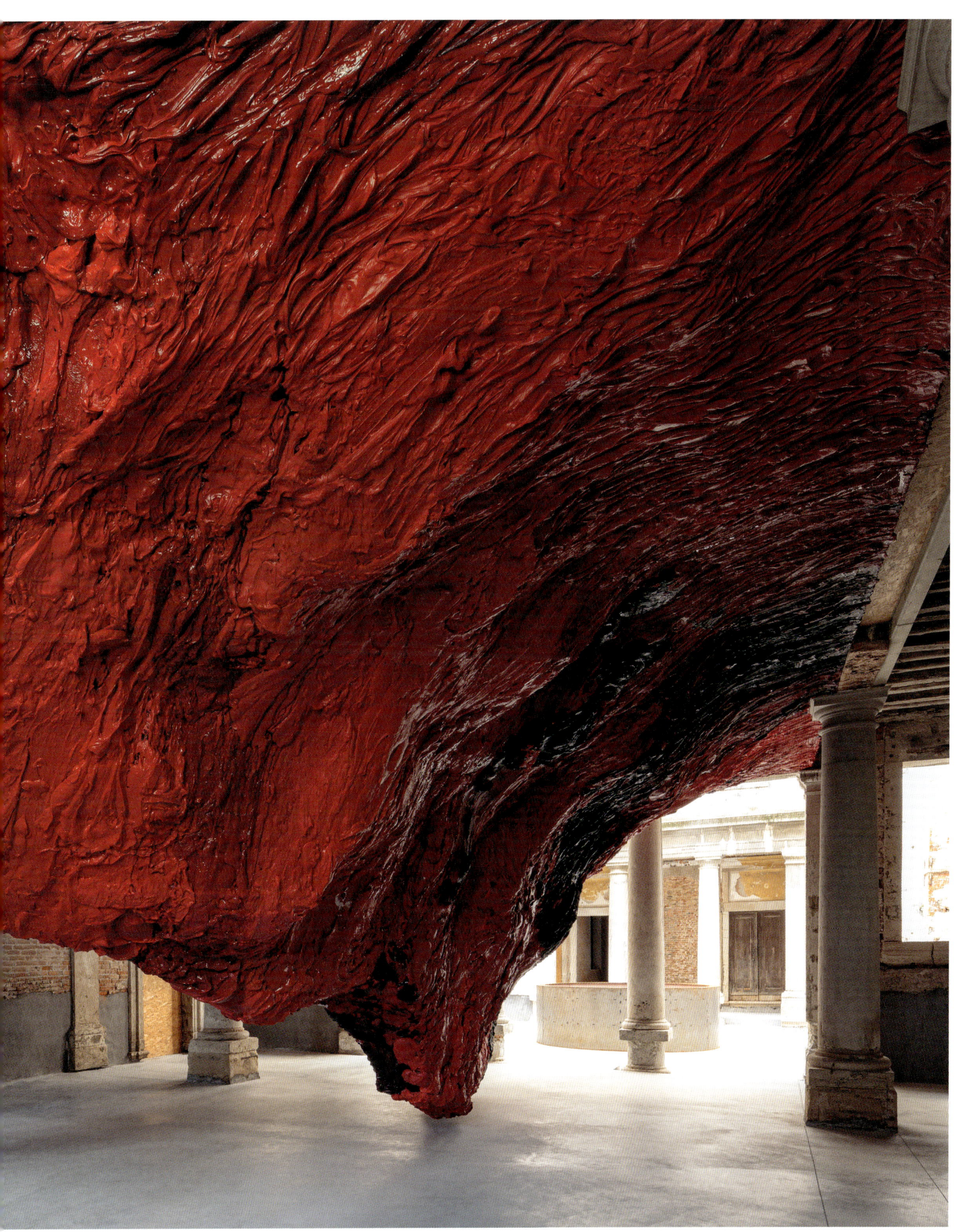

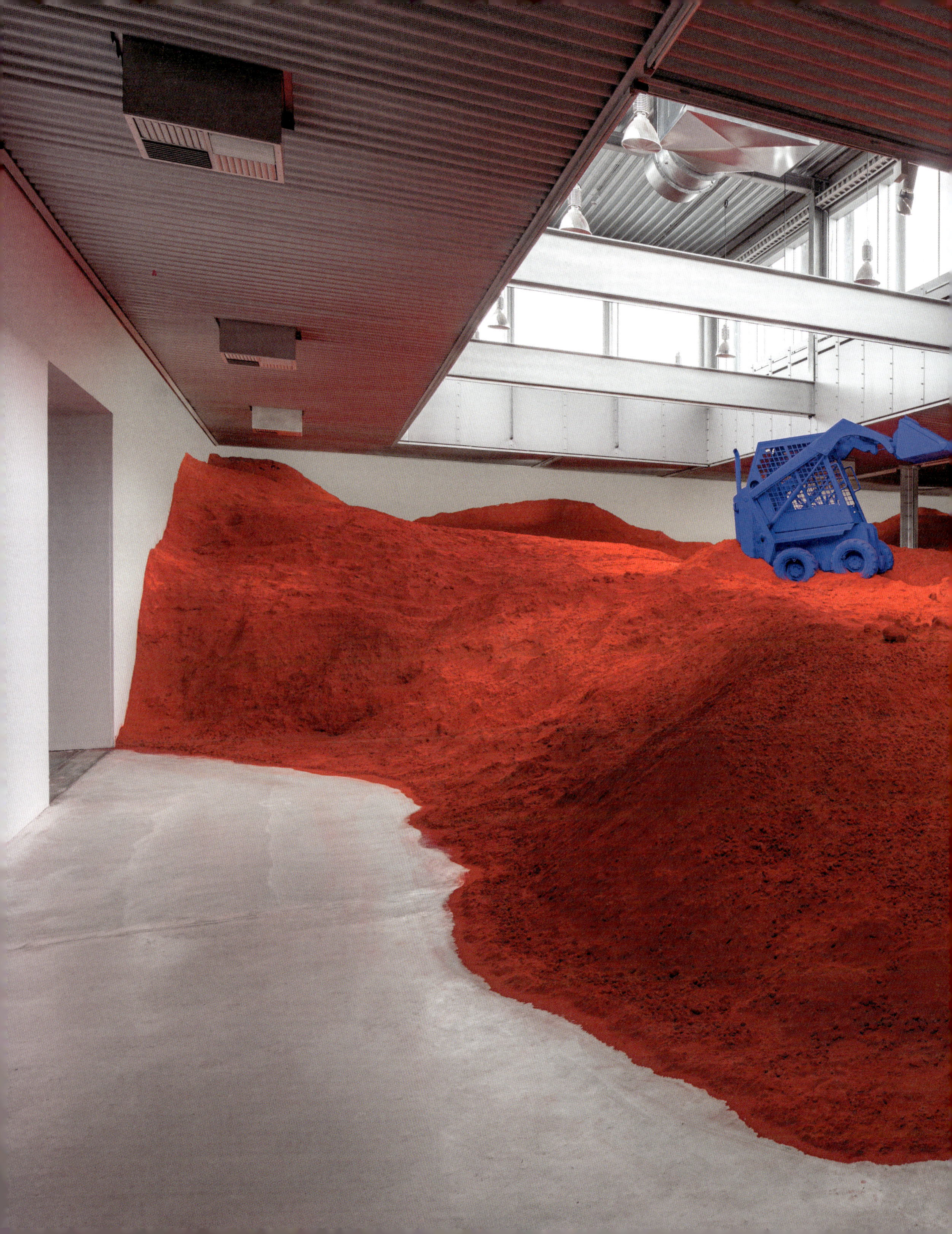

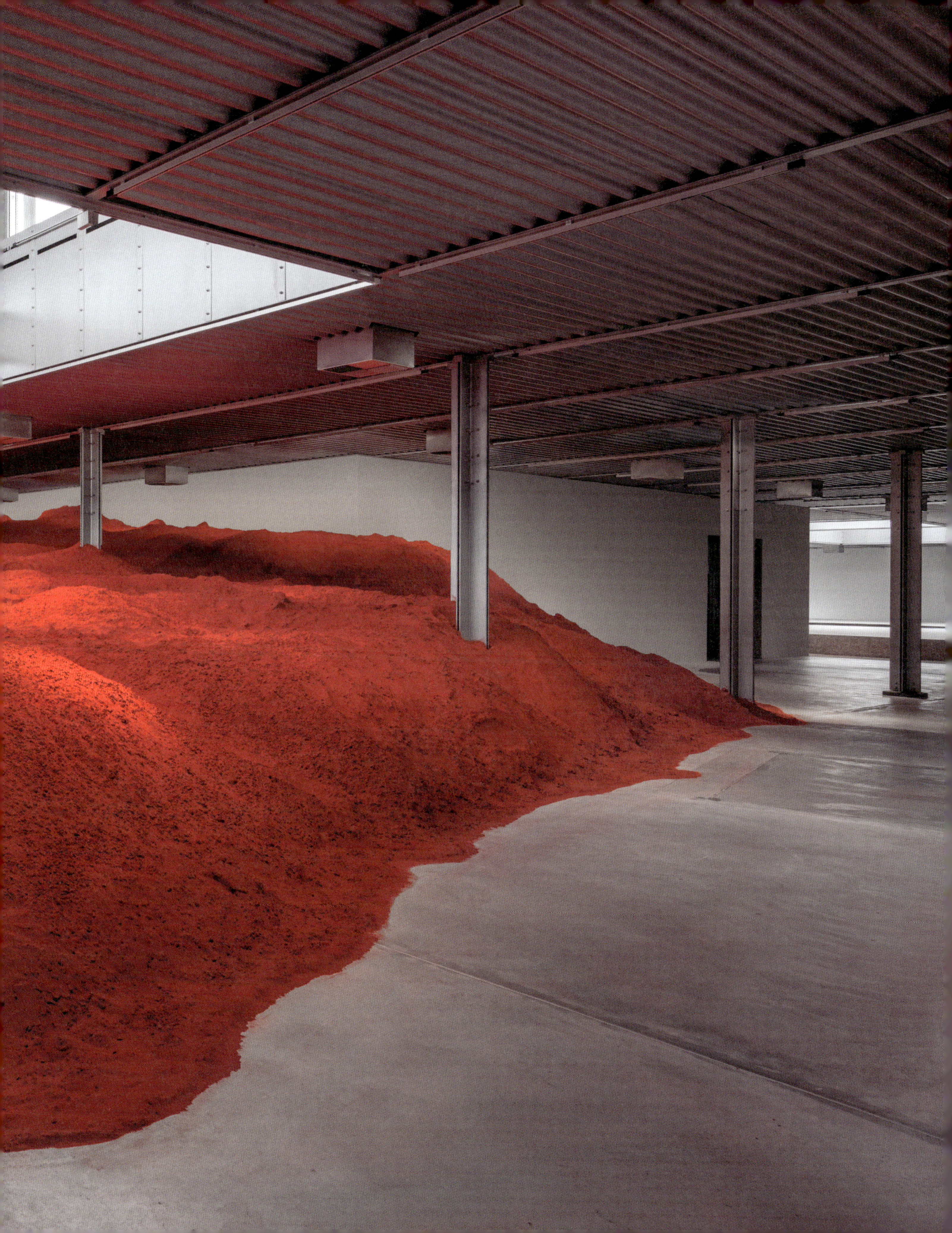

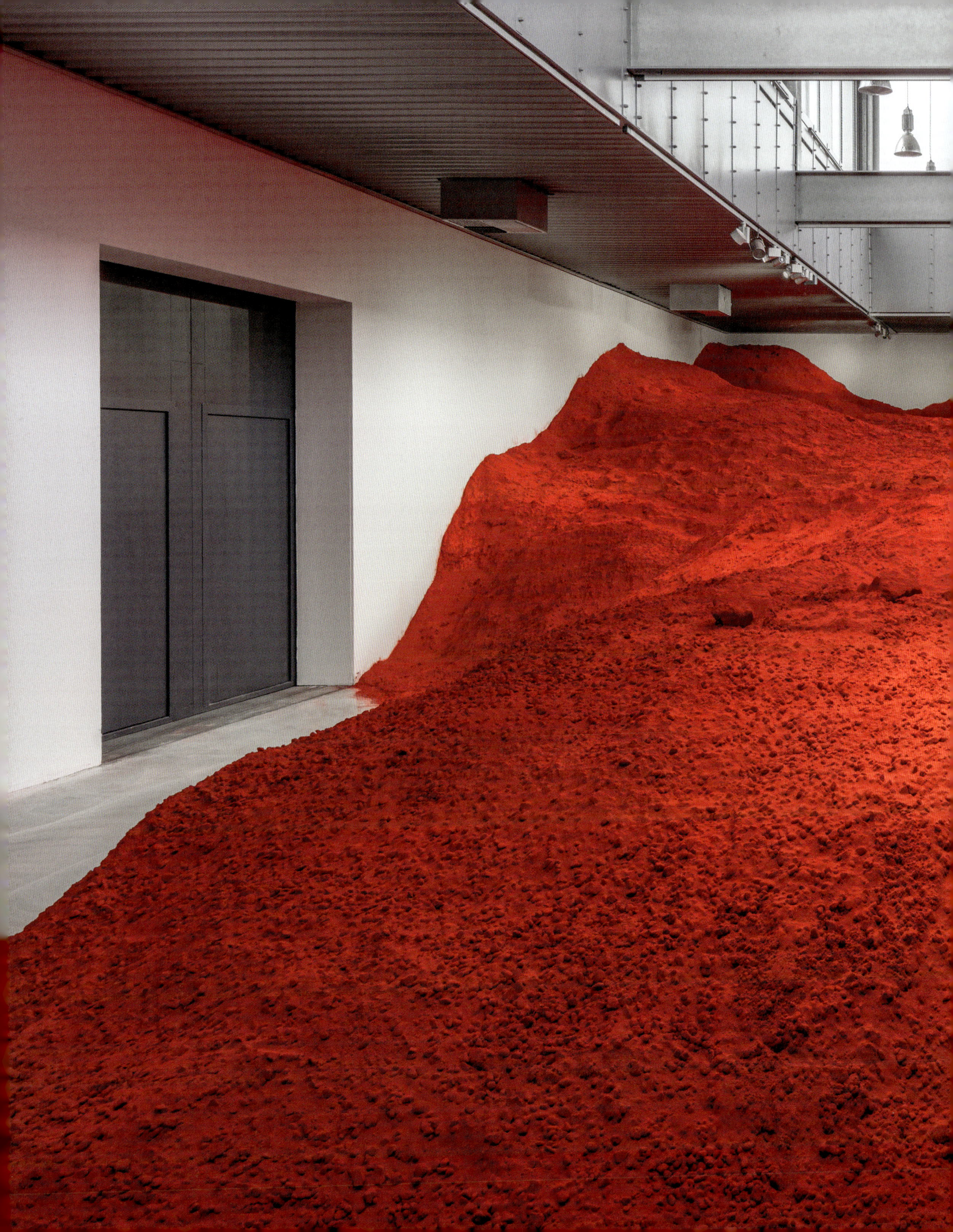

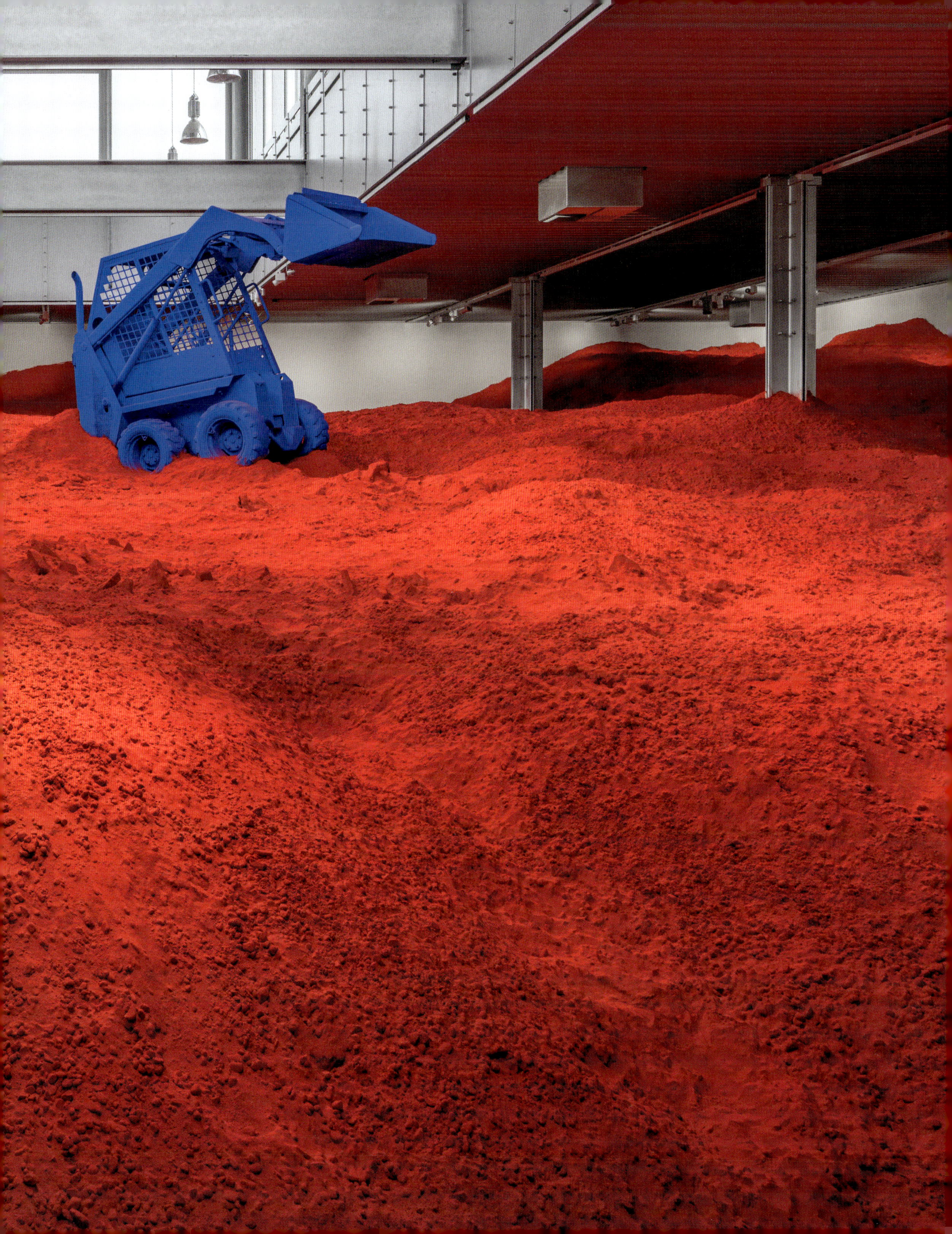

pp. 107-109
Descent into Limbo, 1992
Mixed media
Dimensions variable

pp. 68-71
At the Edge of the World II, 1998
Fibreglass, pigment
300 × 800 × 800 cm

pp. 136-139
My Red Homeland, 2003
Wax, oil-based paint, steel arm, motor
Diameter 12 m

p. 91
S-Curve, 2006
Stainless steel
216.5 × 975.4 × 121.9 cm

pp. 50-55
Memory, 2008
Corten steel
14.5 × 8.97 × 4.48 m
Commissioned by Deutsche Bank
in consultation with the
Solomon R. Guggenheim Foundation
for Deutsche Guggenheim

pp. 122-125
Descension, 2014

pp. 148-151
Destierro, 2017
Earth, pigment, mechanical digger
Dimensions variable

p. 92
Random Triangle Mirror, 2017
Stainless steel, resin
199 × 199 × 35 cm

p. 79
Grave, 2019
Resin, earth, pigment
270 × 250 × 247 cm

pp. 98-101
Mipa Blue no.5 to Cobalt Blue and Black, 2021
Aluminium, paint
214 × 214 × 25 cm
Courtesy the artist and Lisson Gallery

p. 80
Untitled, 2022
Steel, lacquer, paint
300 × 150 × 150 cm

Biography

1954 — Anish Kapoor is born in Mumbai, India, as the eldest of three boys.

1959–66 — Kapoor is a pupil at The Cathedral School, a private school in Mumbai.

1966–70 — The family moves to Dehradun in Northern India, where Kapoor attends The Doon School.

1970–73 — Kapoor moves to Israel and begins to study engineering, but drops out after six months and takes up painting.

1973–76 — Moves to the UK to study at the Hornsey College of Art, London. Becomes familiar with artists such as German Joseph Beuys (1921–1986), the American minimalists Donald Judd (1928–1994) and Sol LeWitt (1928–2007) and the American sculptor Paul Thek (1933–1988).

1974 — Takes part in his first group show at the Serpentine Gallery, London, and in the *Young Contemporaries* exhibition at the Royal Academy of Arts, London.

1977–78 — Studies at the Chelsea School of Art and Design, London.

1979 — Creates his first series of pigment works, *1000 Names* [pp. 12 and 75], a seminal body of work that marks a synthesis of influences in the emergence of his own unique artistic language.

1980 — First solo show at the gallery Patrice Alexander in Paris, France; includes *1000 Names.*

1981 — Kapoor is becoming one of the most highly acclaimed British contemporary artists. Is featured in the exhibition *Objects and Sculpture* at the Institute of Contemporary Arts, London.

Kapoor meets Nicholas Logsdail, director of the Lisson Gallery, London, one of the world's most influential galleries. The Lisson Gallery represents Kapoor from this point on.

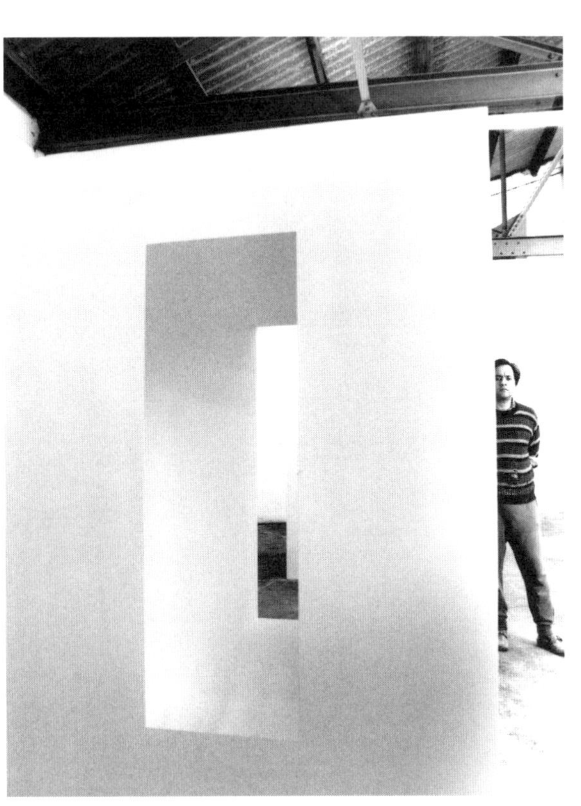

Anish Kapoor behind *White Dark I,* 1995

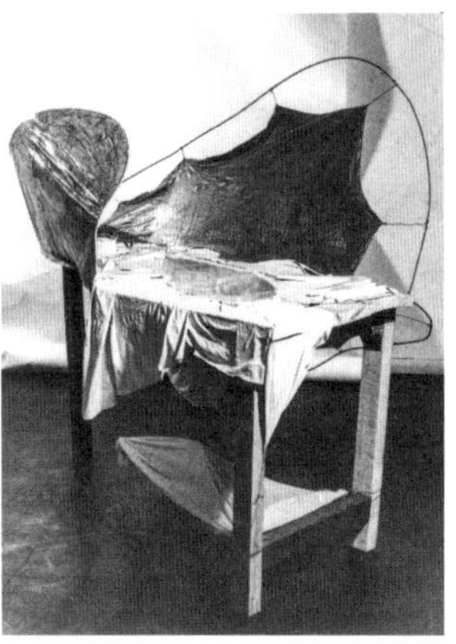

Table of Dreams, 1976
Wood, wire, cloth, paint
213 × 152 × 213 cm

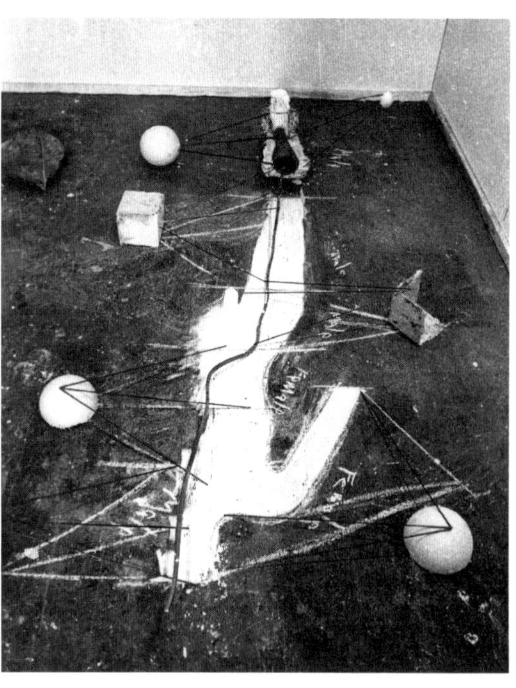

Untitled, 1975
Paint, chalk, steel, plaster
15 × 121 × 274 cm

Has his second show at the Serpentine Gallery, London, and is part of the exhibition *British Sculpture in the 20th Century* at the Whitechapel Gallery, London.

1982 First show at the Lisson Gallery.

Takes part in *British Sculpture Now* at the Kunstmuseum Luzern in Switzerland alongside a number of significant British artists who also work in sculpture.

At *Aperto 82*, an exhibition at the Venice Biennale dedicated to emerging artists, Kapoor shows *As if to Celebrate I Discovered a Mountain Blooming with Red Flowers* (1981). The work is later acquired by the Tate Gallery, London.

1983 Three solo shows and 23 group shows, including at the Hayward Gallery and the Serpentine Gallery, London, and the São Paulo Biennale in Brazil.

1984 First solo show in the US at Barbara Gladstone Gallery, New York, which goes on to represents Kapoor from 1984 to 2016.

1985 Kapoor creates his first works exploring the void, including *Mother as a Mountain* [p. 74].

Solo shows at Kunsthalle Basel, Switzerland, and the Lisson Gallery. Takes part in nine group exhibitions.

1986 Several solo shows in the US, including at the Fine Arts Center, Massachusetts.

1987 *At the Hub of Things* marks the culmination of the development of Kapoor's *Void* works. He begins to work with stone as part of his exploration of voids.

1990 Represents the UK at the Venice Biennale; receives the Premio Duemila prize.

Participates in the exhibition *British Art Now: A Subjective View*, which tours Japan, where Kapoor garners great acclaim.

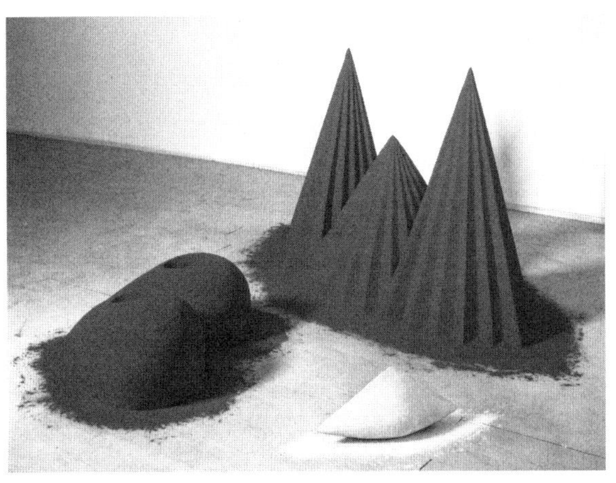

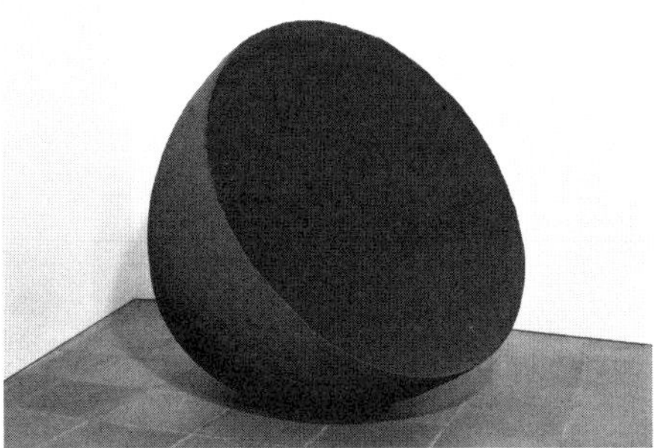

As if to Celebrate I Discovered a Mountain Blooming with Red Flowers, 1981
Mixed media, pigment
107 × 305 × 305 cm

At the Hub of Things, 1987
Fibreglass, pigment
150 × 163 × 141 cm

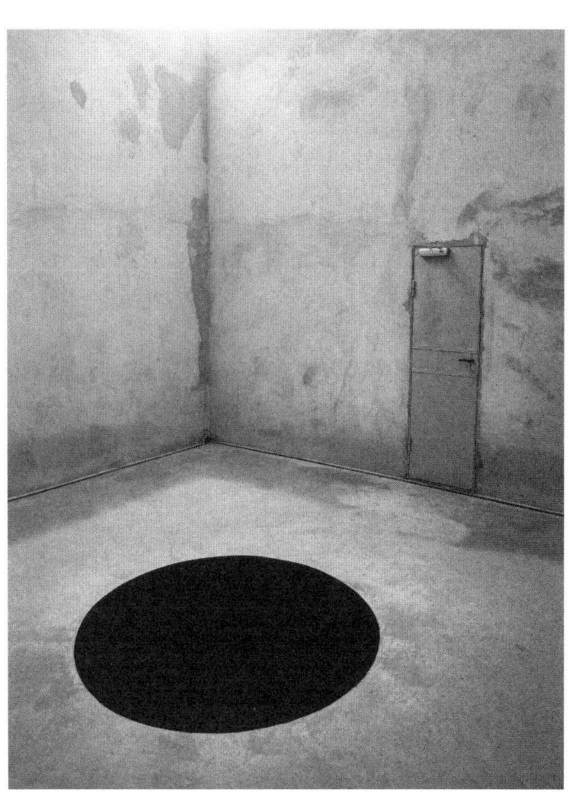

Descent into Limbo, 1992
Concrete, pigment
600 × 600 × 600 cm
Documenta IX, Kassel, Germany

| 1991 | Receives the prestigious Turner Prize.

Begins to work with embedding works within the architecture of the gallery space, for example *Untitled* and *The Earth*, exhibited at the Sixth Ushimado International Arts Festival in Japan. |
| 1992 | Takes part in Documenta IX in Kassel, Germany, presenting a range of works that includes *Descent into Limbo* [preceding page]. |
| 1994–95 | Creates his first permanent outdoor work, *Mountain*, for the city of Tachikawa in Japan.

Begins working with polished limestone, which in turn inspires Kapoor to use polished stainless steel in his works. *Turning the World Inside Out II* is one of his first mirror works created using this material. The work is part of Kapoor's first solo show in Italy, held at the Fondazione Prada, Milan. |
1997	Inaugurates the three-metre-tall granite sculpture *Eye in Stone* on the coast of Lødingen in Norway.
1998	Major solo exhibition at the Hayward Gallery, London, which includes *At the Edge of the World II* [pp. 68-71] and sculptures from his recent body of *White Dark* works.
1999	Creates the colossal sculpture *Taratantara* out of PVC, a commission for the new Baltic Centre for Contemporary Art, Gateshead in the UK.
2001	Kapoor's first permanent outdoor work in the UK, *Sky Mirror*, is installed in front of the Nottingham Playhouse.
2002	Exhibits *Marsyas* [pp. 72-73] in the 320-square-metre Turbine Hall at Tate Modern, London. Extending to a length of 155 metres, it is one of the largest indoor sculptures ever created.

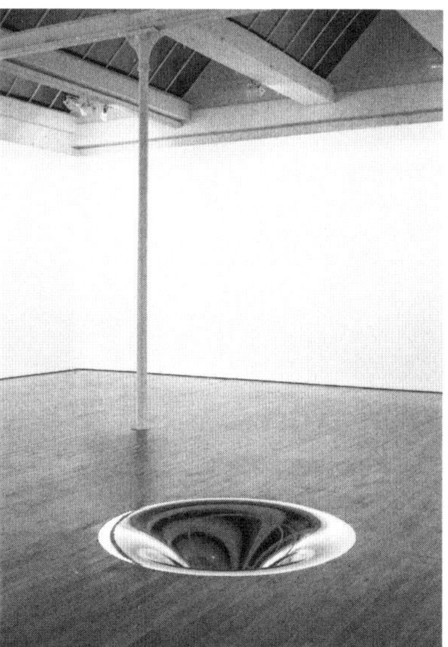

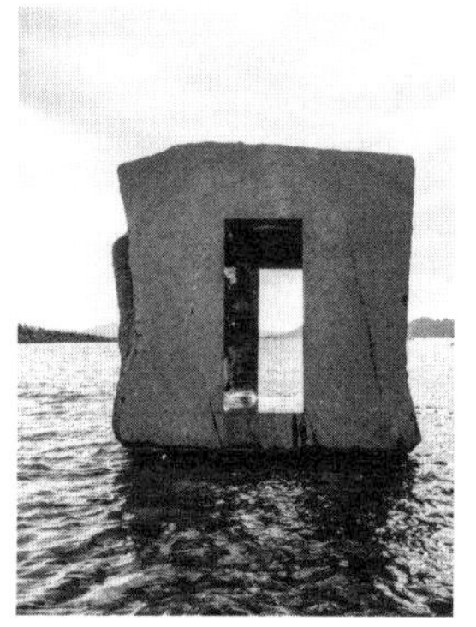

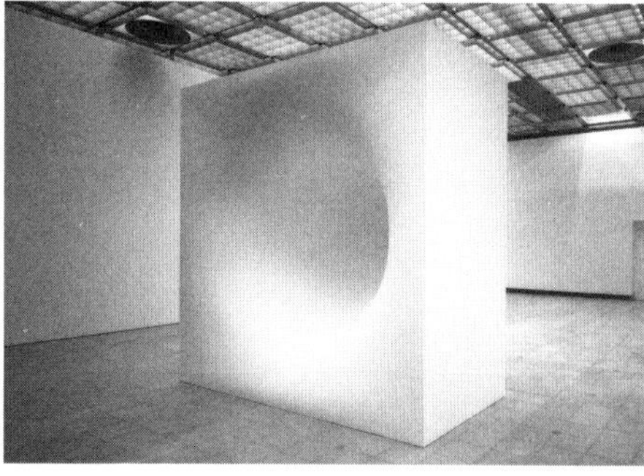

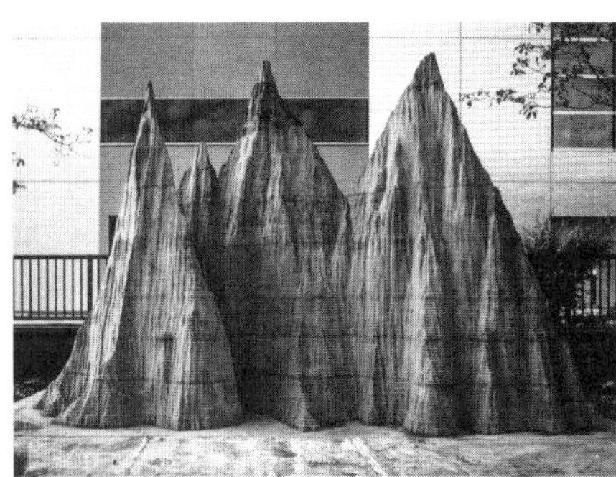

Eye in the Stone, 1997
Granite
300 × 300 × 200 cm
Artscape Nordland, Lødingen, Norway

White Dark VI, 1998
Fibreglass, paint
300 × 300 × 140 cm

Mountain, 1994
Cast iron
285 × 420 × 210 cm

Turning the World Inside Out II, 1995
Chromed bronze
180 × 180 × 130 cm

2003   Solo show at the Kunsthaus Bregenz
in Austria; includes *My Red Homeland*
[pp. 136-139].

2004   Creates the public sculpture *Cloud Gate* in
Chicago, a 110-tonne mirror work popularly
known as *The Bean*.

2006   Creates the huge public artwork *Sky Mirror*
at the Rockefeller Center, New York.

2007   Solo show at the Musée des Beaux-
Arts, Nantes, France, featuring the work
titled *Svayambhu* [pp. 142-143], which is a
Sanskrit word that can be translated as
'autogenerated'. The work consists of a single,
vast mass of wax of the kind also used in
My Red Homeland. Mounted on and riding
along rails, the block of wax is forced through
doorways, leaving trails of red wax as it moves
through the building.

Solo exhibition at the Haus der Kunst, Munich,
Germany.

2008   The first-ever exhibition dedicated to Kapoor's
architectural works is held at the Royal
Institute of British Architects (RIBA), London.

Creates *Memory* [pp. 50-55] as a commission
for the Deutsche Guggenheim, Berlin.
Begins working with computer processes to
create auto-generated works in concrete.

2009   Creates *Shooting into the Corner* [pp. 140-141]
for his solo exhibition of wax works at
the MAK – Museum of Applied Arts, Vienna,
Austria.

Becomes the first living artist to have a solo
show at the Royal Academy of Arts, London.

Exhibits *Memory* (2008) at the Guggenheim,
New York.

Works as artistic director of Brighton Festival,
UK, where he exhibits works around the city,
including *Dismemberment of Jeanne d'Arc*
created for the Old Municipal Market.

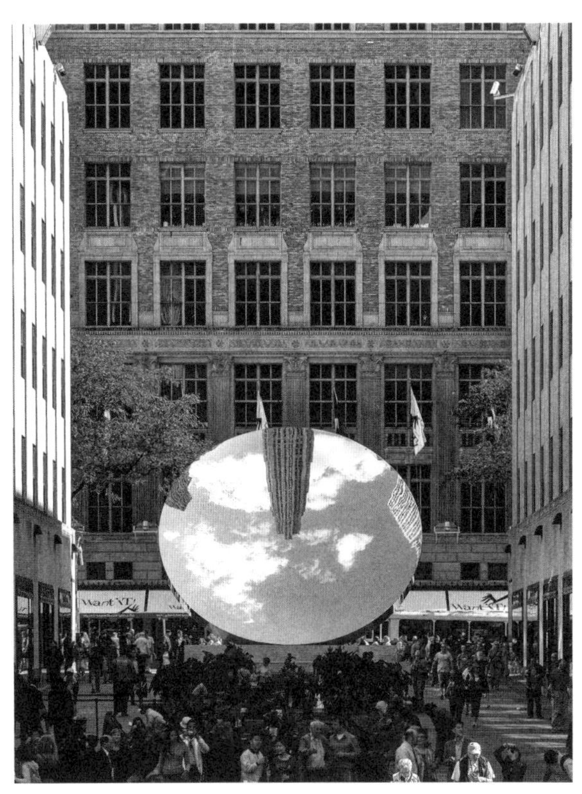

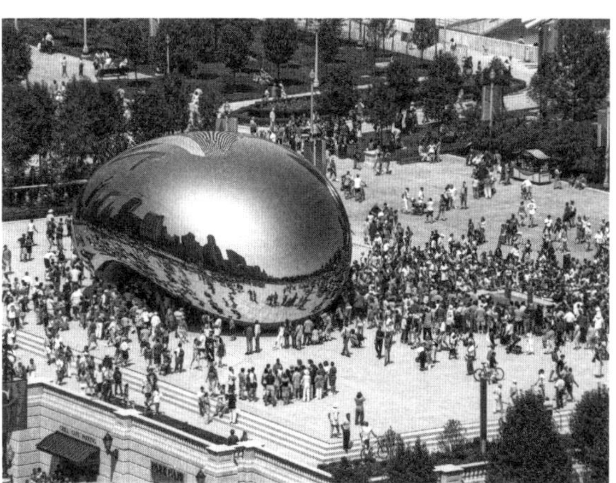

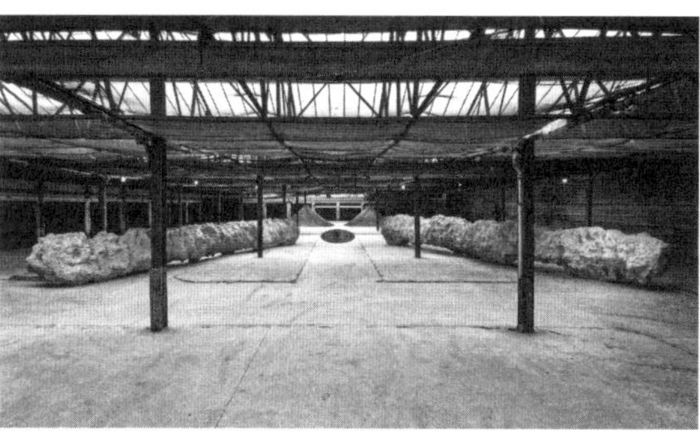

Sky Mirror, 2006
Stainless steel
Diameter 10 m
New York City

Cloud Gate, 2004
Stainless steel
10 × 20 × 12.8 m
Millennium Park, Chicago

Dismemberment of Jeanne d'Arc, 2009
Mixed media
Dimensions variable

2010 First solo show in India, held at the National Gallery of Modern Art, New Delhi and Mehboob Studio, Mumbai.

2011 Becomes the fifth artist to be invited to exhibit at the Grand Palais, Paris, as part of the public art project *Monumenta*. His contribution is the monumental sculpture *Leviathan* [pp. 62-65], which fills the space of the building.

Solo show at Rotonda di via Besana, and the work *Dirty Corner* is presented at the art venue Fabbrica del Vapore, both in Milan, Italy.

2012 Creates *Orbit*, a colossal tower standing 115 metres tall. The work is commissioned by the Queen Elizabeth Park, London, on the occasion of the 2012 Olympic Games.

Solo exhibitions at Museum of Contemporary Art Australia, Sydney; Pinchuk Art Centre, Kiev, Ukraine; Leeum – Samsung Museum of Art, Seoul, South Korea; and De Pont Museum, Tilburg, Netherlands.

Takes part in the exhibition *Klein/Byars/Kapoor* at ARoS, Aarhus in Denmark.

2013 Solo show at Martin-Gropius-Bau, Berlin, for which he creates the work *Symphony for a Beloved Sun* [p. 134] which fills the rotunda of the museum.

With Japanese architect Arata Isozaki (1931–2022), Kapoor creates *Ark Nova*, an inflatable mobile concert hall which tours the regions that, in 2011, were ravaged by the strongest earthquake ever recorded in Japan.

2014 Creates *Descension* for the Kochi-Muziris Biennale in India.

2015 Exhibits six sculptures in the Palace of Versailles Park outside of Paris.

Kapoor takes out a patent for the artistic use of Vantablack, a material using nanotechnology that absorbs 99.8% of all visible light.

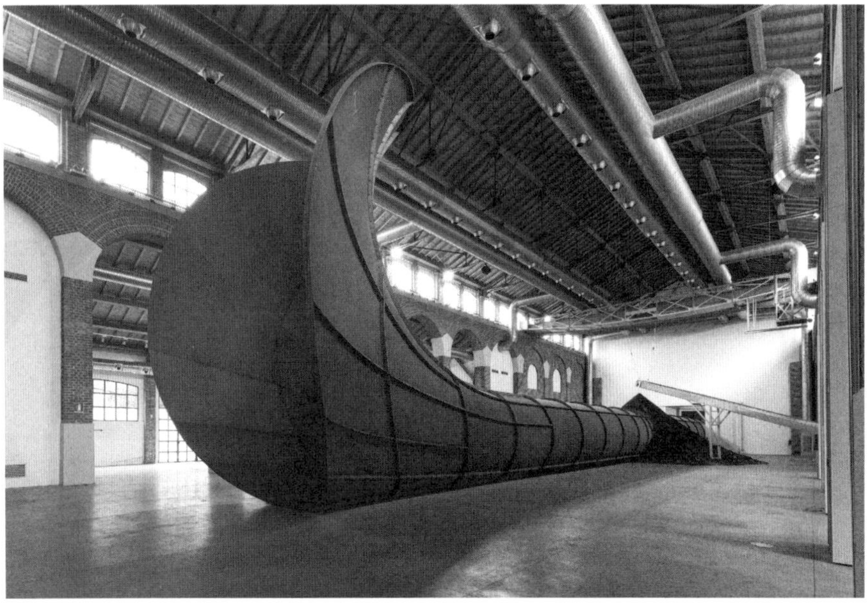

Dirty Corner, 2011
Corten steel, earth, mixed media
8.9 × 6.55 × 60 m

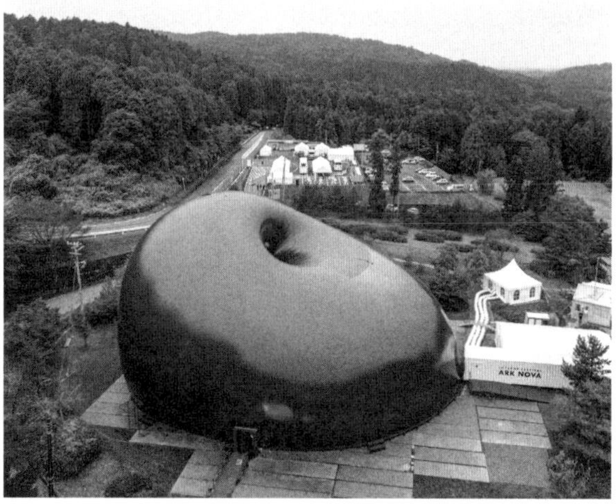

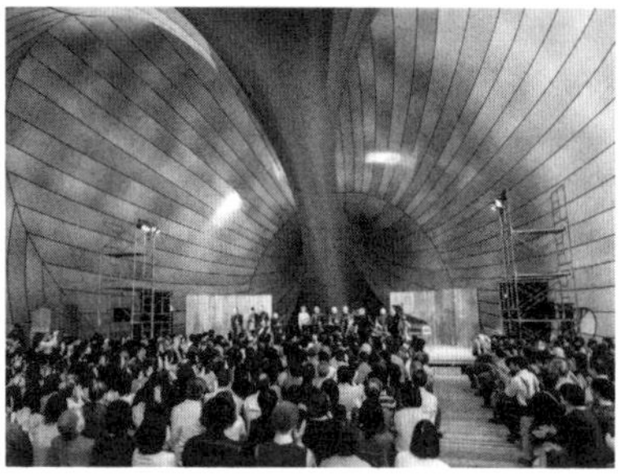

Ark Nova, 2013
PVC
18 × 29 × 36 m
Lucerne Festival in Matsushima and Sendai, Japan, 2013-14

| 2016 | Solo exhibitions at MACRO Museum of Contemporary Art, Rome, Italy, and Museo Universitario Arte Contemporáneo, Mexico City, Mexico. |

2016 Solo exhibitions at MACRO Museum of Contemporary Art, Rome, Italy, and Museo Universitario Arte Contemporáneo, Mexico City, Mexico.

2017 Solo exhibition, *Destierro*, at Parque de la Memoria, Buenos Aires, Argentina.

2018 Solo exhibition at Serralves, Porto, Portugal.

Creates *Void Pavilion VI* [p. 42] for Beppu Park in Japan.

2019 Museum exhibitions in China at CAFA Art Museum and Imperial Ancestral Temple, Beijing.

Solo exhibition, *Surge*, in Santiago in Chile, travelling to PROA, Buenos Aires.

2020 Takes part in the Bangkok Art Biennale, Thailand.

Solo exhibition at Houghton Hall, Norfolk in the UK.

Creates *HOWL* for the Rotunda of the Pinakothek der Moderne, Munich.

2021 Takes part in the exhibition *Light and Space* at Copenhagen Contemporary in Denmark.

Solo exhibition, *Painting*, at Modern Art Oxford, UK.

2022 Extensive solo show at Gallerie dell'Accademia di Venezia and Palazzo Priuli Manfrin in Venice, where the Vantablack works are exhibited for the first time.

2023 First permanent work in New York is unveiled.

Solo show at Palazzo Strozzi, Florence, Italy.

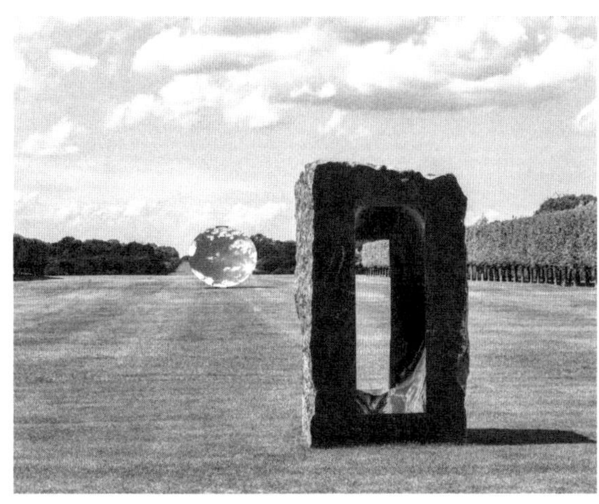

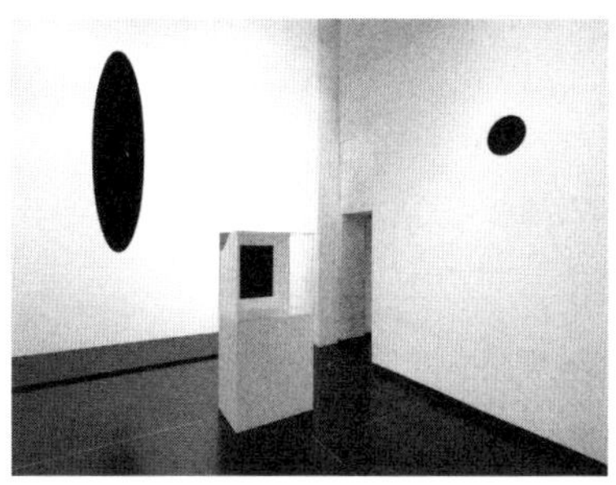

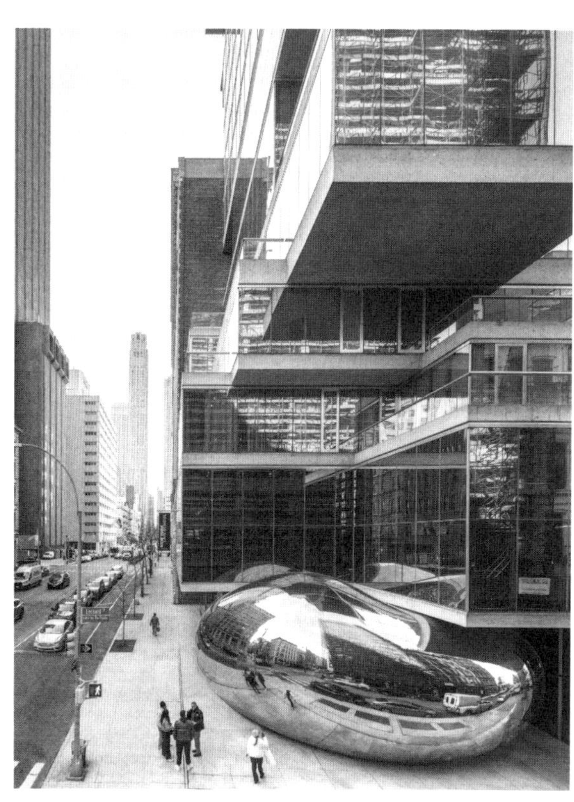

This book has been published on the occasion
of the exhibition

ANISH KAPOOR
UNSEEN

ARKEN Museum of Contemporary Art
11 April – 20 October 2024

© 2024 ARKEN Museum of Contemporary Art
and the authors

Curators:
Marie Nipper, Rasmus Stenbakken, Sarah Fredholm

Curatorial assistant:
Laura Meulengracht Olesen

Exhibition architect:
Michelle Malling

Exhibition design:
Studio Claus Due

Studio Anish Kapoor:
Sophie Baker, Peter Lynch, Clare Chapman, Lucy Adams

Exhibition team:
Jon Almazan, Rory Beard, Angus Miller,
Ektor Rodriguez, Christophe Taundon

Editor:
Sarah Fredholm

Publishing editor:
Pernille Gøtze Johansson

Editorial assistant:
Mie Noer Smedstad

Translation:
René Lauritsen
(Preface, Fredholm, Bille/Sørensen and Biography)

Copyediting, proofreading:
Sarah Quigley

Graphic design:
Studio Claus Due

Paper:
270g Curious Matter, 115g Munken Print White
and 150g Arctic Volume White

Print:
PNB Print

Repro:
Narayana Press

Print run:
3,850

1st edition, 1st print run
ISBN: 978-87-94418-24-9
Printed in Latvia 2024

Sarah Fredholm's article, 'Facing the Void. Effect and
Affect in Anish Kapoor's *Descent into Limbo*', has been
peer reviewed.

The certification means that an independent peer of at
least PhD level has made a written assessment justifying
the article's scientific quality and originality.

Publisher:
ARKEN Museum of Contemporary Art
Skovvej 100
2635 Ishøj
Denmark
Phone: +45 4354 0222
www.arken.dk

Produced by Strandberg Publishing A/S
Book dealer sales: In commission with
Strandberg Publishing A/S
www.strandbergpublishing.dk

International distribution:

North America:
ARTBOOK LLC
D.A.P. | Distributed Art Publishers, Inc.

Rest of the world:
Thames & Hudson Distribution

Published with generous funding from:

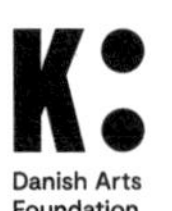

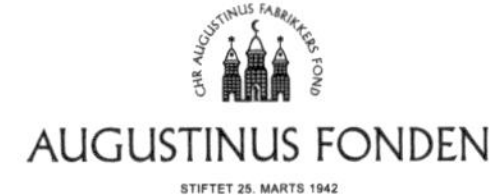

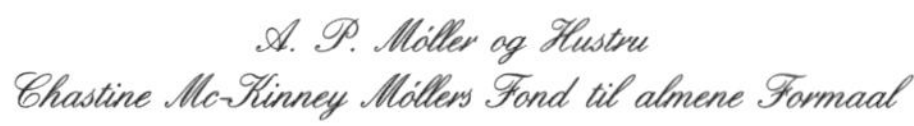

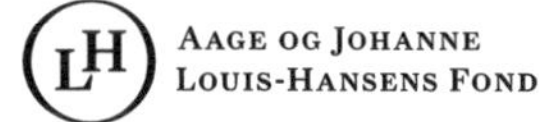

Furi Appel og Gunnar Niskers Fond
til Almennyttige Formål